ISRAEL KNOHL

The Divine Symphony

THE BIBLE'S MANY VOICES

2003   5763
The Jewish Publication Society
Philadelphia

The Jewish Publication Society
2100 Arch Street, 2nd floor
Philadelphia, PA 19103

Design and Composition by Book Design Studio

Manufactured in the United States of America

03 04 05 06 07 08 09 10   10 9 8 7 6 5 4 3 2 1

Library of Congress Cataloging-in-Publication Data

Knohl, Israel.
  The divine symphony : the Bible's many voices / Israel Knohl.
     p. cm.
Includes bibliographical references and indexes.
  ISBN 0-8276-0761-X
  1. Bible. O.T.—Theology. 2. Judaism—History—To 70 A.D. 3. P
document (Biblical criticism) 4. Religious pluralism—Judaism. I.
Title.
  BS1192.5.K545 2003
  221.6—dc21
                    2003012150

In memory of Rivka Knohl and of
Rabbi Dr. Yisrael Olesker

Contents

CONTENTS

Dedication and Acknowledgments

I DEDICATE THIS BOOK TO THE MEMORY OF TWO GREAT SOULS. The first is my beloved wife, Rivka, who died on the first day of the month of Nisan 5763 (April 3, 2003), after three years of heroic struggle with cancer. Rivka studied philosophy and computer science at Bar Ilan University, educational psychology at Rutgers University, and classics and cognitive science at the Hebrew University. She integrated all her various fields of study and knowledge in her work at the International Center for the Enhancement of Learning Potential, where she founded and directed the computer institute.

The book is also dedicated to the memory of my uncle, after whom I was named: Rabbi Dr. Yisrael Olesker, who was killed in Poland during the Holocaust. He was ordained as a rabbi in the Rabbinical Seminary at Vienna and earned his Ph.D. in Jewish history at the University of Vienna.

My late uncle and my late wife both had great love for Torah. They overcame many difficulties during their lives, and had an enormous devotion and strong will that enabled them to surmount these obstacles. Sadly, the two of them died at a young age, before they could fulfill their plans and hopes. I am glad that I can dedicate this study of the Hebrew Bible and early Judaism to their blessed memories.

I could not have brought this book to its final form without the help and excellent work of my editor, Dr. Herb Levine. The book has benefited greatly from his deep knowledge of the Hebrew Bible and his unique editorial skills. My thanks also to my former student and dear friend, Ms. Margot Pritzker, who read the entire manuscript and gave me valuable comments.

I received support in the writing and publication of this book from various foundations and individuals. Parts of the book were translated from the Hebrew by my former student, Dr. Azan Meir-Levi, now Professor of Talmud at Rutgers University. This translation was funded by the Yad Hanadiv Foundation. The publication of the book was subsidized by a dear friend who wants to keep his anonymity and by the Wolfson Foundation at the Hebrew University. The Shalom Hartman Institute and its director, Rabbi Prof. David Hartman, provided me with excellent working conditions and a stimulating environment.

Finally, I would like to thank the Jewish Publication Society; the editor-in-chief, Dr. Ellen Frankel; the publishing director, Carol Hupping; and their staff for their patience and good work.

Israel Knohl
Department of Bible
Hebrew University
Jerusalem

Introduction

"Remember" and "observe" in one utterance
Announced to us the one and only God,
God is one and God's name is one.

THESE VERSES ARE TAKEN FROM "LEKHA DODI" (COME, MY Beloved), the song with which Jews welcome the Sabbath. They refer to the different versions given in the Torah regarding the commandment of the Sabbath. According to the version of the Ten Commandments given in Exodus 20:8, God said at Sinai, "Remember the Sabbath day and keep it holy." However, according to the version of the Ten Commandments given in Deuteronomy 5:12, God said at Sinai, "Observe the Sabbath day and keep it holy." The reader of the Torah is puzzled; what indeed did God say at Sinai: "Remember" or "Observe"?

The Midrash, upon which the quoted verses of "Lekha Dodi" is based, gives the following answer to this puzzle:

One thing God has spoken;
two things have I heard:
that might belongs to God (Ps. 62:12)

According to the Midrash, the divine speech is one, but it has within it many different voices. The human ear can only hear these voices separately—"One thing God has spoken; two things have I heard." God said "Remember" and "Observe" at one utterance, but Israel heard the two words separately.

The Midrash also brings other examples of commandments that were spoken by God at the one utterance:

> "He who profanes it shall be put to death" (Exod. 31:14) and "And on the Sabbath day: two yearling lambs" (Num. 28:9) were both spoken in one utterance. "Do not uncover the nakedness of your brother's wife" (Lev. 18:16) and "Her husband's brother shall unite with her" (Deut. 25:5) were both spoken in the same utterance.

Each pair in this paragraph consists of laws that contradict each other. The commandment in Num. 28:9–10 to bring a sacrifice and burn it every Sabbath day contradicts the prohibition of kindling a fire on the Sabbath day (Exod. 35:3). The commandment to the brother of the man who died without producing a son to marry the widow of his deceased brother (Deut. 25:5) stands in tension with the warning not to have a sexual relationship with one's brother's wife (Lev. 18:16). The Midrash explains that God gave each pair of contradictory laws in the same utterance. The human mind can't easily grasp this dichotomy, so it must seek to reconcile the contradictions.

The evidence for different but parallel traditions in the Pentateuch, or Torah (like the abovementioned difference between the two versions of the Sabbath commandment in the Ten Commandments), and the evidence for contradictory laws within it have been the main basis for critical study of the Torah in the modern period. At the core of this method stands the hypothesis that the Pentateuch was formed by the combination of several different sources, which are designated by the letters P (the Priestly code), J (the Jahwist), E (the Elohist) and D (the Book of Deuteronomy).[1]

The dominant theory in biblical studies regards the Priestly layer of the Pentateuch as the latest stratum of the Torah. This theory, associated with Julius Wellhausen,[2] a German scholar of the nineteenth century, sees the Priestly tradition as a product of the exile to Babylon. In the Priestly source, there is a clear detachment from the needs of everyday life and a high interest in holiness and atonement. According to Wellhausen, this was due to the impact of the exile that cut off the roots of the people in its land and caused tremendous guilty feelings.

Unlike Wellhausen and his school, and following a line of previous scholars,[3] I see the roots of the Priestly source in the pre-exilic period. The loftiness and the aspiration toward sanctity on the one hand and the desire for expiation on the other are in my view not a result of the exile, but rather a reflection of a unique theological concept that prevailed within the priesthood in Jerusalem at the time of composition of the Priestly source, which can also be referred to as the Priestly Torah. I believe that the Priestly Torah was written in the period between the building of Solomon's Temple (tenth century B.C.E.) and the time of King Hezekiah and the prophet Isaiah (second half of the eighth century B.C.E.). During this period, the priests in Jerusalem were an elite group, closeted within the walls of the sanctuary, drawn toward the hidden, noble divinity ensconced within its shrine. However, the great social and religious crisis of the eighth century B.C.E. bore within the priesthood a new desire to transcend the limits of the Temple and to go out into the broad avenues of the nation, even at the price of surrendering the loftiness of the earlier faith and practice of the Priestly elite. The crisis, well recorded in the writings Amos, Isaiah, and Micah, the prophets of this period, was expressed in the detachment between cult and morality. People thought that they might acquire sanctity by meticulous performance of the cultic laws, ignoring at the same time the social-moral commandments. As is well known, this led to the prophets' harsh attack on the Temple and cult. The priesthood was sensitive to the prophetic critique; a new conception of holiness developed within the Jerusalem priesthood, a concept that combined cult and morality under the call, "You shall be holy, for I, the Lord your God, am holy" (Lev. 19:2). Hence, I name the new Priestly school, which was formed in the eighth century B.C.E., "the Holiness school." It is my contention that this school continued its activity for many generations. It is this school that is responsible, in my view, for the redaction of the Torah at the time of the return from Babylon. This Priestly-popular school is to be seen as the precursor of the Pharisaic-Rabbinical movement, as will be shown in this book's final chapter.

Wellhausen argued that the authenticity and vitality of early Israel is best represented in the J source of the Pentateuch and in the historical books Judges and Samuel. He made a distinction between these sources and the Priestly source, which for him represents later Judaism of the time of the exile to Babylon and the return to Zion. A recent trend in biblical studies argues that the J source and the books of Judges and Samuel are also post-exilic.[4] Several of these scholars claim that David and Solomon were not historical figures, but rather purely products of the Jewish imagination of the Second Temple period. I would not like to enter into detailed debate with these arguments here. However, I will say that it is clear to me and many other scholars that J was written in pre-exilic Judea.[5]

In spite of the great diversity among the different biblical schools and conceptions, they are all unified by one principle: the unity of God. They all agree that there is only one God and that this God is the creator of heaven and earth. God is the creator of the world and not part of the world. God is detached from the biological process, neither born, nor dying, without spouse or biological children.[6] While there were views in biblical Israel that lay outside this normative consensus, they did not end up being included in the Bible.[7]

In this book, I will describe the spectrum of diverse religious conceptions and schools that existed in Israel during the millennium from the time of Solomon (970–930 B.C.E.)

until the end of the Second Temple period (70 C.E.). In contrast to the prevalent approach to disconnect the biblical period from later developments in post-biblical Judaism, this book will demonstrate a marked continuity between biblical schools and post-biblical sects. The reader will see that the theological and legal debate among the Jewish sects of the Second Temple period mainly continues the debate that existed between the different biblical schools of the First Temple Period. Through the different biblical sources and schools, we may hear the diverse voices of the divine revelation that started at Sinai.[8] Only by analyzing carefully the different sources in the Bible, and by a meticulous study of what makes each tradition unique, will we be able to finally hear the divine symphony of revelation in all its diversity and unity.

CHAPTER ONE

The Editing of the Torah

D IFFERENT SPIRITUAL CURRENTS AND DIFFERENT LITERARY
works developed within Israel in the period between
the founding of the Temple of Solomon and the return from the Babylonian exile. These various voices were
isolated for a long time and kept separate from each other.
For example, the Priestly teachings were closely guarded
within the ranks of the priesthood, and no one outside this
elite group had access to them.[1] Thus, the people of Israel
were not familiar with the laws formulated in the Priestly circle. Moreover, the rites and customs of the priests were not
widely accepted by the populace, and this situation engen-
dered estrangement and ritual ignorance. No Israelite would
have been familiar with the entire corpus of sacred teachings
as they were evolving. In this essentially closed system, different customs, laws, and norms were created in many realms
of social and religious life. But after the destruction of the
Temple and the exile of the Israelites to Babylonia, it became
necessary to gather together all the spiritual wealth that had
been amassed by the people of Israel and collect it in a single
book. This process culminated after many years in the formation of the Bible, the Book of Books.

The first stage in the formation of the Bible was the editing of the Torah, the Five Books of Moses.[2] The editing process consisted of gathering the different stories that were current among the people and that told of the Creation, the Patriarchs, the Exodus from Egypt, and the events in the desert. In the same way, the editors collected the various legal codices that had developed within the different circles. No attempt was made to blur the differences between them; instead they were bound together in a single book.[3] This is the Torah, which we have before us today.

We do not know precisely when this great enterprise was undertaken, but it doubtless took many years. It reached its apogee with Ezra's reading of the Torah before the assembly of the people, as described in the Book of Nehemiah.

> *The entire people assembled as one man in the square before the Water Gate, and they asked Ezra the scribe to bring the scroll of the Teaching of Moses with which the Lord had charged Israel. On the first day of the seventh month, Ezra the priest brought the Teaching before the congregation, men and women and all who could listen with understanding. He read from it, facing the square before the Water Gate, from the first light until midday, to the men and the women and those who could understand; the ears of all the people were given to the scroll of the Teaching.*
>
> *Ezra the scribe stood upon a wooden tower made for the purpose... Ezra blessed the Lord, the great God, and all the people answered, "Amen, Amen," with hands upraised. Then they bowed their heads and prostrated themselves before the Lord with their faces to the ground... They read from the scroll of the Teaching of God, translating it and giving the sense; so they understood the reading. (Neh. 8:1–6,8)*

Biblical scholars consider this the first occasion on which the Torah was publicly promulgated among the people.[4] We are told that the people wept when they heard the Torah being read (Neh. 8:9), but the reason for their weeping is not stated. We can infer that they heard for the first time laws and commandments of which they had not been aware and which they had not observed until that time.[5] Immediately after the reading of the Torah, the text tells us, the people celebrated the holiday of Tabernacles, Sukkot, as it had never been celebrated before, for they had just been informed of laws that they had not known pertaining to the holiday. For this reason, it is written that "the Israelites had not done so from the days of Joshua son of Nun to that day" (Neh. 8:17).[6]

The people of that generation—the event of the reading of the Torah took place around the year 450 B.C.E.—had to internalize the abundance of information that was laid before them, and this was far from easy. Because it is a collection of many different stories, customs, and laws, the Torah contains contradictions and internal tensions, even with regard to very mundane issues. For instance, on the eve of the Passover, one is commanded to sacrifice the paschal offering. In the Paschal Law in Exodus, the instruction is very particular: "Do not eat any of it raw, or cooked in any way with water, but roasted...over the fire" (Exod. 12:9). The offering, then, should be fire-roasted and not water-cooked. (In English, the meaning of the word "cooked" is broad enough to include both roasted and boiled, but not so in Hebrew.) But in Deuteronomy we find that one is commanded to cook—that is, boil—the offering: "You shall cook and eat it at the place that the Lord your God will choose" (Deut. 16:7).

We see that the Torah, the formative book of laws, contains contradictory instructions on the matter of the Passover sacrifice. Therefore an attempt was made in Chronicles, which is among the later-written books of the Bible, to harmonize these contradictory commandments. In a passage describing the Passover that was held during the days of Josiah we read, "They roasted the Passover sacrifice in fire" (2 Chron. 35:13); that is, the meat was roasted, but the Hebrew verb used to describe the process is בשל, which usually means "to boil."[7]

Another example of contradictory laws in the Torah pertains to the treatment of slaves. According to the Book of Exodus, verses 21:1–11, slaves are to be released after seven years, and if a slave refuses to go free, his ear is to be pierced with an awl. The law code in Exodus says nothing about the piercing of a woman slave's ear (*ama*). In the laws concerning slaves in Leviticus, there is no mention of releasing slaves every seventh year; rather, they go free on the Jubilee, that is, on the fiftieth year (Lev. 25:39–41).[8] And in Deuteronomy we have yet another law. Here, as in Exodus, the slaves are released on the seventh year, but the piercing of the ear is applied to women slaves as well (Deut. 15:12–18).We get the sense that the law in Deuteronomy, which is later than the one in Exodus, took into account the omission of the earlier reference with respect to women.[9]

These are merely two of the numerous contradictions and tensions found in the Torah. Its heterogeneous character makes it very difficult to use as a basis for legislation. And so there was an immediate and pressing need for an oral Torah to interpret and harmonize these contradictions. In this sense, the Rabbis were right in saying that the oral and the written Torahs were given together.[10] The written Torah could not remain as was; it had to be explicated and resolved. Indeed, the explication, Midrash, began immediately after the completion of the Torah.[11] The first beginnings of Midrash are to be found in the latter books of the Bible, especially in the Book of Chronicles.[12] Later on, each group within the Jewish people formed its own Midrash.

The anonymous assemblers and editors of the Torah doubtless could have bequeathed us a different book, free of all contradictions and tensions. Indeed, we find in a later period (around the beginning of the Common Era), in the Dead Sea Scrolls (the writings of the Qumran sect), that an attempt *was* made to produce a harmonized edition of the Torah, free of contradictions.This was their Temple Scroll, which will be discussed in chapter 8.[13] But the editors of the Torah did not choose this path. Instead, they left us a book in which we find a variety of voices. Though the overarching narrative tends to blend, or perhaps even obscure, for most readers the diverse sounds of this chorus, if one listens carefully, one can hear them.

The editors recognized that God's word is not uniform, but that God speaks in many voices and people hear God in many ways. They did not want to mar the divine revelation nor detract from its fullness, so they created a pluralistic book, which contains a variety of conceptions, a variety of customs, and a variety of laws, and passed this rich variety down to us in the process. They understood that the Torah does not have only one entrance, but rather, has many.[14] Their actions paved the way for the continuation of multivocality and variation in later generations.

The multivocal editing of the Torah set the tone for Jewish literature. The Torah starts with a debate *(mahloket)* between two contradictory accounts of Creation: the Priestly tradition (Gen. 1–2:4a) and the J account (Gen. 2:4b–3:24). The editors put them side by side since in each of them there is a divine truth.

The editors of the Mishnah followed suit. This most important legal collection of post-biblical Jewish law starts with a debate about the appropriate time for reciting the *Shema* in the evenings.[15] And the controversies continue, for all rabbinical literature is based on debate. The editors of the Mishnah, and then of the Talmud, followed the model of the Torah. They put, side by side, different and contradictory views. They felt that all of them were the words of the living God.[16]

THE DEMOCRATIZATION OF TORAH STUDY

The editing of the Torah made the customs and laws accessible to the general public. Until that time, they were reserved for elite groups. The priests specialized in problems of Temple ritual, and thus all matters of sacrifice, purity, and impurity were reserved for them.[17] An outsider would have had no comprehension of priestly matters. The prophet Haggai, who was active early in the period of the return to Zion, said: "Seek a ruling *(torah)* from the priests" (Hag. 2:11).[18] If you want to investigate a matter pertaining to purity and impurity, go ask a priest. The scribes in the king's court were another elite group; they were experts in affairs of the state. The civil judges were experts in jurisprudence. Until that time, the average person had no access to the laws. Those who were not priests could not inquire into the esoteric laws regarding the Temple and the Temple sacrifices.

The publication of the Torah democratized the study of Torah. When we look back through Jewish history we see that there was no special house or family of Torah scholars; even the simplest of men from the poorest family could become great Torah scholars. In the succeeding generations we have many examples of scholars who were children of converts, like Sehemaiah and Abtalyon,[19] or whose lineage was anonymous or unknown, like Rabbi Akivah and Rabbi Meir.[20]

In the time of the First Temple, before the publication of the Torah, it was inconceivable that there would be such a person as Rabbi Akivah. Everything then was rigidly set and contingent upon family relations. The publication of the Torah was a revolution that radically changed the structure of Jewish society. It was then that the social standing of Torah learners began to rise. Positions of leadership became accessible to people who gained their status through the study of Torah, not through their wealth or origin. An outstanding Torah scholar could attain the highest level and become the spiritual leader of the nation. This represented a radical shift in the spiritual leadership of the Israel, and it took place in the Priestly circles as well.

In the beginning of the Mishnaic tractate *Avot* (The Sayings of the Fathers), the chain of reception of the Oral Torah is described. Moses received the Torah on Mt. Sinai and transmitted it to Joshua; Joshua transmitted it to the Elders, and so on. The last group mentioned are the members of the Great Assembly (Keneset ha-Gedolah). This is the Great Assembly that was convened by Ezra and Nehemiah, an assembly of the heads of the nation. The very next paragraph in the Mishnah tells us that Shimon the Righteous was one of the members of the Great Assembly (*Avot* 1:2).[21] He was a priest, and the following saying is attributed to him: "The world stands on three things: Torah, Temple service, and acts of lovingkindness."

If we regard these statements as expressing a hierarchy of value-concepts, then the order in which Shimon the Righteous lists these is quite significant. It is utterly inconceivable that a priest in Solomon's Temple would give pride of place to Torah. The priests of earlier times would doubtless have said that the most important thing is the Temple sacrifices; it is on Temple sacrifices that the world stands. The concept of Torah in the Priestly literature is pragmatic and narrowly limited. "Torah" is the word used to describe a set of teachings or laws governing a certain situation and pertaining to ritual.[22] Thus we find verses like: "This is the ritual *(torah)* of the burnt offering" (Lev. 6:2) and "Such is the procedure *(torah)* for [leprosy]" (Lev. 13:59). Shimon the Righteous changes these priorities. "Torah"—here understood as the study of Torah, not in the practical sense in which it is used in Leviticus—is the most valued priority. The Temple sacrifice is second and then come acts of lovingkindness. The words of Shimon the Righteous epitomize the change that had taken place in the consciousness of the priests. In second Temple times, we have a group of priests who value the study of Torah above all else.

I have argued elsewhere that the editing and publication of the Torah were the work of the Priestly group that I have designated as the Holiness School.[23] The Holiness School was that circle within the priesthood that addressed the people as a whole and worked toward an integration of popular and Priestly faiths. This school of thought wanted to break out of the ivory towers of the priesthood and draw closer to the nation and to its spiritual needs.[24] Only the Holiness School, with its integration of both Priestly and popular contents, could have gathered together all the different codes and traditions and forged them into a single book. The Holiness

School alone was both tied to the Priestly heritage and open to the nation as a whole. In this manner, they could act as the bridge reaching across generations to incorporate the various writings.

The editors of the Torah were the first composers of the divine symphony, which is embodied in the Bible and in Judaism as a whole. By transmitting to us the full scale and range of the different—and at times contradictory—voices, they have enabled us to listen to the divine revelation with all its fullness and richness. We now have to learn to listen to the various parts of the symphony, each instrument speaking out from an array of ideological possibilities and often in discord with one another. To that task we turn in the following chapters.

CHAPTER TWO

The Uniqueness of the Priestly Torah

THE PRIESTLY FAITH IS UNIQUE WITHIN THE BIBLE. ONLY IN the Priestly Torah do we find a systematic avoidance of the attribution of any physical dimensions to God and of almost any action of God, save the act of commanding. The Priestly thinkers attained an astounding level of abstraction and sublimity. That such a conception develops at the early stages of Israelite monotheism, long before the rise of Greek philosophy, is indeed startling. The course of Israelite religion is not—as so many writers in the nineteenth century claimed—an incremental evolution from the primitive, coarse, and opaque to the pure and the refined. Rather, it can be argued that the purest and most refined elements appeared right at an early stage. The Priestly Torah is a luminous, sublime flash that appears on the stage of the history of Israel's faith from its antiquity. Research on other cultures has shown that indeed literary and religious creativity can sometimes attain its peak of glory at the very dawn of a new culture.[1]

The Priestly conception is scattered over four of the five books of the Torah. Parts of it are in Genesis, including the

9

first chapter, which tells the story of Creation. Other parts are in Exodus, especially the second half of Exodus, which deals with the Tabernacle. Still other parts are in the first half of Leviticus and in various chapters of Numbers.[2] After gathering together the different chapters that belong to the Priestly writings, we can properly appreciate the profundity and the originality of the work composed by the priests of Israel.

In my book *The Sanctuary of Silence* I have argued that the Priestly Torah, or P, as it is usually designated by Bible scholars, was written by the priesthood of Jerusalem in the period of the Israelite monarchy, sometime beween the founding of the Solomonic Temple in Jerusalem (circa 950 B.C.E.) and the middle of the eighth century B.C.E.[3] The establishment of Solomon's Temple created a new situation in the Israelite cult. For the first time, a royal sanctuary was erected. The priesthood retreated behind the Temple walls and avoided taking part in the life of the people and society. In the traditions about the period before Solomon, we hear of priests who were involved in political and governmental activity.[4] For instance, the priests supported David in the time of the rebellion of Absalom[5] and were involved in court politics in the last days of David.[6] But after Solomon ascended the throne, we no longer hear of priests involved in the affairs of the kingdom, with but one exception.[7] Even the traditional roles of the priesthood in war time, the inquiry of the Urim and Thummim before going out to the battle[8] and the carrying of the ark to the battlefield,[9] are no longer mentioned during or after the reign of Solomon.[10]

I see this retreat as an expression of the Priestly Torah's wish to maintain a separation between its own internal world and the surrounding world. Just as priests stop participating in military campaigns, they also do not participate in the legal system. In other strata of the Bible, we find mentions of the priests serving as the judges of the people.[11] But according to the Priestly Torah, the priests have nothing to do with either teaching or the civil judiciary.

10

We may assume that the establishment of the "King's Temple" of Jerusalem and the creation of a closed, elitist Priestly class dependent on the royal court are essential features leading to the development of the Priestly Torah. It is these elitist Priestly circles that generated the ideology of a faith that is completely detached from social, national, or material needs.In this way, the Priestly Torah reflects the literary activity of a closed literary elite.

Scholars have noted that there is a great literary similarity between the Priestly rules in the Torah and between the Priestly writings and cult of the Hittites. This similarity is seen both in the literary form of the texts and in the details of the rituals.[12] There are hints in the Bible that the Jebusites who inhabited Jerusalem prior to David were of Hittite origin.[13] It is thus reasonable to assume that the priests in the Solomonic temple inherited literary formulas and cultic traditions from their predecessors, the Jebusite-Hittite priests of Jerusalem.[14] These traditions were reworked by the Israelite priests according to the monotheistic beliefs that they held.[15] The close connection between the Hittites' Priestly texts and the Priestly Torah is important evidence for the antiquity of the Priestly Torah.

GOOD AND EVIL IN CREATION

We begin our more detailed study of the Priestly Torah with its well-known verses, the Torah's first account of Creation[16] (Gen. 1:1–2:4a):

> When God began to create heaven and earth—the earth being unformed and void, with darkness over the surface of the deep and a wind from God sweeping over the water—God said, "Let there be light"; and there was light. God saw that the light was good, and God separated the light from the darkness. (Gen. 1:1–3)

The first act of God as Creator was the imperative: "Let there be light" (1:3). "When God began to create heaven and earth" does not describe the order of creation, but rather

serves as a general heading[17] to the account of Creation, or
as a temporal clause subordinate to the main clause in verse
two and three.[18] Otherwise, how could it be that the heavens
mentioned in the first verse are formed according to Genesis
1:6–8 only on the second day! The most striking conclusion
that follows from this observation of syntax is that before
the formation of light, which was the first act of God as Creator, there were already entities that predated God's creation.
These primordial materials consisted of unformed and void
earth *(tohu v'vohu)*, darkness *(hoshekh)*, and deep waters
(tehom).[19] Thus, we do not have in Genesis 1 a claim for creation out of nothing *(creatio ex nihilo)*. We cannot interpret
tohu v'vohu as a designation for formless matter, as it is
often interpreted;[20] rather, it is a reference to some primordial entity that preceded divine creation and that was used in
that process. Elsewhere in the Bible, the word *tohu* means
"desert," "waste," "devastation," and this is also its meaning here.[21] God begins Creation assuming the presence of this
primordial *tohu*. On the first day, God created light as a contrast to the preexisting darkness. On the second day, God
separated the preexisting water by forming the expanse of
heaven. On the third day, God gathered the original waters
that were left under the expanse, and distinguished the earth
from the seas.

This description raises two questions potentially troubling
to monotheism. First, if God did not create the primeval entity, who did? And second, doesn't the claim that there are elements of the universe that predated Creation diminish God's
omnipotence and sovereignty? The answer to the first question is not to be found explicitly in Genesis 1. I believe that
scripture would like us to understand that these materials
were always there, coexistent with God. As to the second
question, it is true that this reading limits God's force and authority as Creator. However, we must understand that there
are deep religious implications behind the argument that
some elements of our universe were not created by God.

The most crucial problem facing monotheistic religion is the source of evil. In polytheistic religions, evil can be blamed on wicked divinities. But if there is only one God and God is perceived as good and merciful, how can we explain the existence of evil in the world?

In my view, the Priestly description of Creation is an effort to solve this fundamental dilemma. The primeval elements *tohu, hoshekh,* and *tehom* all belong to the evil sphere.[22] Hence, the Priestly claim that these entities predated God's Creation is really a claim about primordial evil. The three elements comprising the preexistent cosmic substance are the roots (put another way, the substance) of the evil in the world. At the conclusion of the Priestly account of Creation, it is written: "And God saw all that He had made, and found it very good" (Gen. 1:31). All that God had made was very good. Evil was not made by God. It predated the Creation in Genesis 1! This conception is indeed unique to the Priestly school. In other sources in the Bible, we will find different conceptions about the source of evil.[23]

The Priestly account of Creation can thus be read as an effort to demythologize the ancient myth about the combat between God and evil, a combat alluded to throughout the Hebrew Bible:[24]

> Awake, awake, clothe yourself with splendor.
> O arm of the Lord!
> Awake as in days of old,
> As in former ages!
> It was you that hacked Rahab in pieces,
> That pierced the Dragon.
> It was you that dried up the Sea,
> The waters of the great deep;
> That made the abysses of the Sea
> A road the redeemed might walk. (Isa. 51:9–10)

> In that day the Lord will punish,
> With His great, cruel, mighty sword
> Leviathan the Elusive Serpent—
> Leviathan the Twisting Serpent;
> He will slay the Dragon of the sea. (Isa. 27:1)

These prophetic oracles reflect an ancient myth that was regularly recited among the peoples of the ancient Near East. In their epics, the primeval, serpentine dragon and the sea were combatants against the celestial pantheon. We still see reflections of this combat myth in the duality of the primordial elements retained in the Priestly account. We have on the one hand, "darkness over the surface of the deep," and on the other, "a wind from God sweeping over the water."[25] However, unlike the combat myth, the Priestly account of Creation depicts no struggle between the forces of good and evil. The evil elements are entirely passive.[26] God creates the world peacefully, without any struggle or war. When God says, "Let the water below the sky be gathered into one area, that the dry land may appear" (Gen. 1:9), the water does not rebel. Furthermore, as noted by Cassuto,[27] the fact that the only creatures mentioned by name in the Genesis 1 creation story are "the great sea monsters" (Gen 1:21) should be taken as a polemic. The author of Genesis 1 deliberately rejects the tradition of God's combat against the sea monsters.[28] The sea monsters are not independent evil forces. God creates them just as God creates every other creature; hence, there is no place for a struggle between them and God.

EVIL IN THE FLOOD STORY

_{p. 165}

According to the Priestly conception, God created the world literally out of primordial evil. God did not annihilate the primordial chaos, but rather transformed it.[29] Hence, in Rabbinic literature we find God compared to a king who founds his palace on top of rubbish and garbage.[30] Given enough time, bad smells, rats, and cockroaches penetrate the palace and spoil it. This is exactly what happened to the universe just before the Flood:

> The earth became corrupt before God; the earth was filled with lawlessness. When God saw how corrupt the earth was, for all flesh had corrupted its ways on earth... (Gen. 6:11–12)[31]

At the time of Creation, God seemingly swept primordial evil under the carpet. Looking at the perfect masterwork, God ignored its fundamental evil elements and set forth an ideal plan of peace—and vegetarianism—for all his creatures, saying:

> See, I give you every seed-bearing plant that is upon all the earth, and every tree that has seed-bearing fruit; they shall be yours for food. And to all the animals on land, to all the birds of the sky, and to everything that creeps on earth, in which there is the breath of life, [I give] all the green plants for food. (Gen. 1:29–30)

God presents a vegetarian diet for humans and animals. The lion should eat straw with the ox, and the cow and the bear can graze together. In this scheme, there is no violence, no killing, and no bloodshed. As we know, however, this ideal plan fell apart. Evil, which had been hidden in Eden under the beauty of flowers and trees, bursts out; all creatures become violent and begin to kill each other.[32] At that point God sees that all the earth has become corrupt and God decides to destroy it: "I have decided to put an end to all flesh, for the earth is filled with lawlessness because of them: I am about to destroy them with the earth" (Gen. 6:13).

After the Flood, God realizes that the original divine plan for an idyllic, peaceful existence on earth ignores the fundamental evil elements upon which the world was created. Hence, after the Flood, God allows the killing of animals for the sake of eating them, while forbidding the killing of man, who was created in God's image:

> Every creature that lives shall be yours to eat; as with the green grasses, I give you all these...But for your own life-blood I will require a reckoning...
> Whoever sheds the blood of man,
> By man shall his blood be shed;
> For in His image
> Did God make man. (Gen. 9:3–6)

The nature of the universe does not change after the Flood. The basic duality of good and evil is still present. The only change is God's awareness of the powerful influence of the primordial evil elements. God is now willing to tolerate bloodshed in the world, but God channels and restricts this violence.

YHWH VS. AZAZEL

The rituals of the Priestly cult also embodied this fundamental duality of the universe—the primordial evil along with the created good. The most important ritual in the Priestly Torah is the cleansing of the Tabernacle and the sending of the scapegoat to Azazel.[33] This ritual is to be performed during the holiest day in the year—the Day of Atonement. God commands Aaron:

> Aaron shall take the two he-goats and let them stand before the Lord at the entrance of the Tent of Meeting; and he shall place lots upon the two goats, one marked for the Lord and the other marked for Azazel. Aaron shall bring forward the goat designated by lot for the Lord, which he is to offer as a sin offering; while the goat designated by lot for Azazel shall be left standing alive before the Lord, to make expiation with it and to send it off to the wilderness for Azazel. (Lev. 16:7–10)

Azazel is not mentioned elsewhere in the Bible. In Rabbinic literature, there was an attempt to demythologize Azazel by making his name a geographical reference.[34] A similar point of view probably affected the spelling of the name. The spelling עזזאל,[35] Azaz-el (a mighty god) was transformed into עזאזל, Azazel, thus diminishing the depiction of Azazel as a divine being. Despite this, his image in this chapter in Leviticus is astonishing; he is represented as a counterpart on a par with God. The phrasing indicates a form of equality: "one marked for the Lord and the other marked for Azazel."

One might ask why it is here, in the holiest place and at the holiest time of the year, that the foundations of biblical monotheism are thus shaken. The answer is to be found in the meaning and aim of the Azazel ritual. The purpose of the ritual is atonement—cleansing the Tabernacle and cleansing the people of Israel. In order to purge their iniquities and sins, the Israelites must find an evil persona to accept their sins. The God of Israel, who is the source of good in the created world, could not possibly play this role. An apt representative of cosmic evil had to be found. The lot fell to Azazel and he was thus lifted up from the dust of ancient times and assigned the role of the Lord's counterpart, accepting all of Israel's evils and sins.

Seen in this light, the scapegoat is a tool of transportation. The priest loads the communal impurity and sins upon it: "Aaron shall lay both his hands upon the head of the live goat and confess over it all the iniquities and transgressions of the Israelites, whatever their sins, putting them on the head of the goat; and it shall be sent off to the wilderness" (Lev. 16:21). The ritual resembles rites disposing of impurity or illness known from ancient Hittite culture.[36] This role of the scapegoat is described in verse 22: "Thus the goat shall carry on it all their iniquities to an inaccessible region" The expression "solitary land" is the RSV translation for the Hebrew ארץ גזרה.

The root גזר can refer to the cutting of nonliving things,[37] but it can also refer to the cutting of a life, i.e., the death of a person or an animal.[38] Thus, *eretz gezera* can be interpreted with a material meaning, as a land with sharp and jagged mountains and rocks, or in a more abstract and metaphoric manner, as the "Land of Death."[39] This might support the assumption of scholars who wish to identify Azazel with Mot, the Canaanite god of death.[40] In Canaanite myth there is constant struggle between Baal, the god of fertility and rain, and Mot, the god of withering and death. Mot is characterized as living in the innards of the earth: "A pit is the throne on which (he) sits, / filth the land of his heritage." [41] Baal, by contrast, roams the visible world and takes whatever he delights in as his own:

> He loved a heifer in the pasture(s)
> a cow in the fields by the shore of the realm of death;
> he did lie with her seven and seventy times;
> she allowed (him) to mount eight and eighty times;

and she conceived and gave birth to a boy.
[Mightiest] Baal did clothe him with [his robe]...[42]

The struggle between Baal and Mot reflects the constant struggle in nature between life and death, fertility and withering.[43]

According to the Priestly writings, death is the most severe source of impurity.[44] Thus, if Azazel is to be identified with Mot the god of death, the contrast between YHWH and Azazel in Leviticus 16 can be perceived as a contrast between life and death, holiness and impurity. However, there are sharp differences between the Baal-Mot struggle and the YHWH-Azazel contrast. Unlike Mot, Azazel is a passive figure.[45] He does not fight against YHWH. Furthermore, the contrast between YHWH and Azazel is completely detached from the natural cycle of growth and withering. I have shown elsewhere[46] that in the original form of Leviticus 16 there was no indication of the date of the rite. The date of Yom Kippur, the tenth day of the seventh month (Lev. 16:29), is an addition to the original text.[47] I sugggest that this ambiguity regarding the date of the rite stems from a wish to detach it from the critical times of the agricultural year.

There is, then, a similarity between the general pictures of Genesis 1 and Leviticus 16. In both places we find a duality of good and evil, creative and destructive forces. Yet in both cases, there is neither struggle nor combat. Azazel, like *tehom*, is totally passive; neither is engaged in a war against God.[48]. The Priestly account of Genesis 1 is very much about separation. God separated between the good light and the darkness (1:4); God further separated the upper water from the lower water, and the sea from the earth (1:6–10). Similarly, the ritual of the Day of Atonement is about separation: throughout the entire year, the impurity of the Israelites accumulates within the sacred area of the Tabernacle. On the Day of Atonement, the impurity is driven into the "Land of Death" in the desert, leaving the Tabernacle clean and pure. As has been noted by scholars,[49] the description of Creation in

Genesis 1 parallels the Priestly account of the creation of the Tabernacle.[50] We may conclude by saying that the separation of good and evil, pure and impure, on the Day of Atonement in the Tabernacle, can be seen as a symbolic act reestablishing the original orderliness of the universe.

MORAL GOODNESS VS. EXISTENTIAL AND CULTIC GOODNESS

We have seen that the Priestly conception is marked by fundamental dichotomies: good and evil, light and darkness, holiness and impurity, YHWH and Azazel. How much is this dichotomy to be perceived in a moral sense? Is light morally good? And how about darkness (hoshekh), disorderly waste matter (tohu v'vohu), and watery depths (tehom)? Are they only symbols of chaotic and destructive forces or is there also a moral meaning attached to this symbolism? Finally, does the contrast between YHWH and Azazel bear moral significance, or is it only an existential or cultic opposition? In order to answer these questions we have first to look at the unique schema of revelation in the Priestly tradition.

The thought of the Priestly School centers on a sharp distincton between two essential periods of revelation. The first took place in the time of Creation and in the days of the Patriarchs. The second revelation took place during the Mosaic period.[51] During the most ancient times and down to the days of the Patriarchs, God was revealed through the names "Elohim" and "El-Shadday." Elohim maintains a closeness with creatures, especially with humanity. Elohim is depicted in the Priestly Torah as a personal god, creator of the world and of human beings, who sustains and cares for the created beings (Gen. 1:29–30) and is concerned with the moral behavior of humankind. In the Priestly story of the Flood, Elohim is described as punishing the entire universe, humanity in particular, because the earth had become corrupt (6:9–13). After the Flood, Elohim forges a covenant with Noah and with the entire universe (9:9–17), and later makes another covenant with Abraham.[52] The covenant with Noah expresses Elohim's concern for and commitment to the human race. Throughout this entire early period of humanity's existence, Elohim is painted in anthropomorphic colors. For example, we find in the first chapter of Genesis (1:26–7) the central idea that human beings were created in Elohim's image. The affinity suggested by such anthropomorphism expresses the intimate bond between God and humans in the earliest days of humankind.

When Moses steps onto the stage of history, it is the dawn of a new era, a complete break with all that came before. This change is symbolized by the revelation of a new name, the Tetragrammaton: YHWH. According to the Priestly conception, this name was unknown from the earliest times through the days of the Patriarchs. Thus God says to Moses: "I appeared to Abraham, Isaac, and Jacob as El-Shadday, but I did not make Myself known to them by My name YHWH" (Exod. 6:3).[53] In this chapter of Exodus, God reveals for the first time to Moses, and not the Patriarchs, the divine name. The chapter expresses a new essence of the Divine, one unknown to Noah, Abraham, Isaac, and Jacob. But what is this essence and how does it differ from the divine nature that was revealed to Adam, Noah, and the Patriarchs?

Earlier, we characterized the God of Genesis as a personal, legislating, moral god, who cares for his creatures and is close to them, and who, at times, is depicted in anthropomorphic terms. Here, in the second essential revelation, the picture is completely different. The divine nature associated with the name "YHWH" is impersonal, free of any marks of personality.[54] It is never described anthropomorphically in the Priestly Torah. There are no physical dimensions depicted, such as "the eyes of the Lord," "the hand of the Lord," and the like.[55] But it is not only the physical dimension that is absent; there is also no mention of a personal or psychological dimension. There are no descriptions of divine wrath or jealousy in the Priestly Torah.[56]

In order to see the gap between the Priestly Torah and the other biblical sources in this respect, we must note that the descriptions of divine punishments differ in these sources. Compare the vivid and anthropomorphic picture of God's wrath in 2 Samuel 6:7 ("The Lord was incensed at Uzza. And God struck him down on the spot") to the Priestly description of the death of Nadab and Abihu in Leviticus 10:2 ("And fire came forth from the Lord and consumed them; thus they died at the instance of the Lord"). The Priestly Torah avoids any anthropomorphism or personalized description in its characterization of the punishing agent (fire) and avoids direct attribution of the fire to an action of God.

As a rule, there are almost no positive, precise statements made concerning God in the Priestly Torah. The Priestly writers exhibit a general unwillingness to characterize God with any attributes. Throughout the Priestly writings, from the time of the revelation to Moses and onward, nothing is written about God's essence, nor is God associated with any attribute. Even the adjective "holy," so commonly applied to God in other parts of the Bible, is never applied to God in the Priestly writings. There is, moreover, almost no activity attributed to God. The Lord's only activities concern the giving of commandments: speaking, addressing, commanding. Nothing more. The distinction between these two realms of the Divine, that of the God of Genesis and that of the God of Moses, is extremely strict. As soon as the name "YHWH," the Lord, appears, the previous names disappear; they almost are no longer used. Not once in the Priestly Torah is there a juxtaposition of the names "Elohim" and "YHWH," for they constitute two contradictory manifestations.[57]

The contents of the revelation also differ markedly in the two cases. The names "Elohim" and "El-Shadday" are associated with commandments and moral behavior. The aspect of divinity associated with the name "YHWH," however, is wholly devoid of moral content; it is neither a moral legislator, nor an overseer of morality.[58] Indeed YHWH is not tied to morality at all. This feature is epitomized in the corpus of ritual law that constitutes the heart of the Priestly School's writings. There is not a single moral commandment among them. The priests resort to a discussion of moral-legal values only in Leviticus 5:20–26. This is a unique case in which there is an overlap between moral and sacral issues: a man robs or extorts something from his fellow, and then, in addition to the moral transgression, takes a false oath—that is, commits a cultic transgression. This is the one case in which the priests occupy themselves with moral-legal matters; they force the transgressor to return the stolen property. Were it not for the added element of the false oath, the priests would not have discussed this case; it would have lain beyond the purview of their jurisdiction.[59]

It is important to emphasize that the priests' avoidance of such issues is not a case of moral apathy. According to the Priestly School, the moral aspect of divinity *was* central in the early days of humanity, down through the time of the Patriarchs. In switching to a new name for God in the revelation to Moses, they are making a distinction between two aspects of divinity. On the one hand, we have Elohim, the Creator, who maintains the world providentially and bestows moral instruction, and to whom man feels a closeness and affinity. On the other hand, the Divine can be something mysterious, intangible, standing beyond reason and morality. This feature of divinity, exceeding reason and morality, is designated by the name "YHWH." Rudolph Otto[60] named this latter aspect of the Divine "the Numinous," the element of the Divine that is essentially other and different from human reason and experience.

It appears that the priests considered this mysterious aspect hierarchically superior to the earlier aspect, for they describe a process of gradual revelation. In the beginning, the divine contents symbolized by the names "Elohim" and "El Shadday," such as justice and morality, reveal themselves—contents that are to a certain degree, common to humanity.

According to the Priestly source, humanity forges a covenant with Elohim—God the Creator, the moral overseer who looks after our well-being and sustenance. At a later stage, an additional content is uniquely revealed to Moses and to the Children of Israel, one that stands above the previous manifestation and completes it. This is the aspect symbolized by the name "YHWH."

Knowing this distinction between Elohim and YHWH, we can now return to our questions about the moral significance of the basic dichotomy between good and evil and holiness and impurity in the Priestly Torah. We may see now that the writers posit a difference regarding this issue between the period of Genesis and the period of Moses. In Genesis, there are indeed moral implications to the existence of the primordial evil elements. After all, these elements led to the corruption of the earth in the time of the Flood. This corruption is designated as חמס, a word with a clear moral meaning.[61] However, the contrast between YHWH and Azazel—of holiness and impurity, of life and death—in Leviticus 16 has no moral meaning. The term "Holiness" in the Priestly Torah,[62] is a cultic term only, without any moral significance.[63] In the same way, the contrast between Azazel and YHWH, which is a contrast of death and life, does not pose a moral contrast, but rather an existential one.[64]

MATERIAL VS. SPIRITUAL BLESSING

We can arrive at some understanding of the Priestly Torah's idea of blessing through a brief comparative study of how other elements in Israelite religion took over the Canaanite emphasis on material blessing. We will focus on the image of God's sanctuary as it is transmitted in several prophets and Psalms and contrast these with the image of the Tabernacle in the Priestly Torah. The Cannanite materials show how much Israel's religion owed to an affinity with its neighbors;

but ultimately, I will show how much the Priestly Torah chose to separate itself from this influence.

El, the head of the Canaanite pantheon, is a moral god, full of compassion and mercy. He is like Elohim in that he is also depicted as the creator of earth and of all creatures.[65] But he also bears a similarity to the depiction of YHWH in the Priestly tradition.

The cultic center, where YHWH's presence becomes manifest, is designated in the Priestly writings as "tent" and "Tabernacle." Scholars have long noted that similar terms are to be found in the description of El's residence in Ugarit, which predates the Priestly strand of the Bible by about 700 years:[66]

> Then she set her face,
> Toward El at the sources of the two rivers,
> In the midst of the fountains of the double-deep.
> She opened the domed tent[67] of El and entered,
> The Tabernacle[68] of King, Father of Years.[69]

According to this passage, El's abode is in tent and Tabernacle, as is the abode of YHWH in the Priestly Torah.

The link between the sanctuary and the sea was symbolized in the Jerusalem Temple by the "molten sea,"which stood in the courtyard of the Temple built by Solomon (1 Kings 7:23). The relation of this cultic object to ancient Near Eastern mythology has been described by Bible scholar Jon Levenson:

> We have already had occasion to note the general story in the ancient Near East, which describes the creation of the world and the establishment of cosmic order as a consequence of a god's defeat of the sea. The sea embodies chaos; its defeat and containment constitute order. In fact, they do more than that: they also legitimize the victor's claim to kingship and initiate the construction of his royal palace, his temple. In light of this theory, to which allusions are made in the Hebrew Bible, only with YHWH as the triumphant deity, it is not surprising to find a model of the sea, now utterly tame, within the Temple precincts.[70]

The Temple, in the view being advanced here, gave concrete form to the mythic substructure of Israel's religion, which was derived from the mythological religions of the peoples among whom Israel settled.

The description of El's tent located at the sources of two rivers is also echoed in biblical descriptions of the Jerusalem Temple. In several passages in the prophets, we read about the source, spring, or river that will run out of the Temple at the end of days.

> In that day, fresh water shall flow from Jerusalem, part of it to the Eastern Sea and part to the Western Sea, throughout the summer and winter. (Zech. 14:8)

> And in that day,
> The mountains shall drip with wine,
> The hills shall flow with milk,
> And all the watercourses of Judah shall flow with water;
> A spring shall issue from the House of the Lord
> And shall water the Wadi of the Acacias. (Joel 4:18)[71]

In the Book of Isaiah we have the following passage that similarly looks ahead to a secure future for Israel, in a way that reflects the Tent of El with its setting of stream and waters:[72]

> Look upon Zion, the city of our appointed feasts (קרית מועדנו)
> Your eyes will see Jerusalem a quiet habitation, an immovable tent (אהל בל-יצען)
> Whose stakes will never be plucked up,
> Nor will any of its cords be broken,
> But there the Lord in majesty will be for us,
> A place of broad streams,
> Where no galley with oars can go, nor stately ship can pass. (Isa. 33:20–22)

The Canaanite imagery of El's sanctuary sitting atop a stream becomes an aspect of the Israelite experience of God—as "a place of broad streams," though not for literal boat traffic. And the holy city itself, where God is said to reside, is compared to a tent. Unlike the ordinary variety, it has become "immovable"—that is, steady and secure, full of the blessings attendant upon a stable life. Jon Levenson has noted of this passage that the term קרית מועדנו is parallel to אהל מועד—the "Tent of Meeting."

> *Qiryat mo'adenu* of v. 20 should be translated "the city of our en-
> counter," referring to the encounter with God in the tent in the
> wilderness. Probably, the term *mo'adenu*...means here both "en-
> counter, assembly" and "feast, pilgrim festival....The epic idea of
> the Tent of Encounter, one with deep pre-Israelite roots, has been
> transferred onto the complex of Zion tradition inception.[73]

The tent of the Canaanite El is a source of blessing, fertility, and life. Similarly, Zion and its shrine are depicted in the
Psalms as a source of good and material blessing.[74] Thus
Psalm 128:5 reads, "May the Lord bless you from Zion; may
you share the prosperity of Jerusalem all the days of your
life." This aspect of material blessing is even more fully manifest in Psalm 133:

> *How good and how pleasant it is*
> *that brothers dwell together.*
> *It is like fine oil on the head*
> *running down onto the beard,*
> *the beard of Aaron,*
> *that comes down over the collar of his robe;*
> *like the dew of Hermon*
> *that falls upon the mountains of Zion.*
> *There the Lord ordained blessing,*
> *everlasting life.*

Though the oil on Aaron's head is the oil of Priestly anointment,[75] this psalm does not stem from the circle of the
Priestly Torah. The Psalms were connected to the Levites,
not to the priests, and they generally belong to popular religion and not to the Priestly sphere. The High Priest and his
robes symbolize (for the presumably Levitical author of this
psalm) fertility and blessing. The shrine of Zion is the place
par excellence of blessing, fertility, and life, just as the
Canaanite shrines of El and Baal are.[76]

> While we have drawn some connections between Israelite images
> of the central sanctuary and Canaanite myth, it needs to be re-
> membered that the Priestly Tent of Meeting, as described by the
> Priestly Torah, is very different from either the tent of El, or the
> shrine of YHWH in Zion. In the Priestly tent, to be discussed in
> greater detail in Chapter 5, there is neither river nor spring, nor a

symbol of the sea. Unlike the description of Zion's shrine in Isaiah as "an immovable tent, / Whose stakes will never be plucked up, / Nor will any of it cords be broken,"[77] the very essence of the Priestly tent is its mobility. This tent wanders with Israel in the Sinai desert. The very fact that this shrine is portable and constantly moves from place to place prevents the creation of any myth with regard to its location.[78] As another scholar has written, The Priestly writing has no mention of a particular place, except that YHWH speaks with Israel from above the cover of the ark, from between the two cherubim. The ark with its cover and cherubim is not a place, however, but a piece of cult-furniture, which, like the Tabernacle in which it is set, is portable and moves about with the people. The last vestiges of a Canaanite idea of the divine presence, linked to an earthly dwelling place through which the land is blessed, have now disappeared."[79]

Psalm 133, quoted above, depicts Aaron as a symbol of blessing and prosperity. However, according to the Priestly conception, the cultic rituals performed in the Tabernacle do not contain a single ceremony aimed at attaining human prosperity, whether in the form of agricultural plenty or military victory.[80] The sole purpose of Priestly worship is to comply with God's decree and to attain some proximity to God. It is therefore possible to summarize the essence of the Priestly tent of meeting and its worship with the following verse from the Psalms: "As for me, nearness to God is good; I have made the Lord God my refuge, that I may recount all Your works" (73:28). The goodness of the Lord's proximity, in the Priestly view, is spiritual rather than material.

Here again we see the difference between Elohim, the God of Genesis, and YHWH, the God of Moses, according to the Priestly Torah. While Elohim is the Creator who supports all his creatures with food (Gen. 1:29–30), YHWH is never depicted in the Priestly Torah as a source of material blessing. The shift in the revelation of the divine names actually represents a shift between two types of religious life. The religion of Genesis is what we might call the popular or basic level of faith, where God is the moral creator who establishes social order and sustains life and food. Upon this basis, the

Priestly Torah constructs its higher, or elitist, level of faith, which is characterized by the recognition of the name of YHWH. With the revelation of the sublime dimension of God represented through the name "YHWH," Moses and Israel can attain religious perfection. This aspect of the deity cannot be described through any anthropomorphic imagery, transcends reason and morality, and is independent of reward and punishment. Only with the revelation of this religious truth can the Israelites recognize their true status and be transformed into people who "worship through love" without expecting any material recompense for their deeds.

COVENANT AND PACT

The Priestly Torah reflects the evolution of Israelite religious consciousness—from the basic religious level of the time of Genesis to the higher religious level of the time of Moses—in its shift from the term "covenant" (ברית) to the term "pact" (עדות). Earlier I noted that the term "covenant" is quite commonly used to refer to the period of creation and of the Patriarchs. This term expresses a reciprocal relationship: God promises something to humanity and humanity, in return, is required to maintain moral behavior, which God oversees. When someone keeps moral commandments, God cares for that person, keeps him or her from harm, and so forth. However, when God reveals the name "YHWH" to Moses, the concept of covenant disappears completely from the Priestly writing. According to the Priestly Torah, there was no reciprocal covenant between God and the Children of Israel at Mt. Sinai. As a result, the Priestly Torah does not call the two tablets given at the Sinai revelation "tablets of the covenant," as we find them called in other biblical sources, but rather, 'edut, "the Pact" (Exod. 25:16). The very term "covenant" and "tablets of the covenant" are completely absent from the revelation at Sinai, according to the Priestly tradition.

Different explanations have been given to explain the absence of covenant (ברית) from the Priestly account of Sinai. We may divide them into three main categories:

SOLUTIONS FOCUSING ON THE EDITORIAL LEVEL

According to this theory, the description of the covenant at Sinai was omitted, or never composed, by the writers of the Priestly Torah since the covenant was already described in earlier sources of the Torah.[81] However, as one scholar has asked, is it possible that such an important concept as "covenant" would be dropped from the Priestly account of the revelation at Sinai for technical reasons?[82]

IDEOLOGICAL EXPLANATIONS

Some scholars find that the authors of the Priestly Torah objected fundamentally to the Sinai covenant in favor of the Abrahamic covenant of grace.[83] We may categorically reject this view, since the Abrahamic covenant was not a covenant of grace, according to the Priestly Torah. Abraham was asked by God to "walk in My ways and be blameless" (Gen. 17:1–2) as a condition of the covenant. Moreover, to attribute to the Priestly Torah, which is full of commandments and rules, the opposition to the divine dimension of command would indeed be a great distortion.[84]

Another ideological explanation supposes that the Priestly Torah was composed during the Second Temple Period and argues that the omission of "covenant" was an expression of a desire at that time to detach the laws from their historical context in order to ensure that they withstand the vagaries of time.[85] While I agree with the emphasis on the absolute nature of the laws in the Priestly Torah and their presentation as the incontestable will of God, I find it hard to accept the theory that removing the idea of covenant could ensure the independence of the laws from transient historical institutions. After all, the laws are tied to the cultic Tent of Meeting, an institution far more susceptible to the changes wrought by time than relationship to a divine covenant.

DENYING THAT THE IDEA OF COVENANT IS MISSING FROM THE PRIESTLY TORAH

This theory relies on Exodus 31:13–17, in which the Sabbath is ordained as a sign of the covenant, immediately following the Sinaitic revelation.[86] In my view,[87] these verses in Exodus do not originate in the Priestly Torah, but rather in the Holiness School that has, as we will see below, a different approach to the whole issue of covenant.

THE ASSYRIAN ANALOGY

Thus, we have to look for another explanation for the absence of the covenant from the Sinai in the Priestly Torah. According to the Priestly source, the Sinaitic revelation was the communication of a pact (עדות), which was placed in the Ark of the Pact (ארון העדות),[88] the Priestly term for the Ark of the Covenant. In order to demonstrate the difference between the terms "covenant" and "pact," it is necessary to turn our attention briefly to the history of the Assyrian empire.

For many centuries, the Assyrian kingdom and its rulers, like many other kingdoms in the ancient Near East, made covenants with other rulers. These were made either with kings of equal standing, with whom they formed relationships of reciprocity and equality, or more frequently, with lesser kings, known as vassals.[89] In these vassalage arrangements, the Assyrian ruler—like Hittite and Babylonian rulers—was committed to protecting the the vassal king, if the vassal in turn was loyal and paid tributes to the Assyrian king. Such treaties were fully bilateral.

When Assyria became an empire in the eighth century B.C.E. (in fact it is the first empire we know of in the ancient Near East), its kings ceased making covenants. They became the sole rulers of the region, gaining complete dominion over all the other nations, with the Assyrian king gathering kingdoms, as Isaiah says, "as one gathers abandoned eggs" (10:14). The Assyrians needed a new term to describe their relations with the nations they now governed, and they chose the term *ade*, which they coined from the Aramaic term for pact, עדות.[90]

When the Assyrian king entered into a relationship of *ade* with a certain kingdom, he issued harsh decrees commanding loyalty to the Assyrians, the breaking of which incurred heavy penalties. He did not commit to anything in return. This was an explicitly unilateral agreement, in which the side that issued the *ade* was not bound in any way.[91]

Just as the Assyrians had two kinds of treaties at different periods, depending on their relative power as an empire, so the Priestly Torah distinguishes between the early period of humanity, including the days of the Patriarchs, an era in which there was a bilateral relationship based on mutual commitment by God and man, and the post-Mosaic period, in which there is a unilateral relationship of pact. In the latter period, it is God who decrees, God who demands of human beings the observance of strict commandments. Human beings are not God's partners, and ought not, then, expect any advantage or reward for their deeds. Thus, we do not find in the Priestly Torah any promise of reward for keeping the commandments.[92] The commandments are not part of a commercial deal; God does not commit to give anything to human beings. Instead, God demands that human beings worship God for the sake of worship, without any expectation of future benefit.

In this regard, the Priestly Torah is unlike the other strata of the Bible, in which the concepts of the covenant and of the reciprocity between human beings and God play a central role. The Priestly Torah is unique, in that it grounds the relationship between Israel and God in the concept of pact.[93]

The only exception to this rule, where the term "covenant" appears in the Priestly Torah after the revelation of the name "YHWH," occurs in Leviticus 2:13: "You shall season your every offering of meal with salt; you shall not omit from your meal offering the salt of your covenant with God; with all your offerings you must offer salt." Salt also appears as a symbol of the covenant with God elsewhere in the Bible (Num. 18:19; 2 Chron. 13:5), as well as in neighboring ancient cultures.[94] Because the symbol מלח ברית ("salt of covenant") is itself the reason for the law requiring the salting of sacrifices, the Priestly Torah is compelled to use the term "covenant" here, although it conflicts with its decision to restrict the use of the term "covenant" to the period of Genesis. The Priestly writers were indeed aware of this deviation from their ideology and thus employed here, exceptionally, Elohecha—an inflected form of the name "Elohim"—rather than the name "YHWH," which is used regularly in the period of Moses. Through this choice of divine name, the Priestly Torah expressed its view that the covenant concept properly refers to the relation of God and humanity in the Genesis period, when the name "Elohim" was widely used.

A deep chasm lies between the faith of Genesis and the Patriarchs and the faith of Moses and Israel. According to the Priestly Torah, it was the revelation of the name "YHWH" that resulted in profound changes in religious awareness. It marked a turning point in the development of faith and resulted in a reappraisal of Israel's status before God. The systematic, selective use of certain specific names of God in the Genesis period and others in the period of Moses and the replacement of the term "covenant" by the term "pact" are indications of how the Priestly Torah signals these changes in worldview.

In the level of faith characteristic of Genesis, humanity perceives itself as the summit and purpose of Creation. Contrary to the Babylonian myth which views humans as tools for the use of the gods, the Priestly creation story depicts the submission of heaven and earth and all their array to *human* control; this relationship is the purpose of the creation of the universe.[95] Thus, God is portrayed primarily through divine actions vis-a-vis God's creatures; humans, in particular. God is primarily a creator, supervisor, legislator, and righteous judge. Human beings, the crown of Creation, stand erect before God, engaged in a direct, bilateral relationship with the Creator, based on comprehensible principles of morality and recompense. This closeness between humans and God determines how the encounters between God and humanity are described in the Genesis period: God is depicted as human-like in both image and actions.

The revelation of the name "YHWH" results in a theological Copernican revolution. Moses, and Israel with him, learns to recognize the essence of divine nature, which is unrelated to Creation or to humanity and its needs. This dimension cannot be comprehended fully by humans and surpasses the limits of morality and reason, since morality and its laws are only meaningful in relation to human society and human understanding. The aspect of divine essence that surpasses reason and morality—the numinous element—is represented by the name "YHWH." The divine nature associated with the name "YHWH" is impersonal—free of any marks of personality and anthropomorphic language.[96] Human beings, when faced with the holy, no longer see themselves as the center of the universe, nor do they evaluate God from the narrow point of view of their own needs and desires. Thus, we never find in the sacred sphere any explicit request by humans for the fulfillment of their needs nor any expectation of divine salvation.

Although the Priestly Torah concentrates on how humans can encounter the majesty of the holy and places the revelation to Moses and the sacred enclosure itself in the realm of the numinous, this does not imply alienation from the religious value of morality and social justice. The Priestly Torah represents the Genesis period as a realm regulated by enduring principles of justice and righteousness. Morality is the law of Creation, binding on all created beings and supervised and enforced by God. The revelation of the name "YHWH" to Moses and Israel neither invalidates the moral order of Genesis nor detracts from its importance. According to the Priestly Torah, no new moral command is entrusted to the nation at

Sinai, since the Sinai revelation focuses on the dimension of God that surpasses morality. But this only reinforces the ongoing validity of the universal moral laws of Genesis. Israel, as part of humanity, is subject to these moral laws, just as Abraham, forebear of Israel, was obligated to uphold the moral perfection or "blamelessness" exemplified by Noah, forebear of postdiluvian humanity (Gen. 6:9,17:1). The faith of the Genesis and patriarchal period is the foundation on which the content of the revelation to Moses is built; the later revelation is designed to deepen and broaden religious understanding, not to subvert or negate it.

Unlike the faith of Genesis, which is the heritage of all humanity, the revelation of the name "YHWH" and its faith contents are the possession of Israel alone. According to the Priestly Torah, the Gentiles do not know the name "YHWH" or the divine dimension symbolized by it. This is expressed in the words that the Priestly Torah places in the mouth of the magicians in response to the plague of lice: "This is the finger of God!" (Elohim) (Exod. 8:14) The Egyptian magicians call God "Elohim" even though the name "YHWH" has already been revealed to Moses and Israel. Their choice indicates that the name "YHWH" is unknown to the Gentiles and not for their use. Their description of God's action, employing the extremely anthropomorphic image "the finger of God," accords with the anthropomorphic language used to describe the acts of God in the Genesis period.[97]

The Priestly Torah, thus, has a unique view regarding four fundamental matters: the preexistent evil substance incorporated into Creation, the role of anthropomorphism in our understanding of God, the revelation to Moses, and the covenant.

While other strands of the Bible see God in primeval combat with mythic beings, the Priestly Torah sees preexistent evil elements as unavoidably part of God's repertoire of creation, entirely passive and unable to challenge God for hegemony. All that God created was good, though subject to degradation through violence and cultic impurity. The sphere of evil is completely detached from God and stands in a polar relationship to God. This polarity is reflected in the description of Creation in Genesis 1 and in the Azazel rite in Leviticus 16. In the yearly ceremony for cleansing the Tabernacle, the primordial evil elements are given their due in the representation of Azazel, and Azazel has no choice but to accept the cultic impurity that is transferred to him. The realms of God and Azazel are at that point completely separate and the holiness of the divinely created realm is assured.

While popular legends and prophetic visions attribute images to YHWH, the Priestly Torah avoids all use of anthropomorphism in describing God or God's cult. In contradiction to the other sources of the Pentateuch and the prophetic writings, which claim that the revelation to Moses included a moral code, the Priestly Torah restricts the revelation to the cultic sphere. As opposed to the other strata of the Pentateuch and the prophetic writings, which assert the bilateral relationship between God and Israel based on the making of a covenant, the Priestly Torah espouses a one-sided relationship represented through the term 'edut. But according to the Priestly Torah, the concepts and values absent from the revelation to Moses were presented in the period of Genesis. There we find God described in anthropomorphic terms: God as a moral judge, and God who establishes covenants with his Creation and with the Patriarchs. Thus, the faith concepts prevalent elsewhere in the Pentateuch and in the words of the prophets serve, for the Priestly Torah, as the basic religious experience. Upon this basis, the Priestly Torah constructs its higher level of faith, characterized by the revelation of the name "YHWH." This higher level is expressed in a sphere of devotion and holiness centered in the sacred area of the Priestly Tabernacle.

CHAPTER THREE

Knowing Good and Evil: God and Humanity in J's Story of Beginnings

W HILE THE PRIESTLY TORAH, OFTEN ABBREVIATED SIM-
PLY as P, argues that the name "YHWH" was not
known before the revelation to Moses, the J
source uses the name "YHWH" in the period before Moses.
It seems that the main argument between the two sources is
whether there is a possibility of full divine revelation before
Israel. J argues that God was fully revealed from the time of
Creation, but according to P, the complete revelation did not
take place before the time of Moses and the name "YHWH"
is not known outside of Israel.

In addition to this theological debate, there is also a great
difference between the Priestly and non-Priestly conception
of evil, its source and its role in the universe. We recall that
the Priestly School saw evil as a primordial entity, which
was not created by God and predated God's activity as Creator. Every thing that was created by God was good and perfect. The imperfection of the universe is a result of the
continuing impact of the preexistent evil elements. In J's account of Creation (Gen. 2:4b–24), we have a completely

different picture. God's Creation is imperfect. Whereas in the Priestly account, God looks at his work and sees that it is perfectly good (Gen. 1:31), J tells us that God's first reaction to his Creation was: "It is not good for man to be alone" (Gen. 2:18). According to J, evil, and the serpent, which is the symbol of evil, were created by God. After the statement "it is not good for man to be alone," we would expect that God would then create a mate for man, but instead he formed the beasts and birds and brought them to the man (2:19). Following the insight of the Book of Jubilees,[1] we may assume that God wanted man to be aware of his loneliness by exposing him to the possibilities of companionship for him in the animal world. It is only after the absence of a mate is felt not just by God, but also by the man—"but for Adam no fitting helper was found" (2: 20)—that the woman is created. Here again, we see the difference between P and J. While in P both male and female are created at the same time as a part of the divine plan (1: 27), in J, the creation of the woman is a result of the feeling of some absence in Creation that only she could fill.

Once the man and his wife are together in the Garden of Eden, they walk about the Garden naked, since they are like young children, unashamed of their nakedness (Gen. 2:25).[2] In the following verse, the serpent is introduced to the story: "Now the serpent was the shrewdest of all the wild beasts that the Lord God had made" (3:1). Serpents (נחשים) and sea monsters (תנינים) are sometimes synonymous in the Hebrew Bible.[3] The fact that the serpent is presented here as one of the creatures made by God should be compared to the statement in P's account that the sea monsters were created by God (Gen. 1:21). The cunning serpent seduces the woman to eat the forbidden fruit by telling her: "You are not going to die, but God knows that as soon as you eat of it your eyes will be opened and you will be like divine beings who know good and bad" (3:4–5). The serpent describes the knowledge of good and evil as a divine quality. This statement is affirmed later by God himself who says: "Now that the man has become like one of us, knowing good and bad" (3:22).

What is it to know good and evil and why should it be conceived as a divine quality? Immediately after eating the forbidden fruit, the man and woman become aware of their nakedness: "Then the eyes of both of them were opened, and they perceived that they were naked" (3:7). This might lead to the thought that "knowing good and evil" implies sexual awareness.[4] However, it is difficult to fully identify "knowing good and evil" with sexuality. This term was described in God's own speech as a divine quality. Since the God of Israel is not involved in any real sexual activity as represented in the Bible, how could sexual awareness be described as a divine quality? Yet, we cannot negate the fact that humans' using their sexual awareness appropriately is clearly an important element throughout the Bible in "knowing good and evil." In order to clarify the concept of "knowing good and evil"[5] we must look at other occurrences of this expression.

While describing the sin of the spies, the Book of Deuteronomy says: "Moreover, your little ones who you said would be carried off, your children who do not yet know good from bad, they shall enter it" (1:39). We can infer that the lack of knowledge distinguishing between good and evil is to be associated with childhood.[6] This impression can be supported by the story of Solomon's dream in 1 Kings. Solomon presents himself as a young child "but I am a young lad, with no experience in leadership" (3:7). He then asks God to give him "an understanding mind to judge Your people, to distinguish between good and bad" (3:9). It appears that knowledge of good and evil also includes the ability to make moral judgments, something that young children lack.

We may conclude that before the eating of the forbidden fruit the man and the woman were in an infantile stage. They lacked both sexual awareness and moral judgment. The eating of the fruit is actually a process of growing from childhood to maturity. According to J, it is only through disobedience and rebellion that this maturity can be achieved.[7]

Thus, the Eden story should not be perceived primarily as a story of "fall" or "original sin."[8] It is true that Adam and Eve disobeyed the divine commandment and were punished for their disobedience. However, it is also true that Adam and Eve did not yet have "knowledge of good and evil." When they made their decision to disobey God, they lacked moral judgment and they also had no sexual awareness. We can see them as having the intellectual awareness of very young children.[9] It is hard to believe that God wanted them to stay at this undeveloped stage forever. Otherwise, why had God planted the tree of knowledge in the Garden? Why did God put the serpent in the Garden? It seems that God's hidden wish was to help the man and woman to grow up and become like God, who knows good and evil.

The serpent, the arch representative of evil, is described in J as merely one of "the wild beasts that the Lord God had made" (Gen. 3:1). In J's account, evil is a part of God's Creation. The serpent's role is to lead Adam and Eve to acquire a full consciousness of being human and thus *become* like God. Unlike the Priestly tradition, where human beings are created in the image of God (i.e., were created like God), in J, humans acquire their divine quality only with the help of evil. And so in J, evil is the leaven in the dough, as one of the talmudic Rabbis put it, without which there could be no fermentation.[10]

Why is the knowledge of good and evil perceived as a divine matter? We can get some further insight when we continue to read the story of Solomon's dream mentioned above. Immediately after the dream we are told about the two harlots who came to the king (1 Kings 3:16–27). When Solomon managed to find out which one was truly the mother of the baby, he impressed his people greatly: "When all Israel heard the decision that the king had rendered, they stood in awe of the king; for they saw that he possessed divine wisdom to execute justice" (1 Kings 3:28). The king's ability to discern between good and evil and to render justice is a divine wisdom given to the king in order to enable him to determine and implement justice. We get the same impression from the story of the wise woman of Tekoa, who says to David, "my lord the king is like an angel of God, understanding everything, good and bad" (2 Samuel 14:17). In this story also, the context of the saying about the angelic wisdom to discern good and evil and render justice is a complicated issue.[11]

The idea that the king is chosen and helped by the gods to make justice in the land is a common motif in the ancient Near East.[12] We can also find in these ancient cultures the claim that the king is created in the image of the God.[13] Scholars have noted that the Priestly Torah democratizes this motif, with P describing all human beings as created in the image of God.[14] We see now that J moves along the same democratizing path; the knowledge of good and evil, which is the essence of divine wisdom, is given by the eating of the forbidden fruit not just to a king, but to all humanity.

Yet in the two biblical traditions there is a marked difference in the transference of divine qualities to human beings. In P, this is part of the well-planned creation process, but in the J story, by contrast, it is done through rebellion and sin, and is therefore a cause for continuous tension between God and humans. The fact that humans have acquired the divine knowledge of good and evil is a threat[15] to the heavenly "family," God and his angels:

> And the Lord God said, "Now that the man has become like one of us, knowing good and bad, what if he should stretch out his hand and take also from the tree of life and eat, and live forever!" So the Lord God banished him from the Garden of Eden, to till the soil from which he was taken. He drove the man out, and stationed east of the Garden of Eden the cherubim and the fiery ever-turning sword, to guard the way to the tree of life. (Gen. 3:22–24)

After "the man has become like one of us, knowing good and bad," the only thing that differentiates the human being from God is mortality. This explains why the first humans

41

must be expelled from the Garden—in order to prevent them from acquiring immortality and fully closing the gap between them and the divine beings.

The role of the cherubim in J's story is to separate humans from divinity, to be an entity between them: not God and yet not human. How different this is from the role of the cherubim in P! In P, the cherubim are the symbol of the presence of God among humans. As figurines placed above the Ark of the Pact, they define the location where God meets Moses: "There I will meet with you, and I will impart to you—from above the cover, from between the two cherubim that are on top of the Ark of the Pact—all that I will command you concerning the Israelite people" (Exod. 25:22).

A third image of the guarding cherub is to be found in Ezekiel, where the wise king of Tyre is seen as a cherub who once sat in the Garden of Eden in God's holy mountain:

> *I created you as a cherub*
> *With outstretched shielding wings;*
> *And you resided on God's holy mountain.*
> *You walked among stones of fire. (Ezek. 28:14)*

The prophet blames the king, however, because of his arrogant and pretentious claim to divine status. For the king had proclaimed, "I am a god; I sit enthroned like a god in the heart of the seas" (Ezek. 28:2). In the prophecy that Ezekiel directs against him, the king-cherub is expelled from the Garden because of his sins:

> *By the greatness of your guilt,*
> *Through the dishonesty of your trading,*
> *You desecrated your sanctuaries.*
> *So I made a fire issue from you,*
> *And it has devoured you;*
> *I have reduced you to ashes on the ground,*
> *In the sight of all who behold you. (Ezek. 28:18)*

Despite the differences in context between J and Ezekiel, we can discern a common theme: when a human is trying to obliterate the border between himself or herself and God, that person is expelled from paradise.[16] In Ezekiel, we sense an objection to the tradition of sacral kingship of the ancient Near East; no longer can the king, no matter how wise, claim divine status. In J, it is not a king, but an ordinary man and woman who are precluded from claiming divine immortality for themselves. Ironically, this hard and fast division between God and humans comes into play just after the first humans attain a different kind of quasi-divine stature, by coming into the knowledge of good and evil.

CAIN AND ABEL

One of the main elements of the ideology of sacral kingship was the conception of the king being represented as a son of the gods. In Egypt, the Pharaoh was perceived as being born through the union of his mother, the queen, with a god.[17] In Mesopotamia, the relationship was perceived in a more metaphorical way, and the term "son of the gods" expressed special care and protection, rather than physical parenthood.[18] The Israelite king was also described as a "Son of God."[19] This motif is also democratized in J's story. Immediately after the expulsion from the Garden, the man "knew" Eve, his wife, and she gave birth: "Now the man knew his wife Eve, and she conceived and bore Cain, saying, "I have gained a male child with the help of the Lord" (Gen. 4:1).[20]

This saying of Eve's probably has some mythological origin. According to some scholars, we see here the footprints of the goddess, mother of life, who took part with the supreme god in the production of humans.[21] However, in the context of J's story, Eve's saying should be interpreted in a different way: After the expulsion from Eden, there is no longer any direct connection between humanity and the Divine. God does not speak to Adam and Eve ever again. Eve tries to use the naming of her son to form a new contact between herself and God. She describes a partnership between God and herself in creating the newborn baby, Cain. Her saying can be seen as a reply to the last words that she heard from God:

> *I will make most severe*
> *Your pangs in childbearing;*
> *In pain shall you bear children.*
> *Yet your urge shall be for your husband,*
> *And he shall rule over you. (Gen. 3:16)*

God stresses the pain of childbearing. Eve replies by describing birth as a new, positive creation. God says that she would be subjected to her husband; Eve replies by taking her husband out of the picture; it is God and she who are responsible for the great event of the creation of a new human. She does not mention Adam at all.

The description of Cain as an offspring of God and Eve reminds us very much of the Egyptian conception of the Pharaohs as being born through the union of the queen and a god. J takes this royal motif and applies it to the firstborn human child, who, in a sense, becomes paradigmatic for all future children. With this narrative choice, J democratizes the royal concept of the "Son of God," just as J did with the motif of royal divine wisdom

When the child Cain grows up, he becomes the founder of sacrificial worship[22] by bringing an offering to the Lord. No explicit reason for Cain's sacrifice is given in Scripture. Perhaps Cain wanted to form a relationship with "his father," God, through an offering. As a farmer, he is the one who struggles with the curse that was put on the earth as the punishment upon his biological father, Adam (Gen. 3:17–19).[23] An offering might have atoned for Adam's sin and removed the curse from the earth. But God, playing the typical role of a parent in the Book of Genesis, rejects his offering.[24] God prefers the offering of the younger brother Abel over that of the firstborn Cain. Unlike all the other similar traditions in Genesis, where the elected younger brother continues the dynasty, here the rejected older brother kills the younger in a burst of jealousy. What Esau wanted to do to Jacob is actually done by Cain to Abel.

Ironically, the result of Cain's offering is another curse on the earth. Cain may have wanted to establish a connection with his "father," God, by way of his offering, but now he has to hide himself from God.[25] I fully agree with Harold Bloom[26] that J's Cain is "a tragic rebel and not a villain."[27] "Cain left the presence of the Lord and settled in the land of Nod, east of Eden" (4:16). Just as his parents did after they were expelled from Eden, Cain begins to procreate immediately after his expulsion: "Cain knew his wife, and she conceived and bore Enoch" (Gen. 4:17).

However, Cain's terrible sin leads finally to the development of humanity. Cain, who was expelled from the soil which he tilled, becomes the founder of cities.[28] Among his descendants we find the founders of industry and music.[29] As in J's ironic story of the Garden, sin again leads to the development of human culture.

THE SONS OF GOD AND THE DAUGHTERS OF MAN

Mortality is the clear boundary between man and divinity. J's God says explicitly that the aim of the expulsion from Eden is to prevent man from gaining immortality. This idea is expressed elsewhere in the Hebrew Bible with regard to the heathen kings' claiming divinity for themselves. Isaiah, for instance, denounces the king of Babylon's claim to divinity by saying to him:

> *How are you felled to earth,*
> *O vanquisher of nations!*
> *Once you thought in your heart,*
> *"I will climb to the sky;*
> *Higher than the stars of God*
> *I will set my throne.*
> *I will sit in the mount of assembly,*
> *On the summit of Zaphon:*
> *I will mount the back of a cloud—*
> *I will match the Most High."*
> *Instead, you are brought down to Sheol,*
> *To the bottom of the Pit. (Isa. 14:13–15)*

The claim for divinity is negated by the actual descent of the king to Sheol, the land of death. A similar idea is found in the prophecy of Ezekiel to the prince of Tyre, quoted in part below:

> *Assuredly, thus said the Lord God:*
> *Because you have deemed your mind equal to a god's,*
> *I swear I will bring against you*
> *Strangers, the most ruthless of nations.*
> *They shall unsheathe their swords*
> *Against your prized shrewdness,*
> *And they shall strike down your splendor.*
> *They shall bring you down to the Pit;*
> *In the heart of the sea you shall die*
> *The death of the slain.*
> *Will you still say, "I am a god"*
> *Before your slayers,*
> *When you are proved a man, not a god,*
> *At the hands of those who strike you down? (Ezek. 28:6–9)*

This prophecy has many ties with the story of Eden in Genesis 2–3. The prince is described as being in "Eden, the Garden of God" (28:13), and as in Genesis 2:12, precious stones are also associated with this garden.[30] In chapter 3 of Genesis, the first man and woman become like God after they acquire the divine knowledge of good and evil. The prince of Tyre similarly claims to be a god on the basis of his divine wisdom. The prince is expelled from Eden and he will turn into ashes upon the earth (28:16–18). In the same manner, the man and woman are expelled from the Garden, and are to die and to return to dust. In both images, death is the ultimate negation for the human claim to divinity.[31]

However, the expulsion from the Garden did not put an end to the tension between human beings and God. The story of Cain and Abel is followed in J's narrative by the story of the sons of God and the daughters of men:

> *When men began to increase on earth and daughters were born to them, the divine beings saw how beautiful the daughters of men were and took wives from among those that pleased them.—The Lord said, "My breath shall not abide in man forever, since he too is flesh; let the days allowed him be one hundred and twenty years."—It was then, and later too, that the*

Nephilim appeared on earth—when the divine beings cohabited with the daughters of men, who bore them offspring. They were the heroes of old, the men of renown. (Gen. 6:1–4)[32]

Before the expulsion of man from the Garden of Eden, God had said: "Now that the man has become one of us, knowing good and bad, what if he should stretch out his hand and take also from the tree of life and eat, and live forever" (Gen. 3:22). The plural "us" should be understood as a reference to the members of the divine clan,[33] with whom God in this speech is sharing a fear of human immortality. It is these same divine beings who are designated in Genesis 6:1 as "the sons of God."[34] But these "sons of God," in seeking sexual union with human females, are actively opposing God's will to maintain a clear division between the human and the divine spheres. It would be natural to assume that the children of these unions would be expected to live forever. In this way, the purpose of the expulsion from Eden (3:22) would be overcome,[35] and there would be no more gap between humans and divine beings.

But God sharply rejects this attempted erasure of boundaries, declaring in J's account that all human beings are flesh, even those involved in sexual relationships with the "sons of God," or the fruits of such union. Human life is dependent upon the spirit of God. When God takes away the divine spirit, then humans die.[36] As we saw in the prophecies to the kings of Babylon and Tyre, the human claim for divinity is negated by the decree of death.[37]

The effort of the "sons of God" to annihilate the borders between humans and the divine realm, which had been deliberately marked out by God, deserves special attention. In other traditions in the Hebrew Bible, we hear of the sea as the entity who tries to annihilate the borders, which were laid by God in nature. Job, for instance, says, "Am I the sea or the Dragon, / That You have set a watch over me?" (Job 7:12)[38] In J's account of Creation there is no mention of the sea. Instead of the sea monsters of P from the first chapter of Genesis, we have in J the serpent, a dry-land animal. It is not the sea that rebels against God's order and borders, in J's tradition, but human beings and the "sons of God." The subject of the rebellion is not the border between the land and the sea, but rather, the mark that differentiates human beings from divinity.

THE TOWER OF BABEL

The last human effort to overcome the expulsion from Eden and achieve divine status is described in J's story about the tower of Babel, the Hebrew name for the kingdom of Babylon.[39] The text takes pains to note that the top of the tower, in the mind of the builders, was intended to be in the heavens:

> Everyone on earth had the same language and the same words. And as they migrated from the east, they came upon a valley in the land of Shinar and settled there. They said to one another, "Come, let us make bricks and burn them hard."—Brick served them as stone, and bitumen served them as mortar. —And they said, "Come, let us build us a city, and a tower with its top in the sky, to make a name for ourselves; else we shall be scattered all over the world." The Lord came down to look at the city and tower that man had built, and the Lord said, "If, as one people with one language for all, this is how they have begun to act, then nothing that they may propose to do will be out of their reach. Let us, then, go down and confound their speech there, so that they shall not understand one another's speech." Thus the Lord scattered them from there over the face of the whole earth; and they stopped building the city. That is why it was called Babel, because there the Lord confounded the speech of the whole earth; and from there the Lord scattered them over the face of the whole earth. (Gen. 11:1–9)

The "tower of Babel" or "Babylon" undoubtedly reflects the ziggurat, the lofty and massive temple tower of Mesopotamian cities.[40] The ziggurat was built by the king as the great project designed to assure the monarch's eternal fame.[41]

Once more we see J democratizing monarchic motifs. It is human beings as a collective, rather than in the name of the king, who build the tower. The builders of the tower say: "to make a name for ourselves" (11:4). Like the Mesopotamian kings, they want to assure themselves eternal fame by monumental building.[42] This should be seen as another effort on the part of humanity to achieve divine status.[43]

Up until the building of the tower, all people share the same language and the same words, but from then on, the earth is divided into distinct languages and distinct kingdoms. Humanity is dispersed to the four corners of the earth and each aggregated people forms its own ethnic entity, distinguished from all others by its language. Borders begin to be drawn between different nations.

From this moment on, just as humans treat each other as different from one another in ethnicity, God also no longer treats humanity equally. Immediately following the Tower of Babel incident, God begins a personal relationship with Abraham and his family. God tells Abraham, "Go forth from your native land and from your father's house to the land that I will show you" (Gen. 12:1). God forms a special, intimate tie with Abraham and his progeny.[44] Whatever connection the rest of humanity will have with God must come through the children of Abraham: "And all the families of the earth / Shall bless themselves by [i.e., through] you" (Gen. 12:3). This shift from the universal scope to the particular and national is at the core of the Hebrew Bible.

CHAPTER FOUR

Good, Evil, and Holiness in Isaiah and the Holiness School

G ENESIS DEPICTS A MAJOR CHANGE IN THE RELATIONSHIP of humanity to God's other creatures. According to the Priestly source, God's original plan was for a peaceful, vegetarian world with no violence: "See, I give you every seed-bearing plant that is upon all the earth, and every tree that has seed-bearing fruit; they shall be yours for food" (Gen.1:29). Likewise for the animals, God gives "all the green plants for food" (Gen. 1:30). However, after the Flood, God allows bloodshed for the sake of eating: "Every creature that lives shall be yours to eat; as with the green grasses, I give you all these" (Gen. 9:3). J's account concurs with the Priestly one; in Eden there was no animosity between the serpent and man. This enmity was only decreed as a punishment after the serpent's transgression (Gen. 3:15). In both accounts, those changes are presented as irreversible events. There is no way back to Eden, for the way is blocked by the cherubim and the fiery sword.

The other major change, the shift from universalism to nationalism, is also presented as irreversible. In the pentateuchal sources there is no direct expression of a hope that at some time in the future all humanity will know and worship the God of Israel.

In the last book of the Pentateuch, Deuteronomy, we find a theological framework for utterly separating the other nations from the worship of the one true God. We find this framework in the "Song of Moses," which we know as Deuteronomy 32, but which was probably written earlier than the rest of the book.[1] In this song, we find a description of how the different nations are divided.[2]

> Remember the days of old,
> Consider the years of ages past;
> Ask your father, he will inform you,
> Your elders, they will tell you:
> When the Most High gave nations their homes
> And set the divisions of man,
> He fixed the boundaries of peoples
> In relation to Israel's numbers.
> For the Lord's portion is His people,
> Jacob His own allotment. (Deut. 32:7–9)

In this Masoretic version of the Hebrew Bible, the phrase "He established the borders of peoples according to the number of the sons of Israel" is unclear, and the commentators usually explain it as referring to the number of the sons of Israel who descended into Egypt, the number seventy, corresponding to the number of nations thought to exist in the world.[3] When we compare other versions of the Bible, however, we find illuminating differences. In the Qumran text, we read that God "established the borders of peoples in relation to the numbers of the sons of God (l'mispar bnei Elohim)."[4] A similar version is reflected in the Septuagint.[5] These readings shed new light on the matter. When God gave nations their homes and set divisions among human beings—probably at the time of the Tower of Babel episode—God established the boundaries of peoples by the number of the sons of God, which was seventy, according to this tradition.[6] God gave each nation to a son of God in order that that particular son rule over it. Only one nation was not entrusted to them: "For the Lord's portion is His people, Jacob His own allottment." God took Jacob's descendants for Himself. The other nations, then, do not have direct contact with God, according to the authors of Deuteronomy, for they were turned over to sons of God, to be governed by them; only the people of Israel enjoy an unmediated relationship with God. It follows that it is not incumbent upon the other nations to worship God. They are in the care of the sons of God, other divine beings, which are in another passage in Deuternomy described as heavenly bodies:

> *And beware lest you lift up your eyes to heaven,*
> *and when you see the sun and the moon and the stars,*
> *all the host of heaven,*
> *you be drawn away and worship them and serve them,*
> *things which the Lord your God has allotted to all the peoples*
> *under the whole heaven. (Deut. 4:19)[7]*

The Lord allotted the hosts of heaven to other peoples; they are governed by these heavenly beings, and it may be that they are allowed to worship them. Only one nation was commanded to worship God—the people of Israel, the inheritance of God—and when they stray from God, they are worshiping "gods whom they had not experienced and whom He had not allotted to them" (Deut. 29:25). The other nations may worship their deities, according to Deuteronomy, and Israelites should harbor them no ill unless the nations worship their deities in the land of Israel, which is God's land. However, God's dominion extends over the sons of God, whom the nations worship. God has ordered the world in such an manner that the other nations have been given to the sons of God, and God has no interest in forming a direct bond with them. Deuteronomy presents this situation as a permanent one.

Nowhere in the Torah, or in the historical books, do we have a vision or a hope that humanity will return to the Genesis period, where God had an intimate relationship with all human beings.[8]

THE VISION OF ISAIAH

The first time Scripture mentions a vision that all humanity will search for God is in the Book of Isaiah:

> *In the days to come,*
> *The Mount of the Lord's House*
> *Shall stand firm above the mountains*
> *And tower above the hills;*
> *And all the nations*
> *Shall gaze on it with joy.*
> *And the many peoples shall go and say:*
> *"Come,*
> *Let us go up to the Mount of the Lord,*
> *To the House of the God of Jacob;*
> *That He may instruct us in His ways,*
> *And that we may walk in His paths."*
> *For instruction shall come forth from Zion,*
> *The word of the Lord from Jerusalem. (Isa. 2:2–3)*

Not only Israel, not only Jacob are God's allotment (see Deut. 32:9), but all the other nations shall go to the Mountain of God.[9] As in the time of Genesis, God will again instruct all humanity.

According to the Book of Isaiah, just as the separation of the nations from God is reversible, so too are the other major changes that occurred in the earliest period of human history. Nonviolence will replace violence, and the way back to the peace of Eden will be open again. "In all of My sacred mount / Nothing evil or vile shall be done; / For the land shall be filled with devotion to the Lord / As water covers the sea" (Isa.11:9). When this happens, a change will come about in the relations between humans and other humans and between humans and animals. This is Isaiah's celebrated vision of world peace:

> *The wolf shall dwell with the lamb,*
> *the leopard lie down with the kid…A babe shall play*
> *Over a viper's hole,*
> *And an infant pass his hand*
> *Over an adder's den. (Isa. 11:6,8)*

In essence, this is a return to the state of affairs that existed at the beginning of Creation, a return to the peaceful coexistence of human beings and the serpent in the Garden of Eden.

What was the background of the revolutionary vision of Isaiah? Biblical scholar Yehezkel Kaufmann cautions us about seeking explanations solely in historical causes: "The primary sources of human creativity are beyond our ken and power to explain. An Amos or an Isaiah is not entirely accounted for by historical or social circumstances." Yet, says Kaufmann, "it is true that classical prophecy was born in a certain historical situation. To that extent, then, one may speak of the social and historical conditions which shaped its character."[10] In the time of Isaiah, in the middle of the eighth century B.C.E., a new power began asserting itself in the Near East—the Assyrian kingdom. Assyria was the first true empire in the region. The Assyrians set forth on journeys of conquest and managed to subject nation after nation, kingdom after kingdom, to their rule. The prophet Isaiah attributes to the Assyrian king[11] the boastful claim that: "As one gathers abandoned eggs, / So I gathered all the earth" (Isa.10:14). And indeed, the Assyrian king became the sole ruler of the region. Between the years 732 and 720 B.C.E., the Assyrians succeeded in conquering the kingdom of Israel and ending its independence. They exiled the populace to an assortment of odd lands—to Halah, to the River Habor, the River Gozan, and the towns of Medea (2 Kings 17:6)—and in their stead, the Assyrians brought people from all corners of the empire—from Babylon, Cuthah, Avva, Hamath, and Sepharvaim (17:24)—to Israel. This was the strategy routinely adopted by the Assyrians. Mass exiles were used to uproot inhabitants from their homelands, thus detaching them from old allegiances and transforming them into loyal subjects of the Assyrian empire.[12] In this fashion, the conquered nations were transported from one end of the vast empire to the other. The king of Assyria boasted of his prowess:[13]

> For he thought,
> "By the might of my hand have I wrought it,
> By my skill, for I am clever:

> *I have erased the borders of peoples;*
> *I have plundered their treasures. (Isa. 10:13)*

Indeed, the king of Assyria had erased the borders that divide the nations, jolting the world from one end to the other. The static state described in Deuteronomy 32, namely, that God "established the borders of peoples," no longer existed. The borders of the nations set by God at the end of the Genesis period had been erased.

The reign of the Assyrian king and the deeds he performed—gathering up kingdoms and thoroughly shaking them up—brought about a revolution in Israelite religious thinking concerning the relationship between God and the nations of the world. The world picture was challenged and strained with the rise of the Assyrian kings. Isaiah accepted the new reality of his time, and gave it new meaning. Indeed, the borders between the nations had been erased, but not for the nations to be handed over to the king of Assyria. The borders had been erased so that all peoples would be able to seek out the word of the Lord. Isaiah's vision of all the nations of the world seeking out God's teachings can be seen as a reaction to the words and the deeds of the Assyrian king.

From within this geopolitical crisis, there burst forth a new religious idea. Against the government of the sword that the king of Assyria employs, Isaiah holds up a vision of peace:

> *And they shall beat their swords into plowshares,*
> *and their spears into pruning hooks:*
> *nation shall not take up*
> *sword against nation;*
> *they shall never again know war. (Isa. 2:4)*

The expectation that all nations will be united in seeking the word of God and that there will be peace between nations and between people and animals: This is Isaiah's reaction to the challenge presented by the king of Assyria and his arrogant boasts.

THE ROLE OF EVIL IN ISAIAH

Isaiah prophesies the assured destruction of Assyria through "the Name of the Lord":

> *Behold the Lord himself*
> *comes from afar*
> *In blazing wrath,*
> *With a heavy burden—*[14]
> *His lips full of fury,*
> *His tongue like devouring fire,*
> *And his breath like a raging torrent. (Isa. 30:27)*

The "Name of the Lord" is described here as an independent agent, a convention that is extremely rare in the Hebrew Bible.[15] The "Name of the Lord" has "lips full of fury, his tongue like devouring fire." This image of wrathful lips and tongue is not employed anywhere else in the Bible in reference to God. It is, however, used to describe serpents.[16] The reference to the "thick rising smoke" that issues from the mouth of the "Name of the Lord" fits perfectly with Isaiah's vision of the seraphim, in which the chamber of the Temple that he stands in is filled with the smoke they emit from their mouths.[17] The seraphim are heavenly winged serpents.[18] Hence, we may conclude that the serpentine "Name of the Lord" is, in fact, the angel of God,[19] the winged seraph.

The "Name of the Lord"—the seraph—represents the wrathful, destructive aspect of the divine. According to Isaiah, this aspect is an integral part of God's holiness. It is the seraphim, the fiery serpents, that issue the sublime cry, "Holy, holy, holy" (Isa.6:3). Here we can see the similarity between Isaiah and J's conception of evil. Both see evil as part of the divine. In the J source of Genesis, the serpent, the messenger of evil, is a creature of God. In the same way, Isaiah sees God's destructive forces manifested by the winged serpents, the seraphim.

While looking at the seraphim Isaiah receives a terrible mission:

> *Go, say to that people:*
> *'Hear, indeed, but do not understand;*
> *See, indeed, but do not grasp.'*
> *Dull that people's mind,*
> *Stop its ears,*
> *And seal its eyes—*
> *Lest, seeing with its eyes*
> *And hearing with its ears,*
> *It also grasp with its mind,*
> *And repent and save itself. (Isa. 6:9–10)*

Ironically, Isaiah is being sent to prevent the people from hearing God's words. His task is to hold back any possibility of repentance and salvation. God wants to punish his people horribly, and the prophet is called to help him.[20] When Isaiah asks "How long, O Lord?" God replies:

> *Till towns lie waste without inhabitants*
> *And houses without people,*
> *And the ground lies waste and desolate—*
> *For the Lord will banish the population—*
> *And deserted sites are many*
> *In the midst of the land. (Isa. 6:11–12)*[21]

The god who is enthroned among the winged serpents is the god of destructive anger. Isaiah accepts fully this "dark" side of the divine. Among Isaiah's contemporaries were people who thought that God's fiery anger could be appeased only by sacrificing their children to the Molech, a deity identified by some people in that period with the God of Israel. The place of the Molech cult was called Topheth, and it was located in the Hinom valley near Jerusalem.[22]

Micah, another prophet of Isaiah's time, dramatizes an argument with a person who holds this terrible conception, as follows:

> *With what shall I approach the Lord,*
> *Do homage to God on high?*
> *He has told you, O man, what is good,*
> *And what the Lord requires of you:*
> *Only to do justice*
> *And to love goodness,*
> *And to walk modestly with your God. (Mic. 6:6–8)*

Micah rejects the view that the Lord wants child sacrifice. However, unlike Micah, Isaiah seems to hold the opinion that identifying the God of Israel with the Molech cult is not totally mistaken. Isaiah's prophecy about the "Name of the Lord" ends with this telling oracle regarding the destruction of Assyria:

> The Topheth has long been ready for him;
> He too is destined for Molech—
> His firepit has been made both wide and deep,
> With plenty of fire and firewood,
> And with the breath of the Lord
> Burning in it like a stream of sulfur. (Isa. 30:33)

The Topheth of the Molech serves here as a symbol of God's destructive anger.[23] According to Isaiah the breath of the Lord burns in the Topheth like a stream of sulfur. This close connection between the God of Israel and the burning Topheth in Jerusalem is manifested elsewhere in Isaiah's prophecy with regard to the fall of Assyria:

> Then Assyria shall fall,
> Not by the sword of man;
> A sword not of humans shall devour him.
> He shall shrivel before the sword,
> And his young men pine away.
> His rock shall melt with terror,
> And his officers shall collapse from weakness—
> Declares the Lord, who has a fire in Zion,
> Who has an oven in Jerusalem. (Isa. 31:8–9)

Isaiah's image of fire that burns in the furnace in Jerusalem is the fire of the Topheth in the Hinom valley, and it is this divine fire which will burn the Assyrian army and save Jerusalem.

Scholars have shown that the Molech worship and Topheth were associated with the realm of death.[24] We have seen that according to the Priestly Torah, the realm of death is associated with Azazel, who is connected to the primordial evil elements that existed before God's Creation. Hence for P, evil and death are both independent elements that are not associated with God and God's Creation. But unlike P, both J and

Isaiah do connect evil and death with YHWH. According to J, God created the serpent, the messenger of evil (Gen. 3:1), and death is the punishment given by God to the man (Gen. 3:19). Isaiah sees serpents, the winged seraphim, as the messengers of God. He similarly associates the horrible Topheth with the breath of YHWH.[25]

THE MEANING OF HOLINESS IN ISAIAH

The rise of Assyria happened around the middle of the eighth century B.C.E. Before the rise of the Assyrian power, in the first half of the century, both Israel and Judea experienced a period of military success and economic prosperity. Due to financial prosperity and a series of wars and conquests, in this period a widening social and economic gap appears within Israelite society.[26] In what follows, I refer to the societies of both the northern kingdom, Israel, and the southern kingdom, Judea, as "Israelite society."

The beginning of the eighth century was a time of great conquests in the north. Jeroboam the Second managed to subdue the Arameans and to acquire territory in the Golan Heights. He even succeeded in conquering Damascus. Following these conquests, there emerged a class of nouveaux riches, described by the prophet Amos as living in great luxury and scheming for ways to take from their poor neighbors:

> They lie on ivory beds,
> Lolling on their couches,
> Feasting on lambs from the flock
> And on calves from the stalls.
> They hum snatches of song
> To the tune of the lute—
> They account themselves musicians like David.
> They drink [straight] from the wine bowls
> And anoint themselves with the choicest oils—
> But they are not concerned with the ruin of Joseph. (Amos 6:3–6)

This polarization causes an entire segment of the populace to lose its share of the land and forces them to sell their fields and their ancestral plots in order to subsist.

They then sell themselves into slavery to their wealthy brethren.

At the same time, the nouveaux riches are described by the prophets of the day as being extremely meticulous in their observance of the commandments. We are told that they adhered to the laws of the Sabbath with great fastidiousness. The prophet Amos speaks of a man who eagerly awaits the end of the Sabbath and the passing of the holiday of the New Moon:

"If only the new moon were over, so that we could sell grain; the sabbath, so that we could offer wheat for sale, using an ephah that is too small, and a shekel that is too big, tilting a dishonest scale, and selling grain refuse as grain! We will buy the poor for silver, the needy for a pair of sandals. (Amos 8:5–6)

The merchant satirized by Amos is careful to keep the Sabbath, and also goes to the Temple and offers many sacrifices. But after he finishes offering these sacrifices, he drinks wine, which he confiscated from a poor man who did not repay a debt on time. "And drink in the House of their God / Wine bought with fines they imposed" (Amos 2:8). We see, then, people who take great care in observing the cultic commandments, who view themselves as righteous men doing the will of God, and yet who are completely indifferent to the moral and social aspects of religion. A schism between morality and ritual emerges.

Isaiah, along with his contemporaries Amos and Micah, mounts an unrelenting attack against this schism. The attack is not limited to criticism of sacrificial rites. While Isaiah does say, "'What need have I of all your sacrifices?' Says the Lord" (Isa. 1:11), he also adds:

Your new moons and fixed seasons
Fill Me with loathing;
They are become a burden to Me,
I cannot endure them. (Isa. 1:14)

Not only are the sacrifices and holidays of the people abhorrent in the eyes of God, but God does not want to hear their prayers either:

And when you lift up your hands,
I will turn My eyes away from you;
Though you pray at length,
I will not listen.
Your hands are stained with crime. (Isa. 1:15)

Isaiah calls on his people:

Wash yourselves clean;
Put your evil doings
Away from My sight.
Cease to do evil;
Learn to do good.
Devote yourselves to justice;
Aid the wronged.
Uphold the rights of the orphan;
Defend the cause of the widow. (Isa. 1:16–17)

What God desires is moral behavior and social justice, not rituals such as sacrifices, holy days, and prayer. Amos expresses a similar view. In the Book of Amos we read the harsh words that Amos voiced in the Temple of Bethel, which caused the local priest, Amaziah, to address him with the verse: "Seer, off with you" (Amos 7:12).[27] Amos's criticism undermines the legitimacy and the very foundation upon which the entire Priestly conception rests. Not only does he say, "I loathe, I spurn your festivals, / I am not appeased by your solemn assemblies" (5:21), but he presses on and asks: "Did you offer sacrifice and oblation to Me / Those forty years in the wilderness, / O House of Israel?" (Amos 5:25). The answer to this radical rhetorical question is a resounding "no." Casting doubt on the foundational story of the Priestly cult, Amos points instead to what God truly wants: "But let justice well up like water, / Righteousness like an unfailing stream" (Amos 5:24). Offerings, Amos implies, are not a demand made by God, for there were no sacrifices in the desert.[28] This approach is diametrically opposed to the Priestly conception, according to which a tabernacle was built in the desert, and served as the focus of Israel's religious life. Aaron was the high priest of this Tabernacle, and Moses communed with God from within it, that is, from within the Tent of Meeting. Sacrifices were offered in the Tabernacle, and all manifestations of Israel's religious life revolved around it. Amos undermines the Priestly ideology.[29]

Unlike Amos, Isaiah does not reject the legitimacy and foundations of ritual or the Temple cult. After all, Isaiah himself has a vision in which he is sanctified and shown his mission within the Temple.[30] What Isaiah wants to remove is ritual unconnected to social justice and righteousness. There can be no ritual when "Your hands are stained with crime" (Isa. 1:15). Morality is the central demand of the Lord. The destiny of the people of Israel will rise or fall according to their moral behavior. If they sin and neglect social justice and righteousness, the nation will come to an end.

A seminal verse in Isaiah reveals how profound Isaiah's conceptual revolution was: "And the Lord of Hosts is exalted by judgment, / the Holy God proved holy by retribution" (Isa. 5:16). We have here a new approach to the concept of holiness. Before Isaiah's time, the concept of holiness is mentioned in the Priestly Torah only with regard to ritual matters: the holy Temple, the holy days, the priests as holy people.[31] Not once in the Priestly Torah is holiness tied to moral behavior, to upholding social justice, and to behaving righteously. Some scholars claim that through prophecy the notion of holiness took on moral meaning,[32] but Isaiah is the only one of the eighth-century prophets who infuses holiness with morality.[33] Isaiah's new idea of holiness is also reflected in the writings of a new Priestly school, called the Holiness School, which was most likely founded at about this time.

THE HOLINESS SCHOOL

The Priestly Torah, as I have shown, maintains a distinction between morality and ritual, two realms of religious life which, according to this view, are in no way interrelated. Morality is universal, while the divine revelation to the people of Israel is wholly in the realm of religious ritual and worship.[34] It is clear that anyone who adopts this position could not easily respond to the moral critique leveled by the eighth-century prophets. The people of Israel were in deep crisis. The social polarization of rich and poor was manifest in exploitation and immoral behavior on the part of the rich. This point of view was made worse by the people's observance of ritual without morality, a distinction that could be supported, albeit somewhat ironically, by P's insistence on a strict separation between these spheres. P's separation between morality and religious ritual makes it impossible for that school of Priestly thought to offer a solution to the crisis which the people of Israel underwent in the eighth century B.C.E.

There was therefore a need for creative and powerful innovation from within the Priestly camp, both in order to heal the ills of the people and to respond to the prophetic critique. And indeed, we find that Priestly thinking undergoes a profound change in the latter half of the eighth century. There arises a new school of thought, the Holiness School,[35] which produces a spiritual work of utmost importance, and leaves its mark on the future development of the religion of Israel.

The most central aspect of this innovation has to do with the relations between morality and religious ritual. Whereas the classical Priestly conception maintained a rigid distinction between the two, the Holiness School combines morality and ritual. The main corpus of the writings of the Holiness School, the Holiness Code,[36] is found in the second half of Leviticus, from chapter 17 through the end of the book. The signature section in this corpus begins with a call to the people of Israel as a whole:

> Speak to the whole Israelite community and say to them:
> You shall be holy, for I, the Lord your God, am holy. (Lev.19:2)

It is not only the priests but the entire people of Israel who are called upon to be holy. How can they attain this level of holiness? How can the people become holy like God? The chapter enumerates a long list of commandments that will raise whoever observes them to holiness, thus becoming like the holy God. Let us examine the content of this list.

According to the classical formulation of the Priestly Torah, holiness is tied exclusively to matters of religious ritual: sacrifices, holidays, the Temple, and so forth.[37] These elements also appear in the Holiness Code. But alongside them, we find explicitly ethical commandments, which could never have appeared in the earlier Priestly Torah: "Love your fellow as yourself" (Lev. 19:18), "You shall not falsify measures . . . You shall have an honest balance, honest weights, an honest *ephah*, and an honest *hin* [units of measurement]" (Lev. 19:35–6). These ethical commandments are found adjacent to ritual commands: the offering of sacrifices, alongside an interdiction against defrauding and prohibitions against unfair commerce;[38] a command to keep the Sabbath and the holy days alongside decrees to honor one's father and mother and to care for the needy.[39] The underlying idea is that if pracitioners want to be holy, they must simultaneously maintain the ritual commandments and pay attention to the moral injunctions. Working for social justice, caring for the poor and the weak, loving fellow human beings, all these are part of the concept of holiness, according to the Holiness School.

It was the prophet Isaiah who said: "The Lord of Hosts is exalted by judgment, the Holy God proved holy by retribution" (Isa. 5:16). We cannot determine which of the two came first. Did the priests of the Holiness School hear Isaiah prophesying in Jerusalem, pick up on the idea and give it a fuller expression, or was it perhaps the other way around? Whatever the historical answer, there is clearly a great affinity between the two.[40] The main difference is that Isaiah, like the other prophets of his era, is thoroughly critical of the religious rituals of his time. The Holiness School, on the other hand, does not criticize the ritual aspect of religion at all; on the contrary, its adherents fully embrace the ritual, but emphasize the close affinity of ritual and morality as components of holiness.

Over the man described by the prophet Amos, who awaits the end of the Sabbath so that he may resume selling his wares with a tilted balance,[41] the Holiness School places the commandment of Sabbath observance and the prohibition against deception in commercial dealings in the same chapter (Lev. 19:3,36). The Holiness Code instructs the rich man resting on his ivory bed[42] that the end of the Sabbath is not a time to begin cheating with false measures; an adherent of the Sabbath must also observe the adjacent commandment, "You shall have an honest balance."

The Holiness School also attempts to rectify the wrongs of its day by putting forth a program of reform, which features the law of the jubilee. The jubilee, the year occuring after seven cycles of sabbatical years (i.e., every fiftieth year), is to be a time in which all social inequity is redressed.[43] The people of that generation enslaved their poor brethren, selling a needy person for a pair of shoes. The Holiness School counters them by saying that none of the people of Israel can enslave their brethren, because all the children of Israel are enslaved only to God. So says God: "For they are My servants, whom I freed from the land of Egypt; they may not give themselves over into servitude....for it is to Me that the Israelites are servants" (Lev. 25:42,55). In the redemption from Egypt, the Israelites did not pass from slavery to freedom, but from slavery to slavery. They are now God's slaves rather than Pharaoh's, with this corollary: whomever God has acquired as a slave cannot be enslaved by another. On these grounds, the Holiness School rejects the concept of slavery within Israelite society.[44] It recognizes instead the possibility of a person working for another for remittance—"He shall remain with you as a hired or bound laborer" (25:40)—but not as a slave.

Another widespread phenomenon of the day was the eviction of the poor from their fields. Anyone who could not repay a debt could be forced to sell his field to the rich. Isaiah attacks the greed underlying this cruel economic practice: "Ah, / those who add house to house / And join field to field, / till there is room for none but you / to dwell in the land!" (Isa. 5:8). The Holiness School seeks to redress the eviction of people from their ancestral plots of land. Here again they use the law of the jubilee, which claims that no Israelite can sell his land to another because according to the Lord, "the land is Mine; you are but strangers resident with Me" (Lev. 25:23). While God permits people to reside on the land, all are equally tenants. As such, no tenant is permitted to deal in land as though it were his. That is why in the jubilee year anyone who had been forced by debt to sell his or her plot receives it anew. "In this year of jubilee, each of you shall return to his holding" (Lev. 25:13). In that year, all those who work for other people return to their homes, all slaves go free and return to their homes, and all who sold their land receive it back, with no remuneration necessary. The lot of one's forefathers was given to a person by God; every individual is a protected tenant of the Lord.

It seems that this sweeping reform was never implemented. There are indications that the authors of the laws were not thinking in utopian terms,[45] but intended the law to have practical effects. Still there is no evidence to suggest that this goal was attained. But the sublime vision of morality shaping all aspects of Israelite life, which was put forth by the Holiness School, certainly must have effected a change for the better on the people of Israel.

The elitist and esoteric thinking of the Priestly Torah grew from within the confines of the Temple. While it is true that the Priestly Code reached new heights of abstraction and sublimity in thinking about God, its message about God was aimed at a select few. Only a handful of people could reach the religious summits of the Priestly Torah. The Holiness School, however, bursts the walls of the sanctuary and turns to the people as a whole. It relinquishes religious sublimity and embraces popular customs.

The Priestly Torah treats popular customs with a modicum of skepticism, as in the case of the people who come to offer their first fruit in order that they be granted a bountiful year. According to the Priestly Torah, this custom is not a mandatory ritual.[46] For the Holiness Code, on the other hand, the law of the first fruit is thoroughly developed. It is a great religious obligation to bring one's first fruit to the Temple, as well as the Omer offering that signals the beginning of the grain harvest; great festivities were held in the Temple on that day (see Lev. 23:9-21).

What we have here is a complete acceptance of the popular forms of worship and a synthesis of popular customs with the Priestly ritual.[47] This exemplifies the willingness to relinquish the Priestly elitism and to accept popular customs, even if the people do not match up to the Priestly standard of religious sublimity. The Holiness School wants to influence the people as a whole, to create an integration of the priesthood and the nation, and for this purpose it calls upon the entire nation to lead a life of holiness. According to the Holiness School, all the people of Israel are priests of sorts.

The symbol of a life of holiness is the commandment of *tzitzit*, a blue cord which is to be attached to the corners of the garment (Num. 15:38). The high priest, who stands at the pinnacle of the religious hierarchy, wears special clothes that are not worn by any of the other priests.[48] One of these garments is a frontlet (*tzitz*) of pure gold which adorns the head of the high priest and which is fastened to him with a blue cord. The parallel is evident. A cord of blue and a frontlet (*tzitz*), a cord of blue and a fringe *(tzitzit)*.[49] On the frontlet of the high priest it is written "Holy to the Lord" (Exod. 28:36), while the fringe indicates to its wearers that they should be "holy to your God" (Num. 15:40). The Holiness School is in effect saying to every Israelite: If one observes the commandments, ritual and moral alike, one can attain a level of holiness akin to that of the high priest. The high priest is "holy to the Lord" while the follower of commandments will be "holy to your God." There is a democratization of the Priestly symbols, an equal opportunity for all of the people of Israel to be holy.[50]

The Holiness School claims that all the people of Israel are called upon to lead a life of holiness, which is not limited in time, somewhat akin to the life of a priest. Thus began a revolution in the religious life of the people of Israel. The effects of this revolution can be traced to the religious and spiritual development of Israel, not only in the time of the First Temple, but to the Second Temple as well.[51]

CHAPTER FIVE

Israel's Debate over God's Sanctuary

T HE CENTER OF HOLINESS IN ANCIENT ISRAEL WAS THE sanctuary, but there were different forms and locations of sanctuaries. In this chapter we deal with the different models of the sanctuary that are to be found in the Torah, starting with the Priestly sanctuary: the Tabernacle.

The theological uniqueness of the Priestly Torah is reflected in the special description of its Tabernacle. The outstanding characteristic of this sanctuary is the holy silence within it. In stark contrast to what was common in the temples of the Near East, and indeed to other temples in Israel, the Temple described in the Priestly Torah is a sanctuary of silence. In other temples, it was customary to sing hymns and pray during the sacrifices. In Babylonian, Hittite, and Egyptian texts describing the temple rituals of these lands, we find that when the priests offer sacrifices, burn incense, or light candles, they are accompanied by verbal activity.[1] This activity would at times consist of incantations and magical formulas, and, at other times, of prayers requesting some favor from God or hymns describing God's glory. Surprisingly, the Priestly corpus in the books of Exodus and Leviticus—which contains detailed accounts of most of the Temple ritual—does not mention any form of verbal activity[2] that accompanies the ritual. The priest performs his actions in utter silence.

Yehezkel Kaufmann, who was the first to call attention to this phenomenon in his book *The Religion of Israel*,[3] provided an additional proof from the Psalms. Many individual psalms are attributed to Levites,[4] but there is not a single psalm that is attributed to a priest, nor is there a psalm to be recited during the lighting of the lamps or the burning of incense.

Kaufmann thought this phenomenon stemmed from a desire to combat pagan mythology and magic. As one recent scholar describes this view, "Magic was seen as invoking the direct control by human beings of the forces of nature, while religion was the propitiation of these and higher powers."[5] The prayers and the hymns of the pagan temples were viewed as instruments to control nature. According to Kaufmann, the Israelite religion adopted a Sanctuary of Silence[6] as a protest against this magical form of speech, or in contradistinction to it.

I find this explanation unsatisfactory, for two reasons. First, not every form of temple-centered speech would necessarily be magical. The Psalms contain many prayers and hymns which do not contain the slightest trace of magic or mythology. Instead, they are an expression *par excellence* of the Israelite belief in the unity of God. Why not take a psalm of this sort and recite it while offering sacrifices or burning incense? The second difficulty is that there are two exceptional cases in which speech *is* employed in the Priestly texts, and both are linked to the world of magic.[7] The first is the confession that the high priest recites over the scapegoat, before it is sent off to the wilderness: "Aaron shall lay both his hands upon the head of the live goat and confess over it all the iniquities and transgressions of the Israeites, whatever their sins, putting them on the head of the goat" (Lev. 16:21).[8] Here, the magical element is seen in the transfer of sin to the goat, who deposits the sin in the wilderness, the domain of

Azazel.[9] The second instance is the ceremonial adjuration of the wayward or suspected wayward woman.[10] Here the magical element lies in the effect of the "water of bitterness" that the woman must drink. Dissolved into the water are a series of written curses, spoken by the priest;[11] in the rite, it is presumed that the imbibing of these potent words by the woman will either confirm or disprove her guilt (Num. 5:19–22). If the Priestly silence is motivated by a fear of pagan magic, we should not expect to find forms of speech in rituals which have magical elements. It would appear that it is not the struggle with paganism and magic that engenders the Sanctuary of Silence.

In my opinion, this silence is an expression of the priests' particular conception of God. According to Priestly theology, the aspect of the divinity signified by the name "YHWH" is above and beyond any form and any personality. The Priestly tradition attributes neither characteristics nor actions to YHWH. Within this conceptual framework there is no room for hymns of praise to God, for once we reject the possibility of saying anything about God, or ascribing any attribute to God, what is there to praise? The same holds true for prayers of supplication. The relationship that exists in the Temple is not one of covenant or dependence. Rather it is a unilateral pact. If the priests do not expect God to act on human behalf, then prayers of supplication lose their significance. For this reason, there are no rain ceremonies or ceremonies for victory in battle in the Priestly Torah. Silence characterizes the human being's presence before the sublime and mysterious Divinity that dwells in the Priestly Temple. In this sense, the state of affairs constituted by the Priestly writings envisions an island of silence in a sea of hymn and prayer. We know with complete certainty that the world outside the delimited Priestly confines, outside this enclave of silence, was rich with prayer and hymn. The Levites sang the praises of God, and the people of Israel as a whole used to come to the outer courtyard of the Temple and pray for their daily needs: for their health, for political and military success, and so forth.[12] All these circles of supplicant voices, of hymn and entreaty, surrounded the inner, silent center. Inevitably, there was a tension between the silent inner circle and the outer circles, a tension between the Priestly theology concentrated upon the sanctity of God and the popular religion that cared for the satisfaction of everyday human needs. At the same time, the different beliefs gave rise to a single, unified, holy system, where sound and silence found their place in harmony.[13]

THE PRIESTLY TABERNACLE VS. THE OUTER TENT OF MEETING

The silent sanctuary described in the Priestly Torah is actually not a temple, but rather a wandering tent. This Tent of Meeting, or Tabernacle, is described at length in the second part of the Book of Exodus (chapters 25–30 and 35–40). To understand the role of the Tent of Meeting in the Israelite system of holiness, the Priestly model of the Tabernacle should be compared to other models of shrines written about in the Pentateuch.

Exodus 33 reads, "Now Moses would take the Tent and pitch it outside the camp, at some distance the camp. It was called the Tent of Meeting" (Exod. 33:7). Moses would then go out to the tent where God would be revealed in a pillar of cloud that would descend to the entrance of the tent. When the revelation ended, the cloud departed from the tent and Moses returned to the camp (Exod. 33:9–10). The potential for coming into contact with God in the Tent of Meeting was not exclusively Moses'. It is written that "whoever sought the Lord would go out to the Tent of Meeting that was outside the camp" (Exod. 33:7). Any seeker of the Lord could go to the tent to communicate with God.[14]

This image of the Tent of Meeting is vastly different from the description and function of the Priestly tent. The Priestly

Tent of Meeting, the Tabernacle, is not situated outside the camp, but rather in its center (Num. 2:17), and serves as the focal point of sacrificial ritual (Exod. 29:1–42). Only the priests can enter it, for "any outsider who encroaches shall be put to death" (Num. 3:10). Within the Priestly Tabernacle reside the Ark and the cherubim and it is from amidst the cherubim that the divine revelation takes place (Exod 25:22). The Tent of Meeting described in Exodus 33:6–11 is diametrically opposed to the Priestly Tabernacle; no sacrifices are performed in it, nor do any priests regulate behavior in it. In fact, Joshua the son of Nun, Moses' servant and not a priest, seems to reside in the Tent of Meeting permanently: "His attendant, Joshua son of Nun, a youth, would not stir out of the Tent" (Exod. 33:11). Even with Moses' and Joshua's presence there, this tent is still open for all to enter to seek the Lord.

There is a vast divide separating the two paradigms of the Tent of Meeting, and a great tension between them. The Priestly paradigm requires the presence of God in the midst of the people. "Let them make Me a sanctuary that I may dwell among them" (Exod. 25:8) is the Priestly rendering. In this tabernacle home of God, there is a daily ritual intended to serve the Lord. According to the Priestly conception, it is God's constant presence among the people—anchored in the ritual—which allows one to reach the summit of religious life. In order to preserve the purity and the sanctity of the ritual space, it is necessary to restrict entrance to the tent-tabernacle to the select few who are trained in worship, namely, the priests.

In sharp contrast to this model, the outer Tent of Meeting can be viewed as an antiestablishment, perhaps even anarchistic conception. It places the tent outside the camp, completely cut off from the established order. There are no priests and no Levites in it, no Ark and no cherubs. No ritual takes place in it. The tent is open to all that seek the Lord. The outer Tent of Meeting also figures prominently in the Book of Numbers, chapters 11–12.[15]

These different views of the Tent of Meeting reflect differing approaches to God's place and the nature of God's relationship to Israel. The Priestly tradition emphasizes the immanence of God. Religious certainty is attained by the fixed presence of God within Israel. The purpose of the cultic system practiced within the Tabernacle is to facilitate God's continued presence among the people. In contrast, the tradition of the outer Tent of Meeting claims that God's place is in the heavens, and it is only for purposes of revelation that God descends, momentarily self-revealing in a cloud at the entrance of the Tent of Meeting. At the conclusion of the revelation, God reascends.[16] The power of the religious experience lies not in its constancy, but in the intimacy of the fleeting encounter: "The Lord would speak to Moses face to face, as one man speaks to another" (Exod. 33:11).[17] In this way, the outer Tent of Meeting is clearly associated with prophecy. The situation is identical in the Book of Numbers, where a group of seventy elders goes out to this tent and the spirit of the Lord comes upon them all, and they prophesy (Num. 11:24-5).[18]

It is important to note that the opposition between God's immanence in the Priestly tradition and God's transcendence in the tradition of the prophetic Tent of Meeting has nothing to do with the debate I described earlier between abstraction and anthropomorphism. On the contrary, it is precisely the Priestly tradition, which stresses the immanence of God, that reached the highest level of abstraction in its relationship to God. By contrast, the encounter between the transcendent God and Moses, as described in the prophetic tradition of the Tent of Meeting, is blatantly anthropomorphic. "With him I speak mouth to mouth" (Num.12:8). It seems that because of the marked anthropomorphism in the depiction of God in this tradition, there was an urgent need to achieve a spatial difference between God and human beings, i.e., to make God transcendent. Even though God is perceived with a human shape, there is still a marked border between humans who sit on earth and God who dwells in heaven. However, the Priestly Torah, with its non-anthropomorphic conception, can allow for an immanent God without fear of blurring the difference between God and humanity.

In the Genesis period of the Priestly Torah, when God is depicted in an anthropomorphic manner, the mode of revelation is similar to that in the prophetic Tent of Meeting. The end of the revelation to Abraham reads: "When He was done speaking with him, God was done with Abraham" (Gen. 17:22). We infer that God descended from heaven to speak with Abraham and returned when finished speaking. The same picture occurs at the end of the Priestly version of the revelation to Jacob in Beth-el: "God parted from him at the spot where He had spoken to him" (Gen. 35:13).

In order to understand the background for the development of the prophetic Tent of Meeting, we must turn our attention to Beth-el, to inspect the religious life in the northern kingdom, Israel.

BETH-EL, THE CALVES, AND THE PROPHETIC TENT

According to the story in 1 Kings, Jeroboam rebels against the authority of Rehaboam, the son of Solomon. Jeroboam creates the independent kingdom of Israel in the north, encompassing the northern tribes whose religious center was located in Beth-el. When Jeroboam founds this religious center, he institutes in it a system of worship competing with the one in Jerusalem.

Beth-el is known from the traditions of the Patriarchs in the Book of Genesis. According to these traditions, Abraham passes through this city (Gen 12:8). It is also in Beth-el that Jacob dreams his famous dream of a ladder whose base rests on the ground and whose head reaches to the sky, while angels ascend and descend it. When Jacob awakens from his sleep, he says, "This is none other than the abode of God (bet el), and that is the gateway to heaven" (Gen. 28:17).[19] Thus the sanctity of Beth-el was founded mainly upon divine revelation through dream.[20]

In the traditions about Jacob in the Book of Genesis, we have another component of the sanctity of Beth-el—the angel. This angel, who is designated as "The God of Beth-el," appears to Jacob in a dream in order to save him from Laban, saying: "I am the God of Beth-el, where you anointed a pillar and where you made a vow to Me. Now arise and leave this land and return to your native land" (Gen. 31:13).[21] He is mentioned further by Jacob as "the angel who has redeemed me from all harm" (Gen 48:16).[22] Thus the divine revelation of Beth-el was connected to what the Greeks called *genius loci*, an angel of the place.[23]

The object of worship in Beth-el was the calf. The Bible tells us that Jeroboam formed two calves and presented them to the northern tribes, saying: "This is your God, O Israel, who brought you up from the land of Egypt" (1 Kings 12:28). Was calf worship a way of worshiping foreign deities? Not in the least. The Bible never indicates anything akin to this. On the contrary, we find religious festivities and celebrations of YHWH taking place before a calf in both Exodus 32:5 and 1 Kings 12:32. Even people who zealously defended YHWH and the worship of YHWH worshiped the calf. An outstanding example is Jehu, king of Israel, anointed by Elisha. Jehu killed all the worshipers of Baal and abolished Baal worship from Israel. On his way to destroy the Temple of Baal, he sees Jehonadab, son of Rehab, and says to him: "Come with me, and see my zeal for the Lord" (2 Kings 10:16). And the Bible reveals that, for all his zeal, Jehu worshiped "the sinful objects," the golden calves that Jeroboam had instituted at Beth-el and Dan (2 Kings 10:29). Even Elijah, who fought zealously against the priests of Baal, does not say a single word against the calves.

It is reasonable to conclude that the tradition in the Book of Genesis that speaks in favor of Beth-el about the dream of Jacob and the angel of Beth-el originated in circles of people like Jehu, people who were devoted to the worship of the God of Israel. They accepted the sanctity of Beth-el and its cultic symbols as a manifestation of the holiness of YHWH.[24]

Yet there were other circles in the north who opposed Beth-el and its religious institutions. A northern prophet who fiercely attacks the worship of calves is Hosea. Hosea prophesied in the Kingdom of Israel in the middle of the eighth century B.C.E., until the sacking of Samaria by the Assyrians in 722–721 B.C.E.[25] His rebuke is uncompromising:

> And now they go on sinning;
> They have made them molten images,
> Idols, by their skill, from their silver,
> Wholly the work of craftsmen.
> Yet for these they appoint men to sacrifice;
> They are wont to kiss calves! (Hos. 13:2)

Apparently people would kiss the calves as one kisses a holy object.[26] Hosea also attacks religious ritual in general, as well as the manner in which the people of his generation worship God. His words bear testimony to a profound detachment between God and the people. The Lord does not desire the modes of worship adopted by the people, does not desire their manifold sacrifices: "Then they will go with their sheep and cattle / To seek the Lord, but they will not find Him. / He has cast them off" (Hos. 5:5). God has cast them off, risen to the heavens, and left them below. God says, "I will return to My abode" (Hos. 5:15). Hosea's message is clear: Though the people search after God with their sacrificial animals, they will not find God in this way.

As part of this religious polemic, the angel of Beth-el also comes in for its share of Hosea's criticism. Hosea tells a story about a combat in Beth-el, which evokes the story in Genesis about the struggle between Jacob and an angel in Penuel (Gen. 32:24–32), after which Jacob's name is changed to Israel, meaning, "one who strives with God." Hosea's combat story reads:

> In the womb he tried to supplant his brother
> Grown to manhood, he strove with a divine being,

> *He strove with an angel and prevailed—*
> *The other had to weep and implore him.*
> *At Beth-el [Jacob] would meet him,*
> *There to commune with him. (Hos. 12:4–5)*

The angel of Beth-el, called here "the other," is represented as a weak being, who had to weep and implore Jacob in order to receive his mercies. This picture contradicts Jacob's own claim in the Book of Genesis that the angel of Beth-el was his savior, the "angel who has redeemed me from all harm" (Gen. 48:16)![27]

Hosea's criticism of the calf and his less-than-flattering depiction of the angel has a parallel in Exodus: the making of the Golden Calf. The calf episode follows hard upon the giving of the Law at Mt. Sinai; Moses ascends to the top of the mountain and remains there forty days and forty nights. When the people of Israel see that he is tarrying, they turn to Aaron, saying: "Come, make us a god who shall go before us, for that man Moses, who brought us from the land of Egypt— we do not know what has happened to him" (Exod. 32:1). Aaron does their bidding and fashions the Golden Calf. The Israelites cry out before the calf, "This is your god, O Israel, who brought you out of the land of Egypt" (Exod. 32:4)—the very same cry that comes from the mouth of Jeroboam. Moreover, we find another crucial similarity between Aaron and Jeroboam that has been noted by a number of scholars. Aaron's two eldest sons, Nadav and Abihu, die a sudden, tragic death while they are still young men (Lev. 10:1). Jeroboam had two sons, Nadav and Abiah, and they too died at a very young age (1 Kings 14:17,15:28).

The two sets of names so clearly linked and the two identical annunciatory phrases show that the story decrying the calf worship in Exodus is actually meant as a criticism of Jeroboam and his calves.[28] The story's goal is clearly to communicate to the Israelite reader that this is an unacceptable way of worshiping the Lord. Rituals such as these can only lead to a rupture between God and the people. Just as Hosea says that God "cast them off," so God says to Moses after the Golden Calf, "I will not go in your midst" (Exod. 33:3). Instead, God says, "My angel shall go before you" (Exod. 32:34). Being led by an angel is described here as a part of the punishment for the sin of the Golden Calf. Those who do not deserve to be led by God will henceforth be led by an angel. It seems that we have here a notable criticism of the second component of the Beth-el religious system, the angel.[29]

The question then arises, if we reject the calf, its accompanying sacrifices, and the angel, what is left of the northern Israelite practice? What is the correct way to worship God? At this point, the Book of Exodus suggests a completely different model for the bond between God and the people of Israel. We are told that after the incident with the Golden Calf, Moses erected the Tent of Meeting outside the borders of the camp (Exod. 33:7–11).[30] This is the outer, prophetic Tent of Meeting that is discussed above.

The Exodus text makes clear that there is an ever-present option for any seeker of the Lord to go to this tent outside the camp to communicate with God. We saw that Hosea said of the calf worshipers that "they will go with their sheep and cattle / To seek the Lord, but they will not find Him. / He has cast them off" (Hos. 5:6). God does not desire their sacrifices: "When they present sacrifices to Me, / It is but flesh for them to eat: / The Lord has not accepted them" (Hos. 8:13). But in Exodus, we are told how one can seek God and indeed find God at the outer Tent of Meeting, which is suggested as an alternative to the sacrificial ritual of the calf.[31] God does not want the calf nor its sacrifices; God wants a direct connection with all those who seek the Lord through prayer or prophecy.

The Exodus tradition of the prophetic Tent of Meeing includes, then, an explicit critique of the centerpiece of the Beth-el cult, the golden calves. It also includes an implicit rejection of a second aspect of Beth-el's worship tradition, the angel. The third component of the Beth-el religious system, the dream, is critiqued in the parallel tradition of the prophetic Tent of Meeting in the Book of Numbers. When Miriam and Aaron complain against Moses, God answers them saying:

> When a prophet of the Lord arises among you, I make Myself known to him in a vision, I speak with him in a dream. Not so with My servant Moses. . .with him I speak mouth to mouth, plainly and not in riddles. (Num. 12:6–8)

In sharp contrast to the Beth-el tradition, the dream is represented here as an inferior way of revelation.[32] It appears that some circle, located most likely in the northern kingdom of Israel, developed a theological conception in opposition to the religious system of Beth-el. This opposition is expressed in the story about the Golden Calf in Exodus 32, and in the traditions about the outer Tent of Meeting[33] in Exodus 33 and Numbers 11–12.[34]

THE PRIESTLY TORAH VS. DEUTERONOMY

The Book of Deuteronomy advances a conception of God's place, which is similar to that of the outer Tent of Meeting. In Deuteronomy, God does not dwell within the Tabernacle and is not enthroned upon the cherubim; rather, God resides in the heavens. God does, however, place the divine name in one selected earthly location: "The site where the Lord your God will choose to establish His name" (Deut. 12:11).[35] As a result, the Ark described in Deuteronomy is without cherubim. It is a simple wooden structure in which the Tablets of the Law are placed (Deut. 10:1–5).[36] God resides in the heavens: "Look down from Your holy abode, from heaven" (Deut. 26:15). It is only God's name that resides in the Temple. Only in exceptional situations (Deut. 7:21, 9:3, 20:4, 23:15), such as times of war, is God present among Israel[37]. There are some scholars who see in this conception an attempt to make God abstract.[38] But this approach is unconvincing, for in other verses the Deuteronomist speaks of God in extremely anthropomorphic terms. Thus we read: "the Lord's anger and passion rage against that man" (Deut. 29:19) or "Since the Lord your God moves about in your camp" (Deut. 23:15). It appears that the main motivation is not abstraction, but rather a desire for transcendence. God can be depicted in very anthropomorphic terms, yet in order to mark a clear border and difference between God and man, there should be a spatial gap between the two; therefore, God is in the heavens and human beings are on earth.

Looking back, we can easily see a resemblance between this approach and the idea of the outer Tent of Meeting. There, too, God is not physically present at all times; God descends in a pillar of cloud, appears, and recedes. It seems, then, that there is a connection between the conception of the outer Tent of Meeting and that of the Book of Deuteronomy. Not surprisingly, a passage about the prophetic Tent of Meeting is included in the Book of Deuteronomy:

> The Lord said to Moses: "The time is drawing near for you to die. Call Joshua and present yourselves in the Tent of Meeting, that I may instruct him." Moses and Joshua went and presented themselves in the Tent of Meeting. The Lord appeared in the Tent, in a pillar of cloud, the pillar of cloud having come to rest at the entrance of the tent. (Deut. 31:14–15)[39]

Furthermore, Deuteronomy condemns the calf cult: "I saw how you had sinned against the Lord your God: you had made yourself a molten calf; you had been quick to stray from the path that the Lord had enjoined upon you" (Deut. 9:16). These parallels lead us to assume that Deuteronomy's origins go back to the circle of those who objected to the worship of the calf in the northern kingdom.[40]

It is helpful to distinguish between two different modes of the exaltation and sanctification of God in the Torah literature. In one model, God is perceived in anthropomorphic terms. The gap between God and humanity exists on a spatial plane. The outer Tent of Meeting and Deuteronomy represent this model. In the second model, we have the conception of YHWH as an immanent God who is constantly present in the

Tabernacle, as represented in the Priestly Torah. The exaltation of YHWH in the Priestly Torah is evident not by a spatial gap, but rather by what we might call a conceptual gap: Other than speaking and commanding, YHWH is never described in anthropomorphic terms.

The tendency of the traditions of the outer Tent of Meeting and Deuteronomy to exalt God by means of spatial distance led them to minimize the importance of cultic worship, which is, after all, connected with the constant presence of God in the shrine. This tendency is probably to be understood as a result of the struggle against the calf worship in the northern kingdom. We can also see here the beginning of a major development in the history of Israelite religion. Both the outer Tent of Meeting and Deuteronomy paved the way for a new perspective regarding the connection between God and humanity that reduced the importance of cult and introduced new ideas in its stead. Significantly, the scroll of the Torah is set, according to Deuteronomy, beside the Ark of the Covenant (Deut. 31:26). One might say that the words of God that are in the Torah now come to symbolize the Divine and replace the cherubim that had previously symbolized God's presence in the Priestly Torah. Hence, the importance of Torah study, which is stressed throughout Deuteronomy:

> Take to heart these instructions with which I charge you this day. Impress them upon your children. Recite them when you stay at home and when you are away, when you lie down and when you get up. Bind them as a sign on your hand and let them serve as asymbol on your forehead; inscribe them on the doorposts of your house and on your gates. (Deut. 6:6–9)[41]

Fixed prayer attains a more central role as well: "Look down from Your holy abode, from heaven, and bless Your people Israel and the soil You have given us, a land flowing with milk and honey, as You swore to our fathers" (Deut. 26:15). It is well known that the prayer of Solomon (1 Kings 8:22-53) reflects the conception found in Deuteronomy, according to which God sits in the heavens but places the divine name in the Temple.[42] In this prayer, we find the most prominent

ISRAEL'S DEBATE OVER GOD'S SANCTUARY

description in the historical books of the Temple as the people's house of prayer:

> *May Your eyes be open day and night toward this House, toward the place of which You have said, "My name shall abide there"; may You heed the prayers which Your servant will offer toward this place. And when you hear the supplications which Your servant and Your people Israel offer toward this place, give heed in Your heavenly abode—give heed and pardon. (1 Kings 8:29–30)*

Note that, like Deuteronomy's prayer, this passage also contains anthropomorphic language regarding God: "Your eyes may be open," "when You hear," "heavenly abode," and, in the continuation, "Your mighty hand and Your outstretched arm" (1 Kings 8:42).

The house of prayer envisioned by Deuteronomy and the later Deuteronomistic writers is a shrine whose purpose is to enable human beings to bring their needs and requests before God. The outer Tent of Meeting, which is open to all seekers of the Lord, and the Deuteronomistic house of prayer[43] should be seen as the forebears of the synagogue, while the central Jewish prayer, the *Amidah*, which is said in a silent voice, might be seen as a replacement of the Priestly worship of the Sanctuary of Silence.[44]

CHAPTER SIX

Israel's Debate over King and Messiah

T HE THEOLOGY THAT A SOCIETY CREATES IS ALWAYS A reflection of how that society envisions itself. As a monarchical society, it was natural for Israel to imagine God as king. This chapter will be concerned with that premise, and also with its opposite: to what extent can a human being, exalted by heredity, rank, or power, assume a connection with the Divine? In this chapter, I will discuss three distinct trends with regard to these questions. These trends range along a wide spectrum, from virtual deification of the king to a severe limitation of the king's prerogatives and powers on the assumption that God alone is king.

THE IDEOLOGY OF DIVINE KINGSHIP IN ANCIENT EGYPT

Conceptions of the king and kingship were similar throughout the ancient Near East. We choose as our starting point the image of the king in Egypt, since according to biblical tradition, Israel was formed as a nation in Egypt. Early in its history, Egypt had developed a rich ideolgy regarding its ruler, the Pharaoh: "Pharaoh was not a mortal, but a god. This was the fundamental concept of Egyptian kingship, that Pharaoh was of divine essence, a god incarnate; and this view can be traced back as far as texts and symbols can take us."[1] The Pharaoh was also represented as a "son of the gods."[2] The most literal descriptions of the king's physical siring by a deity are to be found in the parallel accounts of the coronation of Hatshepsut and Amenhotep III. According to these texts, the god Amon took the form of the reigning king, had intercourse with the queen, filled her with "his dew," and thus begot the new ruler.[3] The Pharaoh was perceived as a source of blessing and justice to the land of Egypt and its people. In a song composed for the accession of the Pharaoh Marenptah we read:

> Rejoice, thou entire land, the goodly time has come.
> A lord is appointed in all countries....
> O all ye righteous, come and behold!
> Truth has repressed falsehood.
> The sinners are fallen on their faces.
> All that are covetous are turned back.
> The water standeth and faileth not,
> The Nile carrieth a high flood.
> The days are long, the nights have hours,
> The months come aright.
> The gods are content and happy of heart, and
> Life is spent in laughter and wonder.[4]

The fertility of land and cattle was a main issue in the festivals celebrated in ancient Egypt, and the Pharaoh had a major role in the performance of the rituals that took place in these festivals.[5] In this way, the Pharaoh was perceived as the one who ensured the blessing of the land.

KING AND MESSIAH IN THE PROPHETS AND THE ROYAL PSALMS

It is clear that the Bible could not fully accept the ideology of divine kingship of ancient Egypt. No human being, not even the king, could be seen as a god sired by another god, without violently contradicting the basic premise of biblical monotheism with regard to the uniqueness of the one and only God and the separation between God and the world. Yet in some parts of the Hebrew Bible, we can nevertheless see a clear impact of the divine kingship ideology on the representation of the Israelite king. Both in the historical books and in the Book of Psalms we find the description of the king as the son of God: "I will be a father to him, and he shall be a son to Me" (2 Sam. 7:14). In this covenantal promise to David, God announces an intended adoption of one of David's sons and "establish his royal throne forever" (7:13). In the ritualized atmosphere of the royal psalms, God goes still further in concretizing the divine bond with the king: "You are My son, I have fathered you this day" (Ps. 2:7).[6]

The notion of divine sonship is reflected also in the prophecy of Isaiah at a time of extreme vulnerability for the southern kingdom, Judah:

> For a child has been born to us,
> A son has been given us.
> And authority has settled on his shoulders.
> He has been named
> "The Mighty God is planning grace;
> The Eternal Father, a peaceable ruler." (Isa. 9:5)

Several scholars have shown that this prophecy is based on the model of the Egyptian enthronement rite. Writing in this vein, one scholar has recently claimed that the speakers who announce the birth of the newborn child are the angels, the members of the divine family.[7] The future king is presented as a new member of the divine family and as such he is given the title "Mighty God."

In addition to the divinity of the king, another legacy of the ancient Near Eastern ideology of divine kingship is the idea that the king is centrally involved in establishing righteousness and justice in the land. In the psalms, for instance, we find that the main mission of the king is juridic.

> O God, endow the king with Your judgments,
> the king's son with your righteousness;
> that he may judge Your people rightly,

Your lowly ones, justly. (Ps. 72:2)

Kings such as David and Solomon hear suits of the people in the historical books, but it is the psalmist who connects the king's justice to God's.[8]

Many of the prophets similarly describe the king who will rule at the end of days as executing divine justice.[9] In the prophecy of Jeremiah, this mission is formulated in a unique way:

> See, a time is coming—declares the Lord—when I will raise up a true branch of David's line. He shall reign as king and shall prosper, and he shall do what is just and right in the land. In his days Judah shall be delivered and Israel shall dwell secure. And this is the name by which he shall be called: "The Lord is our Vindicator." (Jer. 23:6).

Jeremiah follows his predecessor Isaiah, who had titled the "Newborn Son" as "Mighty God." Jeremiah goes one step further and applies the Tetragrammaton to the name of the eschatological branch of David: ה' עדקנו "The Lord is our righteousness."[10]

We know from the history of religion that this eschatological king came to be associated with the term *Messiah*. This later practice in Christianity and Judaism had its origin in the Book of Daniel, which uses Messiah as a title.[11] But in its literal connotation, the word "messiah" (*Moshiach*) means "the anointed one"; whoever was King of Israel at a given moment was anointed by a prophet with holy oil.[12] Similarly, in the psalms, the ruling king is said to be anointed with "oil of gladness."[13]

It was a common concept in the ancient cultures of this region to give the king Priestly rights and functions. Often, the king served as a High Priest on important cultic occasions. In Israel too God's anointed is often given Priestly rights, as indicated in both the historical books and the Book of Psalms. Kings function as priests especially in the dedication of new cultic sites. When David brought the Ark to Jerusalem, he offered sacrifices and blessed the people like a priest: "David sacrificed burnt offerings and offerings of well-being before the Lord. When David finished sacrificing the burnt offerings and the offerings of well-being, he blessed the people in the name of the Lord of Hosts" (2 Sam. 6:17–18).[14] It is also said that the sons of David were priests (8:18).

We find a similar combination of priesthood and kingship in the royal psalms. In order to justify this combination, the author of Psalm 110 reverts to a pre-Israelite image of kingship: "You are a priest forever after the manner of Melchizedek" (Ps. 110:4).[15] Melchizedek, King of Salem, is known from Genesis as "a priest of God Most High," who brought out bread and wine and blessed Abraham in God's name (Gen. 14:18). In these two roles, Melchizedek can be seen as the local Canaanite representative of the broader conceptions of the ancient Near East, to which I have been alluding. It is also apropos that as king of Salem, the precursor of Jerusalem, he rules from the same seat of power where the Judean kings later exercised their version of the region's ideology of divine kingship.

Finally, in the psalms we find one more connection to the reigning ideology of the ancient Near East. The King is the embodiment of the fertility of the land:

> O God, endow the king with Your judgments, ...
> Let him be like rain that falls on a mown field,
> like a downpour of rain on the ground, ...
> Let abundant grain be in the land, to the top of the mountains;
> (Ps. 72:1,6,16)

All the elements of the ideology of divine kingship are present. There is a divine status (through birth or adoption) and a set of divine or sacred actions: the king as dispenser of divine justice, the king as priest of the Most High, the king as fructifier of the land. Against this background of usurpation of divine prerogatives, we will see other Israelite ideologies shaping their own versions of kingship.

KING AND MESSIAH IN THE TORAH

When we turn to the Torah, we see an absolutely different description of the king and his status. In the king's law in Deuteronomy (17:14-20), we read:

> *When he is seated on his royal throne, he shall have a copy of
> this Teaching written for him on a scroll by the levitical priests.
> Let it remain with him and let him read in it all his life, so that
> he may learn to revere the Lord his God, to observe faithfully
> every word of this Teaching as well as these laws. Thus he will
> not act haughtily toward his fellows or deviate from the Instruc-
> tion to the right or to the left, to the end that he and his descen-
> dants may reign long in the midst of Israel. (Deut. 17:19–20)*

How different is the atmosphere of these verses from what
we have seen in the Book of Psalms! There is nothing divine
or sacred about the king. The king should fear God and obey
God's commandments. In this sense, he is just like all other
Israelites.

The Torah has a different "Son of God" than the king. According to the Torah, the people of Israel as a whole are the
son and firstborn of God. Through Moses, God says this directly to Pharaoh (Exod. 4:22), and Moses repeats it to the
people: "You are children of the Lord your God" (Deut.
14:1). As scholars have noted,[16] we see in the Torah a tendency to democratize all royal titles and attributes that originated in the culture of the ancient Near East. We already
noted instances of this tendency in the first chapters of Genesis. Thus, in Assyrian writing, we find the idea that the
king has the image of the god Bell, while in the book of
Genesis, it is said that all human beings are created in the
image of God (Gen. 1:26–27, 5:1, 9:6).[17] Similarly, we have
seen that the knowledge of good and evil, which was per-
cieved as a divine and royal quality, is applied by Genesis 3
to all humanity.[18]

Nothing is said in the law of Deuteronomy about the
king's responsibility for justice. His only mission, according
to this law, is to keep the commandments of the Torah like
all "his brethren." This picture differs greatly from the description of kings both in the ancient Near East and in other
parts of the Hebrew Bible. There is even a sharp difference
between Deuteronomy and the later history of kings, written

under the influence of Deuteronomic theology. The books of Samuel and Kings, which form the main part of the Deuteronomistic history, have a sharply different image of the king: his status as "God's anointed" in 2 Samuel 7:14 earns him the right to be considered an adopted "son of God," and, as such, he has a central role in both judgment and cult.

In Mesopotamian literature, we find the concept of *andurarum* that gives the king the ability to release people from slavery and debts.[19] A similar concept is to be found in the law of the jubilee year in Leviticus.[20] However, in this law the king is not mentioned, and the calling of דרור, *deror,* the Hebrew parallel of *andurarum,* is the function of the whole people (Lev. 25:10), not of the king:[21] "You shall proclaim liberty throughout the land for all its inhabitants." This must be seen as yet another indication of the democratization of royal terms in the Torah.

The Hebrew word "messiah" appears in the Torah in the book of Leviticus, in relation to the high priest who is anointed with the holy oil. But it is very clearly intended not as a title, but rather as a term of description. Thus, we read in the law of the sin offering in Leviticus: "If the priest, the anointed one [in the Hebrew Bible, הכהן המשיח] sins, bringing guilt on the people..."[22] The anointed one of Leviticus, the high priest, is only a cultic leader. He has no political role. The Priestly writings of the Pentateuch reject any combination of political and Priestly rights. (This also the case in Deuteronomy, where no cultic role whatsoever is assigned to the king.) Thus, the two hundred fifty chieftains of the community who claimed Priestly rights were destroyed by fire: "And a fire went forth from the Lord and consumed the two hundred fifty men offering the incense" (Num. 16:35).

Scholars understand that this story from the Torah reflects a later period, when the priests strenuously objected to Israelite kings's claim on the right to perform cultic roles.[23]

The best example for such a clash between the priests and the king is the story of King Uzziah in 2 Chronicles, which also reflects the later views of the priesthood.[24]

> When he was strong, he grew so arrogant he acted corruptly: he trespassed against his God by entering the Temple of the Lord to offer incense on the incense altar. The priest Azariah, with eighty other brave priests of the Lord, followed him in and, confronting King Uzziah, said to him, "It is not for you, Uzziah, to offer incense to the Lord, but for the Aaronite priests, who have been consecrated, to offer incense. Get out of the Sanctuary, for you have trespassed; there will be no glory in it for you from the Lord God." Uzziah, holding the censer and ready to burn incense, got angry; but as he got angry with the priests, leprosy broke out on his forehead in front of the priests in the House of the Lord beside the incense altar. When the chief priest Azariah and all the other priests looked at him, his forehead was leprous, so they rushed him out of there; he too made haste to get out, for the Lord had struck him with a plague. (2 Chron. 26:16–20)

To understand this story's climax, we need to recall that the high priest bore on his forehead a frontlet of pure gold engraved with the inscription, "Holy to the Lord" (Exod. 28:36–38). Uzziah wants to act as a high priest, but he is struck by God and his forehead becomes leprous. Instead of the Priestly symbol of holiness, his forehead receives a symbol of impurity.[25]

According to the Torah, no Israelite can be both king and priest. Only outside Israel could priesthood and kingship be combined in the same personality. The exemplar mentioned in the Priestly Torah is the same person alluded to in the royal psalms: Melchizedek, the Canaanite King of Salem-Jerusalem, who was at the same time a priest of God Most High, the God of Abraham (Gen. 14:18).[26]

THE DISPUTE OVER THE KING AND THE MESSIAH

We may now summarize our findings: In the historical books and in the psalms, the term "anointed" or "Messiah" is applied to the king. It is a figure of speech, a metonymy for kingship, which (especially in poetry) can serve as a title.

The king has both royal and Priestly rights and functions. The mission of the king is to make justice and righteousness. In the historical books, in the psalms, and in the prophets, the king is described as a member of the divine family and is given divine names. This may attest, in my view, to the deification of the Israelite king. Most scholars have noted a clear difference between Israel and its neighbors in this matter. In other cultures of the ancient Near East, and later on in the classical world, the king was many times identified with a god and became an object of worship. However, in Israel the king was never identified with God and was never worshiped.[27] Yet, as we have shown, the conception of the king in several biblical sources is nevertheless very much influenced by the model of kingship in the ancient Near East.[28]

When we turn to the Torah we see a dramatically different picture. "Messiah" is not a title, but simply a word to describe the anointment of the high priest. There is a total separation between priesthood and kingship, and the king is not given juridic functions. The title "Son of God" is not given to the king, but rather to the people of Israel. There is no word about the divine character of either the throne or the king's name.

How shall we understand this remarkable difference between the Torah and the other parts of the Hebrew Bible? Any explanation must involve both political and theological concerns. The fact that the Torah denies any cultic role to the king is probably the result of a power struggle between the priesthood and the king. The story of Uzziah mentioned above is a clear example of such a dispute.[29] The objection of the Torah to the service of the political leaders in the cult should not be seen only as a reflection of Priestly power interests. It also reflects a wish to refrain from deification of kings. According to the Torah, the political leaders are not allowed to enter into the temple, neither to bring incense before the Lord, nor to sacrifice (Num. 16:35). These limitations of power and authority and delimitation of the sacred sphere make clear that the king is a human being without a sacred function.

The theological difficulty in the perception of a human king as having divine status was pointed out by Y. Kaufmann:

> God is supreme over all...He is utterly distinct from and other than the world...[30] it is impossible, in the biblical view, to become God. The king has sanctity...poetry styles him a "son" of God (Ps. 89:28), meaning that God is his guardian and help. But deification of kings is mentioned only as a heathen custom. Had it existed in Israel the prophets would certainly not have failed to denounce it.[31]

A similar view is expressed by H. Frankfort, who writes:

> The absolute transcendence of God is the foundation of Hebrew religious thought...The transcendentalism of Hebrew religion prevented kingship from assuming the profound significance which it possessed in Egypt and Mesopotamia....The Hebrew king normally functioned in the profane sphere, not in the sacred sphere...He was emphatically not the leader in the cult.[32]

Yet both of these prominent scholars fail to take into account the variety of sources in the Hebrew Bible touching on this subject. In the Torah, indeed, the king has no role in the cult. However, as we have seen, according to the historical books kings are reported as leading the cult in the most important rites.[33]

The Torah negates any divine status of the king, yet as we have seen, the Book of Psalms provides significant evidence for the deification of the king. Kaufmann's argument that had the deification of kings "existed in Israel, the prophets would certainly not have failed to denounce it" cannot be sustained. The prophets could not very well denounce the deification of the kings, because they based their conception of the deified eschatological king on the model of the sacred king in Psalms. The Torah rejects both eschathology and messianism. For the Torah, the world is never going to be changed dramatically. The wolf and the sheep will never live together as friends, nor will the human child and the serpent play together. According to the Torah, there is no way back to Eden.

In spite of this sharp controversy between the Torah and the other parts of the Bible, there was later an effort to combine some of the ideas of both writings. In the period of the return from Babylonian exile, there was an attempt to validate both sorts of divine anointment in Zechariah's vision:

> *"And what," I asked him, "are those two olive trees, one on the right and one on the left of the lampstand?" And I further asked him, "What are the two tops of the olive trees that feed their oil through those two golden tubes?" He asked me, "Don't you know what they are?" And I replied, "No, my lord." Then he explained, "They are the two anointed dignitaries who attend the Lord of all the earth." (Zech. 4:11–14)*

"The two anointed dignitaries" (literally, "the sons of oil") refer to the high priest Joshua, and the descendant of royalty, Zerubabel, who had been appointed by the ruler in Babylon to lead the people. It is as if the Torah's model of an anointed priest is being combined with the psalmic-prophetic model of an anointed king. The conception of two messiahs, one royal and one Priestly, was later adopted among the sectarians of Qumran.[34]

HUMAN KINGSHIP VIS-A-VIS THE KINGDOM OF HEAVEN

Besides the two trends described so far, there is a third trend in the Bible that negates in principle the very idea of human kingship in Israel. When the men of Israel ask of Gideon, "Rule over us—you, your son, and your grandson as well; for you have saved us from the Midianites," Gideon replied, "I will not rule over you myself, nor shall my son rule over you; the Lord alone shall rule over you" (Judg. 8:22–23). According to Gideon's view, there is no place for the establishment of a royal dynasty in Israel. The people of Israel should be ruled only by God, not by a human king or ruler.

A similar ideology is reflected in 1 Samuel. The Elders of Israel came to Samuel and said to him:

> You have grown old, and your sons have not followed your ways. Therefore appoint a king for us, to govern us like all other nations." Samuel was displeased that they said "Give us a king to govern us." Samuel prayed to the Lord, and the Lord replied to Samuel, "Heed the demand of the people in everything they say to you. For it is not you that they have rejected; it is Me they have rejected as their king. Like everything else they have done ever since I brought them out of Egypt to this day—forsaking Me and worshiping other gods—so they are doing to you. Heed their demand; but warn them solemnly, and tell them about the practices of any king who will rule over them. (1 Sam. 8:4–9)

It is not crucial to our discussion whether or not these stories about Gideon and Samuel are historical.[35] What matters most is the fact that both express a thoroughgoing ideological rejection of human kingship. Both stories depict the appointment of a human king as a rebellion against the kingdom of heaven. This view represents an extreme trend in Israel that saw human kingship in its essence as an invalidation of the religion of Israel.[36]

POST-BIBLICAL DEVELOPMENTS

The three major trends of the biblical period that refer to kingship can also be found in the last generations of the Second Temple period. The first of these trends, the total negation of human kingship, based on the conception that God is the only legitimate king of Israel, was the ideological basis of the party of the Sicarri who fought against the Roman government in the Galilee, in Jerusalem, and in Masada.[37]

The second of the trends, the ideology of the Messiah who has divine status, is found in the messianic Hymns of Qumran.[38] I have argued elsewhere that this ideology was the basis for the formation of Christianity.[39] We have seen that in the biblical period, there was indeed a large impact of the regional ideology of divine kingship on the conception of the Israelite

Messiah. It seems that a similar process took place in the last generations of the Second Temple period. In that period, the source of external influence was the ideology of the divinity of the Roman emperor, developed by Augustus after he defeated Mark Anthony and Cleopatra in 31 B.C.E.[40]

The third trend begins with the fact that Hillel was a contemporary of Augustus.[41] As we will see in detail in chapter 8, Hillel was aware of the worship of the Roman emperor as a god. However, Hillel reacted to the imperial cult by stressing the principle that human beings are created in the image of the divine. Every person, he taught, is partly divine because that person is made in the image of God.[42] In this sense, Hillel continues the trend of the Torah to democratize royal symbols and ideology.[43]

CHAPTER SEVEN

New Conceptions of Evil and Suffering during the Period of Exile and Return

I N THE LAST TWO CHAPTERS, WE DISCUSSED THE MAIN
INSTITUTIONS of ancient Israel: sanctuary, priesthood, and
kingship. But all these institutions ceased to exist at the
beginning of the sixth century B.C.E. At that time, the Babylonians destroyed the kingdom of Judea, razed the Temple in
Jerusalem, and exiled a sizeable portion of the populace to
Babylon. The destruction raised doubts in the hearts of many
Judeans, especially as it followed closely on the heels of the
people's return to an untainted religious faith and purified
worship during the time of Josiah. How could such a religious
awakening be followed by so terrible a crisis as the destruction of the Temple and Jerusalem?

The generation of the destruction claimed that they were
being punished for the sins of their fathers, the contemporaries of King Manasseh, who had placed an idol in the Temple.[1] The Scroll of Lamentations records this saying: "Our
fathers sinned and are no more; and we must bear their guilt"
(Lam. 5:7). We find a similar claim in the book of Ezekiel.
Speaking to the people of his generation, he says, "What do

you mean by quoting this proverb upon the soil of Israel, 'Parents eat sour grapes and their children's teeth are blunted'?" (Ezek. 18:2). The previous generation's sour, unripe grapes refer to sins, for which the next generation is punished. The Book of Second Kings also claims that Jerusalem was overrun and razed because of Manasseh's sins. In other words, everything that Josiah did was fit and proper and found favor in the eyes of God, but it did not suffice to atone for the sins of Manasseh.[2] But the people who experienced the destruction found this explanation difficult to accept; did punishment, exile, and the destruction of the Temple really follow from the deeds done by their forebears? Their voices repudiate and challenge this conception, as we have seen in the quotations from the Scroll of Lamentations and the Book of Ezekiel, cited above.[3]

EZEKIEL'S RESPONSE

Ezekiel takes issue with the proverbial saying, "Parents eat sour grapes and their children's teeth are blunted," saying instead, "As I live—declares the Lord God—this proverb shall no longer be current among you in Israel. Consider, all lives are Mine; the life of the parent and the life of the child are both Mine. The person who sins, only he shall die" (Ezek. 18:3–4). Ezekiel goes on to discuss at length the principle of individual sin and punishment passing from one generation to another. In making this assertion, he argues against a conception already found in the Ten Commandments, according to which God visits the sins of the fathers upon the children (Exod. 20:5).[4] No, says Ezekiel, "The person who sins, only he." At the end of his oration, Ezekiel addresses his contemporaries, telling them that if they have been punished, if they are suffering great pains and exile, their own sins—not the sins of their forebears—have brought this upon them. He calls out to them: "Be assured, O House of Israel, I will judge each one of you according to his ways...Repent and turn back from all your transgressions; let them not be a stumbling block of guilt for you" (Ezek. 18:30). Do not blame your forefathers' actions; things must be rectified by your own hand. "Cast away all the transgressions by which you have offended, and get yourselves a new heart and a new spirit" (Ezek. 18:31). Mend your hearts and spirits: this is Ezekiel's call to his contemporaries.

The view that punishment is visited upon the sinners themselves and is not the result of sins committed by earlier generations requires an alternative explanation for the destruction of the Temple. And indeed, we find in 2 Chronicles the statement that Jerusalem was destroyed not because of the sins of Manasseh (who repented before his death, according to this source), but on account of the transgressions of Zedekiah—the last king of Judea—and his contemporaries.[5]

We have, then, a dispute within the Bible as to the reasons for the destruction of Jerusalem and the razing of the Temple: 2 Kings places the blame squarely on the shoulders of Manasseh, while 2 Chronicles claims that Manasseh repented and that Jerusalem was destroyed on account of the deeds of Zedekiah and his contemporaries. This debate is not motivated by disagreement on the factual level, but by a conceptual–theological dispute. At bottom, the question is between "The person who sins, only he shall die," and "Parents ate sour grapes and the children's teeth are blunted." Ezekiel raises questions that pertain to the fate of the nation as a whole,[6] but he does so through a detailed examination of an individual's action and relationship with God, without regard for ancestors or descendants. Ezekiel emphasizes that one can alter one's destiny. A person who has been wicked throughout life can alter this behavior, and God will disregard the earlier behavior and judge that individual exclusively on the merit of present behavior. The opposite is true as well: if a person has been righteous throughout life but becomes wicked during the latter years, God takes only the present behavior into account.[7] These ideas greatly enhance the autonomy and the responsibility of the individual. An individual can alter fate by altering personal actions.

EZEKIEL'S DETERMINISM

It is very surprising, then, to find also in the book of Ezekiel an approach diametrically opposed to the one described above. According to this deterministic approach, everything was ordained in the distant past, and there is nothing one can do to change one's fate and lot in life. In chapter 20, Ezekiel surveys Israelite and Judean history and states that the whole history is rooted in sin. Already in Egypt, the Israelites sinned and cleaved to idols: "They defied Me and refused to listen to Me. They did not cast away the detestable things they were drawn to, nor did they give up the fetishes of Egypt" (Ezek. 20:8).[8]

According to Ezekiel, the wanderings in the desert were also an era of idolatry, of repeated desecrations of the Sabbath, and of terrible transgressions. The generation that perished in the desert, as well as those who were born in the desert and later entered the Land of Israel, were all sinners and criminals. God bestowed upon them good rules and laws, but they desecrated them and dutifully transgressed them, generation after generation. Moreover, Ezekiel claims that the punishment of exile was ordained for them from the time of their wandering in the desert, under the leadership of Moses.

> However, I swore to them in the wilderness that I would scatter them among the nations and disperse them through the lands, because they did not obey My rules, but rejected My laws, profaned My Sabbaths, and looked with longing to the fetishes of their fathers. (Ezek. 20:23–24)

The stamp of exile was impressed upon the Children of Israel even before they entered the Promised Land. The fate of all the Israelites who crossed into the land and all the generations that were to inhabit the Land of Israel from the days of Joshua down to Zedekiah: their fate of ultimate exile was sealed.

Ezekiel expresses another extreme idea in the same chapter. He writes, "I gave them laws that were not good and rules by which they could not live: When they set aside every first issue of the womb, I defiled them by their very gifts—that I might render them desolate, that they might know that I am the Lord" (Ezek. 20:25–26). In other words, God punished the Israelites by giving them laws that were even more terrible than their earlier transgressions had been—the laws of child sacrifice. Apparently, Ezekiel was of the opinion that when God commanded the Israelites, "You shall give me the first-born among your sons" (Exod. 22:28), God intended by this the sacrificial death of the firstborn.[9]

The prophet Micah attacks this idea in his condemnation of the man who says, "Shall I give my firstborn for my transgression?" (Mic. 6:7). Jeremiah too decries this approach in saying: "And they have built shrines to Topheth in the Valley of Ben-hinnom to burn their sons and daughters in fire—which I have not commanded, which never came to My mind" (Jer. 7:31).[10] According to Jeremiah such a thing never occurred to God, but Ezekiel disagrees. Indeed it did occur to God, Ezekial claims, and in fact was commanded by God—as a form of punishment. In the midst of this dispute between prophets, we cannot help but think of the story of the Binding of Isaac, wherein God commands Isaac to be sacrificed, and then says, "Do not raise your hand against the boy" (Gen. 22:12). The issues that the prophets and the Genesis narrative address are closely related.

CHILD SACRIFICE AND THE BINDING OF ISAAC

The story of the Binding of Isaac, the *Akedah*, is not the first incident in the Book of Genesis involving an offering to God. It is preceded by the offerings made by Cain, Abel, and Noah.[11] These offerings are brought at the initiative of the one bringing them, so as to draw close to and appease God. The nature of the sacrificial object was similarly determined by the individual making the offering, rather than dictated by God. Thus, the command to bind Isaac deviates from the voluntary model of sacrifices known from earlier generations. For the first time, God demands a sacrifice and dictates what to offer.

In this sense, the act of the *Akedah* differs not only from what precedes it, but also from what follows. Throughout the period of the Patriarchs and Matriarchs, we do not find any other command to offer a sacrifice. The only sacrifice God asks for in the entire Book of Genesis is a human sacrifice. In demanding that Abraham bind his son to the sacrificial pyre, Abraham is asked essentially to bind and slay his deepest feelings as a human being. "Take your son, your favorite one, Isaac, whom you love... and offer him there as a burnt offering" (Gen. 22:2).

And yet, this unique cultic command is not executed. The moment Abraham puts forth his hand to slaughter his son, the angel of God calls to him from heaven and commands him to desist from the very act commanded by God. We can explain the literary and theological problems raised by this sudden change in the divine will on the basis of another literary element—the divine names used in the story. In the initial commandment to bind Isaac, the name "Elohim" is used (Gen. 22:1); in contrast, the order to refrain from carrying out the offering is associated with the name "YHWH" (Gen. 22:11). The whole story of the binding seems to stem from one source,[12] so we can not explain the change of the divine names as a result of combining different sources. Instead, we need to see that the narrator deliberately used these two different divine names in order to say something about God and the manner of God's revelation.

Earlier I demonstrated that the Priestly Torah reads the name "Elohim," which is used at the time of Creation, as specifically expressing the rational and ethical dimensions within God. The name "YHWH," which according to the Priestly Torah was revealed only in the time of Moses, expresses the numinous or nonrational dimension of the God-head. But the *Akedah* story reverses the symbolic meaning of these two divine names. Within the story, the numinous, irrational, and amoral dimension of God is signified by the name "Elohim," while the rational–moral aspect is signified by the name "YHWH." The terrible command to bind the son, a command that is beyond the realm of ethical under-standing, stems from Elohim. Through this command, God both contradicts the divine promises to Abraham concerning the proliferation of his seed and requires him to perform a deed that violates the norms of justice and righteousness, for the observance of which God has singled out Abraham.[13] Moreover, Abraham is called upon to do violence to his deep-est feelings and thereby negate his own self in the face of God. Through his willingness to carry out this comand, Abra-ham reveals that he "fears Elohim" (Gen. 22:12)—that is, he is willing to submit totally to the command of the numinous Godhead, while contradicting his own personality and con-signing his personal feelings to oblivion.

But before Abraham can carry out this terrible act, that di-vine element symbolized by the name "YHWH" intervenes and prevents him from doing so. In this story, YHWH, or the angel of YHWH, represents the rational and ethical dimen-sion within the Godhead. It is YHWH, through an angel, who prevents Abraham from offering his son and who confirms to him the fulfillment of the promises regarding his descendants and the inheritance of the land. In this story, the rational and ethical dimensions of God, symbolized by the name "YHWH," overrule the numinous dimension, symbolized by the name "Elohim." The demand to Abraham to erase his self and to obliterate his fatherly emotions is negated, and in its place come the blessings of life and fertility.

The story appears to have it both ways: God both com-mands child sacrifice and negates the command. In effect, the author of the story uses the command from Elohim to refer to a phase in Israelite history when there were those who perceived such a divine obligation, but then juxtaposes it with the later command from YHWH's angel to refer to the author's conviction, disavowed by Micah and Jeremiah, that such commandment was no longer to be construed as legitimately stemming from God. Abraham is explicitly praised for his willingness to carry out Elohim's command, but God's promise to him is reaffirmed when he is able to ascertain the unique commanding voice of YHWH's angel. At that point in the story, the child intended for the sacrifice is replaced by the ram, and understanding the import of the story more broadly, the practice of child sacrifice can be replaced in Israel by animal sacrifice. The *Akedah* story can thus be seen as an allegory of this momentous change in the religion of Israel.[14]

THE PROPHETIC DISPUTE BETWEEN FREEDOM AND DETERMINISM

The material we have surveyed in this chapter serves as witness to an ancient dispute regarding child sacrifice. In response to those Israelites who claim that God wants such sacrifices, Micah and Jeremiah claim, in the strongest possible terms, that God by no means commanded such acts. Genesis 22 takes a different rhetorical path, using a story highlighting the two names of God to overturn the practice of child sacrifice. Ezekiel takes what we might call a middle path with regard to this issue. He admits that God had once commanded the Israelites to sacrifice their firstborn, but did so only in order to punish the sinful nation. God gave the people of Israel "laws that were not good and rules by which they could not live" (Ezek. 20:25).

If we pose to Ezekiel the questions "Why was Jerusalem destroyed?" and "Why were the Israelites exiled to Babylon?" radically different answers would come from from the Exzekiel of chapter 18 and the Ezekiel of chapter 20. According to the latter, exile and destruction come not on account of the sins committed at the time of Zedekiah, as 2 Chronicles would have it, nor on account of the sins committed during the generation of Manasseh, as 2 Kings would have it, but rather on account of the sins committed in the desert by the generation of Moses and the children of Israel. We might call this an ideology of ever-receding determinism. The ultimate extension of this idea is found in the Christian concept of Adam and Eve's original sin. If one views the destruction in these deterministic terms, if the sin runs so deep and hundreds of years of sin and depravity have accumulated within the people of Israel, what could possibly bring about a change in this situation? The people of Ezekiel's generation could do nothing; they wallow in sin and only divine intervention can effect a change.

Indeed, chapter 36 of Ezekiel speaks of a new creation of human beings. The Children of Israel in their present form are unredeemable; they cannot save themselves. God must change the character of human beings in order for redemption to come about. "I will sprinkle clean water upon you, and you shall be clean: I will cleanse you from your uncleanness and from all your fetishes" (Ezek. 36:25). It is God who will sprinkle water upon the people, for they cannot purify themselves through their own agency. "And I will give you a new heart and put a new spirit into you: I will remove the heart of stone from your body and give you a heart of flesh" (Ezek. 36:26). It is God who removes the stone heart and plants in human beings a new heart, a heart of flesh, for according to the view advanced in this chapter, only God can correct the corrupt nature of human beings. "And I will put My spirit in you. Thus I will cause you to follow My laws and faithfully to observe My rules" (Ezek. 36:27). God must reprogram the Children of Israel to observe the necessary rules. They cannot be given free choice. That path was tried and they failed generation after generation. If human beings are to succeed, then God must place in them a new heart—a heart of flesh— that will force them to walk in the path of the Lord.[15]

However, besides this view, we hear in other chapters of the book of Ezekiel a completely different tone. In chapter 18, the prophet promotes an active role on the part of the people, who are called upon to "get yourseleves a new heart and a new spirit" (Ezek. 18:31).

The Book of Ezekiel thus contains an astonishing range of views. On the one hand, Ezekiel enhances the freedom and responsibility of the individual, and places emphasis on an individual's capacity to choose a new way, to alter the future by becoming self-redeeming. On the other hand, he despairs of human nature completely. There is no hope, no possibility short of divine intervention that can change the character, the heart, and the spirit of humanity and bring about re-demption. These two polar opposites are found in the same book.[16] In some way, this may remind us of the modern de-bate between different schools of psychologists over how much of human behavior and potential is dependent upon ge-netics and cultural environment, and how much can yet be changed by human effort and will.

Apparently, Ezekiel was torn between the two possibilities and voiced both in an extreme fashion. Interestingly, these two possibilities recurred in future generations within Ju-daism, each appealing to a different group. We shall see that the polarity found in the book of Ezekiel paved new paths in the development of Jewish faith in the time of the Second Temple.

THE SUFFERING SERVANT IN SECOND ISAIAH

A highly significant effort to give meaning to the exile and to the suffering of the Jewish people is to be found in the prophecy of the so-called Second Isaiah. This anonymous prophet lived around the time of King Cyrus of Persia's dec-laration[17] of the Jewish return to Zion. Second Isaiah's prophe-cies are contained in the second part of the Book of Isaiah, from chapter 40 through the end of the book.[18]

An important and mysterious figure in the Second Isaiah is the figure of the suffering servant. Chapter 53 of Isaiah describes the suffering servant: He was despised, shunned by men,

> A man of suffering, familiar with disease.
> As one who hid his face from us,
> He was despised, we held him of no account. (Isa. 53.3)

The speakers, who are not identified by the prophet, look at the suffering servant and realize that he suffers for their own sins:

> Yet it was our sickness that he was bearing,
> Our suffering that he endured.
> We accounted him plagued,
> Smitten and afflicted by God;
> But he was wounded because of our sins,
> Crushed because of our iniquities.
> He bore the chastisement that made us whole,
> And by his bruises we were healed.
> We all went astray like sheep,
> Each going his own way;
> And the Lord visited upon him
> The guilt of all of us. (Isa. 53:4–6)

Who is the suffering servant? The answer to this question is hotly debated. Some scholars think that the servant is an individual. Several suggestions have been given regarding his identity. Some think of an historical figure,[19] while others believe that the historical elements are interwoven with messianic expectations,[20] or that the figure is purely messianic. Other scholars argue that here, as elsewhere in the prophecies of Second Isaiah, the servant is a collective figure who represents the people of Israel.[21] Y. Kaufmann claimed that the servant represents a group of righteous people within Israel.[22] Following this path, we can see the speakers as the rest of the Isrealites. According to another view, the speakers in chapter 53 are the nations who finally understand that Israel suffers because of the other nations' iniquities.[23]

I accept the view that the servant is Israel; in order to understand this interpretation fully we must read Isaiah's prophecy against the background of the literature and the spiritual reality of that time. Deuteronomy, for instance, had warned the Israelites against worshiping idols, for idolatry, the book argues, would lead to the destruction of the land and the deportation of the people. Deuteronomy describes the response of the gentiles who will observe all the adversities that happen to Israel:

> Foreigners who come from distant lands and see the plagues and diseases that the Lord has inflicted upon that land, all its soil devastated by sulfur and salt, beyond sowing and producing, no grass growing in it, just like the upheaval of Sodom and Gomorrah...which the Lord overthrew in His fierce anger—all nations will ask, "Why did the Lord do thus to this land? Wherefore that awful wrath?" They will be told, "Because they forsook the covenant that the Lord, God of their fathers, made with them when He freed them from the land of Egypt; they turned to the service of other gods and worshiped them, gods whom they had not experienced and whom He had not allotted to them. So the Lord was incensed at that land and brought upon it all curses recorded in this book. The Lord uprooted them from their soil in anger, fury, and great wrath, and cast them into another land." (Deut. 29:21–27)

The reference to "all curses recorded in this book" points to a list of curses that culminates with the exile: "The Lord will scatter you among all the peoples from one end of the earth to the other, and there you shall serve other gods, wood and stone, whom neither you nor your ancestors have experienced" (Deut. 28:64).

The picture that emerges from these verses fits the Deuteronomic conception that only the people of Israel, the elected people, are called to worship the Lord in the land of Israel that is the inheritance of God. To the other nations, God allotted other divine beings whom they can worship in their own lands. When the Israelites serve the gods of other nations, which are not allotted to them, they will be punished harshly. Their land will be ruined and they will be exiled to the lands of the other nations. Since those lands are not under the direct dominion of the Lord, it would be natural for the exiled Israelites to adopt the local deities and to worship them.

These verses in Deuteronomy were written probably at the end of the seventh century B.C.E. or even later.[24] While they claim to speak of the future, it is much more likely that they are based on actual historical experience. One hundred years earlier, the Assyrians had conquered the northern kingdom, the kingdom of Israel, and deported its population to different provinces of their empire.[25] The Israelites who were exiled by the Assyrians were probably instructed by the Assyrian officials "to fear god and king," that is, to accept the Assyrian government and religion.[26] By doing this, they would have been quickly assimilated in their lands of captivity and would have disappeared from the stage of Israelite history. Deuteronomy forecasts the same fate for the tribe of Judah if they, too, forsake their covenant with God.

Deuteronomy's forecast, however, was not fully carried out. The land of Judea was conquered by the Babylonians. Jerusalem and the Temple were ruined, and the people of Judea were deported to Babylon. But unlike their brothers the Israelites, the deported Judeans did not adopt the local religion. Instead, they stayed loyal to their national and religious identity.[27] This loyalty was continued by their children who were born in the exile. These natives of the Babylonian captivity are the audience to whom Second Isaiah speaks. The prophet has to give meaning to the suffering of their exile. As we saw early in this chapter, previous attempts to explain the exile as a punishment for the idolatry of Manasseh were rejected by the people. Second Isaiah comes forward with an entirely new idea.

Like Deuteronomy 29, Second Isaiah draws a picture of the gentiles looking at the suffering of the Jewish people. However, his picture is dramatically different. In the Deuteronomic scene, the gentiles who worship their gods are innocent, because they are not expected to know the Lord, whereas the Israelites are blamed for worshiping the gods of the nations. Second Isaiah rejects the Deuteronomic conception that the other nations are detached from the Lord of Israel. Following his predecessor and namesake, Isaiah the son of Amoz, Second Isaiah calls upon all nations, in the name of the Lord, to abandon their idols and to worship the God of Israel.

> Come gather together,
> Draw nigh, you remnants of the nations!
> No foreknowledge had they who carry their wooden images
> And pray to a god who cannot give success....
> Turn to Me and gain success,
> All the ends of the earth!
> For I am God, and there is none else.
> By Myself have I sworn,
> From My mouth has issued truth,
> A word that shall not turn back:
> To Me every knee shall bend,
> Every tongue swear loyalty. (Isa. 45:20–23)

In the view of Second Isaiah, the idolatry of the gentiles is an error of blindness. They worshiped idols because until this time they did not know the true God. It is Israel, the servant of the Lord, who is called to become a "light for nations" and to save the gentiles from their religious blindness:[28]

> I the Lord, in My grace, have summoned you,
> And I have grasped you by the hand.
> I created you, and appointed you
> A covenant people, a light of nations—
> Opening eyes deprived of light,
> Rescuing prisoners from confinement,
> From the dungeon those who sit in darkness. (Isa. 42:6–7)

However, Israel was sent not only to bring light to the nations, but also to atone for their sins. This is the message of Isaiah 53. The prophet describes the nations' understanding of the reason for Israel's suffering. In sharp contrast to the above mentioned scene in Deuteronomy 29, here the gentiles are the sinners and Israel the innocent. But the nations committed their sin of idolatry out of blindness; they did not know the Lord. According to the Priestly law, a sin committed unwittingly is to be atoned by a guilt offering:

> And when a person, without knowing it, sins in regard to any of
> the Lord's commandments about things not to be done, and then

realizes his guilt...he shall bring to the priest a ram...as a guilt of-
fering. The priest shall make expiation on his behalf for the error
that he committed unwittingly, and he shall be forgiven. (Lev.
5:17–18)[29]

Second Isaiah sees Israel, the suffering servant, as a ram of
guilt offering:[30]

> *He was maltreated, yet he was submissive,*
> *He did not open his mouth;*
> *Like a sheep led to slaughter,*
> *Like a ewe, dumb before those who shear her,*
> *He did not open his mouth....*
> *He made himself an offering of guilt. (Isa. 53:7,10)*

The nations realize now that Israel suffered in order to
atone for *their* guilt:

"But he was wounded because of our sins, / Crushed because of our iniquities" (Isa. 53:5).

The notion that one person can atone with suffering for
sins that others have committed unwittingly stems from the
Priestly legislation of Israel. The law in Numbers 35 deals
with a murder that was committed unintentionally. According to this law, the killer must flee to the city of refuge and to
remain there until the death of the high priest, but "after the
death of the high priest, the manslayer may return to his land
of holding" (Num. 35:28). We can explain this by virtue of the
fact that the high priest's death atones for the unintentional
sin of murder.[31]

Second Isaiah sees Israel the suffering servant as the high
priest of the nations.[32] Through Israel's affliction, suffering,
and death, Israel brings expiation to the gentiles who had committed idolatry without knowing that it was a sin. In this way,
the prophet gives new meaning to the suffering of Israel.[33]

THE BOOK OF JOB

Unlike the prophecies of Isaiah and Ezekiel, which deal with
the collectivity of Israel, the Book of Job deals with the fate of
the individual. Job is stunned by the blows that rain down

upon him in quick succession. All his propety is stolen or destroyed, all his children die, and he is afflicted with terrible skin disease. His wife tells him to "blaspheme God and die" (Job 2:9), but he refuses to commit blasphemy and maintains his faith and integrity. He does, however, speak harshly to God. He asks how it can be that a righteous man like himself should suffer so much? His friends, attempting to console him, try to convince Job that perhaps, despite everything, he has committed some transgression that has escaped his notice. God would not strike him so harshly, so cruelly, for no reason. But Job professes his innocence and refuses to accept their explanations, saying: "Far be it from me to say you are right; / until I die I will not put away my integrity" (Job 27:5).

Finally, God appears to Job in a storm, and in a long discourse describes the wonders of Creation. Amazingly, at the end of God's oration, Job is calmed and says, "I had heard You with my ears, / But now I see You with my eyes; / Therefore, I recant and relent / Being but dust and ashes" (Job 42:5–6). God's revelation puts Job's mind at rest, but what about the nature of this revelation achieves this repose? The answer given by God appears to be a non sequitur involving a discussing of the creation process, while Job's question is about why he is being punished, if he has not sinned? God does not answer in the manner of Job's companions, telling Job that though he may think he is righteous, he has actually sinned. God does not even relate to Job's question at all. Instead, God shows Job the creation of the world and all its wondrous creatures, such as Behemoth and Leviathan. What have these to do with Job's complaint? Why does this comfort Job and elicit the response, "I recant and relent"?

The revelation that Job receives alters his perspective. It is a revolutionary epiphany that radically changes his point of view, and in this revolution he finds the solution to his problem. Job was raised in the belief that there is a direct correlation between human behavior and the behavior of the Creator. This theology posits that if one keeps God's commandments, the heavens will open and provide abundant rain. "If, then, you obey the commandments that I enjoin upon you this day...I will grant the rain for your land in season, the early rain and the late" (Deut. 11:13–14). According to this conception, there is a direct proportional relationship between human righteousness and natural abundance.

This approach might lead a person to think that the rain falls for his or her sake. If someone acts justly, the floodgates of heaven will open and prosperity will result. God broadens Job's perspective by saying: "Who cut a channel for the torrents / And a path for the thunderstorms, / To rain down on uninhabited land, / On the wilderness where no man is, / To saturate the desolate wasteland, / And make the crop of grass sprout forth?" (Job 38:25–27). There are vast uninhabited areas throughout the earth, but the rain nevertheless falls there and brings forth plants. Does Job think that everything was created just to serve him? The world is much greater, much vaster than Job, with his limited perspective, can imagine.[34]

Job's original understanding of the human place in the universe is paralleled by the first chapter of Genesis, the passage that opens the Priestly Torah. In this chapter, the creation of the universe is presented as an ordered, gradual process, proceeding step by step, level upon level, culminating in the creation of humanity. Human beings are the last of God's creatures, and it is for their benefit that the world was created. God entrusts the entire universe to them and says to them, "Be fertile and increase, fill the earth and master it; and rule the fish of the sea, the birds of the sky, and all the living things that creep on earth" (Gen. 1:28). Humanity believes that everything revolves around it, that the whole Creation is for its glory and honor, and that humankind stands in the center of the universe. It follows that if all was created for human beings' sake, then everything should function according to how human beings behave.

But in the Book of Job, God effectively says that the picture presented in Genesis 1 is partial and limited. Take the wild ox, for example. "Would the wild ox agree to serve you? / Would he spend the night at your crib? / Can you hold the wild ox by ropes to the furrow? / Would he plow up the valleys behind you?" (Job 39:9–11). The wild ox is not a domestic animal, who will eat from a manger; he will not be tied up or put to work for human beings. He is one of the many animals that refuse to do humanity's bidding. This is even truer of the great monster, the Leviathan. "Can you draw out Leviathan by a fishhook? / Can you press down his tongue by a rope? / Can you put a ring through his nose, / Or pierce his jaw with a barb? / Will he make an agreement with you / To be taken as your lifelong slave? / Will you play with him like a bird, / And tie him down for your girls?" (Job 40:25–29) Can humans use Leviathan for their own pleasure? No. Quite the contrary: "There is no one on land who can dominate him, / Made as he is without fear. / He sees all that is haughty; / He is king over all proud beasts" (Job 41:25–26). The human being is not the crowning glory of Creation. The crown is taken off the human head and placed upon that of a terrible sea monster.

The Leviathan, the wild ox, and other animals described in these chapters serve as a demonstration to Job that there are things in Creation that cannot be put to work for humankind's advantage; from a human perspective, they serve no purpose. If one believes that the world was created for humans and revolves around their needs, thoughts, and actions, then the creation of these animals could not be justified, for they offer no advantage to humanity. But given their existence and the importance that God's speech places upon them, one is led to conclude that the world is a far more diverse and variegated place than previously imagined, and that God is not humanity's superintendent, supplying people with food and rain and supervising human behavior. God's fullness far surpasses humanity and its needs.

On hearing God speaking to him from within the storm, Job undergoes a process of maturation; he ascends to a higher level of faith. God speaks to him via this astonishing revelation: "Your bookkeeping is perfect, you made all the proper entries in the right order. Do you really want to know why things occur? Because there is a reality far more vast than the ledger. Leave the protective constraints of book-keeping and examine the spaces beyond. When you gaze upon the infinite vastness of Creation, you will be calmed, for you will no longer feel cheated or betrayed." This per-spective causes an individual to forget private woes. That is not to say that private woes are not terribly painful, but that when looking at the grandeur of Creation, one acquires a cer-tain modesty.

It is true that there are certain things in human existence that humanity can understand, but not everything lies within the human grasp. The world is full of wondrous mysteries for which one has no answer. That is the answer to Job's ques-tion.[35] God's revelation brings Job to an awarness of human-ity's true position in the world, and Job expresses the illumination he has gained by declaring, "I had heard You with my ears, / But now I see You with my eyes; / Therefore, I recant and relent / Being but dust and ashes" (Job 42:5–6).

The Book of Job depicts a dynamic process: the refinement of an individual's faith–consciousness similar to that which takes place on a national scale in the Priestly Torah. Within the Priestly Torah, there is a transition from the elementary faith of the Genesis period to the elevated theology of Moses and Israel. In the Genesis period, faith was founded on a worldview that placed humanity at the center of the universe; religiosity was grounded in the laws of morality and a belief in reward and punishment. The faith of Moses and Israel, ac-cording to P, was founded on an awareness of the centrality of God, a consiousness deriving from the discovery of a divine dimension beyond the moral, beyond reward and punishment.

The author of the Book of Job depicts his protagonist, a non-Israelite, as a figure who attains the highest degree of faith. The author says, in essence, that all people can fully recognize God. All people can attain the experience of revelation and can understand the true place that humanity occupies in relation to God. It has nothing to do with the nation or tribe into which one is born, or with the land in which one lives. Job lived in "the land of Uz" (Job 1:1). We do not know exactly where Uz is,[36] but even in the land of Uz, one can see God and hear God speak from within the storm. One need not be in the Land of Israel to receive revelation. One does not have to offer sacrifices to see the Lord. Job is depicted as offering sacrifices in his early days, when he is terribly concerned about his bookkeeping with the Lord. It is written that his sons held feasts, each time in a different house, and at the end of the feasts, Job would offer sacrifices. He was anxious lest one of his sons might do or even think something in the lax atmosphere of the feast, which would find disfavor in the eyes of God. Job offered sacrifices in the hope of keeping the books balanced.[37] After attaining the highest revelation, however, he is no longer depicted as offering sacrifices. God is revealed to him through nature, through Creation. The power of this revelation is not mediated by a certain family, a specific type of religious ritual, or a set location. The Book of Job tells us that the experience of standing before God cannot be limited or confined. No one is ineligible for this experience; it is open to all humanity.

Here we see the great difference between the Book of Job and the Priestly Torah. According to the Priestly Torah, the numinous element in divinity and the exalted faith–insight bound up with it find expression only through the complex of ritual and sanctuary that came into being after the revelation of the name "YHWH" to Moses and Israel. In the pre-Mosaic period, the Priestly Torah placed humanity at the center of the universe and emphasized the rational and the moral dimension of divinity. This is conveyed by the structured description of the Creation in Genesis 1, with human beings as its crowning achievement, and by the portrayal of God as the source of providence and a judge of morality. According to the Book of Job, however, one can discover the numinous dimension of divinity and attain an exalted faith–consciousness even if one does not belong to Israel. Access to this dimension can be gained through a reflection on the divine Creation without any connection to a sanctuary or its system of sacrifice.

This divergence explains the striking difference in the way the two works portray Creation: In Genesis 1, the Creation is built up step-by-step, with every stage having a purpose and defined meaning. In the divine revelation to Job, however, the mysterious, bizarre, and unfathomable elements of Creation are emphasized. While in Genesis 1, the Priestly Torah presents a picture of the Creation in which human beings are the apex of the divine work, the Book of Job makes no mention at all of the creation of humanity.

From the language and style of the Book of Job, it is clear that the author wished to evoke the atmosphere of Genesis and the time of the Patriarchs.[38] This serves to emphasize the author's differences with the Priestly Torah, since the implication is that the most exalted religious conception had already come into the world before the appearance of Moses and the revelation of the name "YHWH,"[39] and it took place outside Israel. Thus, according to the Book of Job, the attainment of an exalted faith–consciousness is not dependent on national identity; it is tied neither to the revelation of a particular divine name, nor to the observance of a Temple ritual. Rather, any person can, by reflecting on God's Creation, attain insight into the fullness of God's being and arrive at an understanding of humanity's true standing before God.

The Book of Job, then, offers the most universal explanation of evil and suffering that we have encountered. Suffering is part of the inescapable fabric of life, and the suffering of Israel requires no special explanation that distinguishes the Jewish people's experience from the rest of humanity. The writer of Job addressed the Jewish people from within the traditions of wisdom literature, which are part of the cultural inheritance of the ancient Near East. Writing in the period of the Restoration, the concerns that the author of Job brings to the fore are those of an intellectual elite and bear the stamp of a universalism that is the exception rather than the rule in ancient Jewish writing. The prophets Ezekiel and Isaiah speak from within vastly different literary conventions. They speak to and for the people in a moment of existential crisis and attempt to interpret the people's pain and suffering in ways that will bring solace, understanding, and a new direction for both Israel and the nations. Like the writer of Job, the prophets also glimpse revolutionary possibilities—a new heart and spirit for Israel, a new openness to the one God from the nations. The newness, richness, and depth of their collective theologies are a testimony to the formative questions that they asked as they struggled in their time with the problem of suffering and evil.

CHAPTER EIGHT

The Emergence of the Sects in Ancient Judaism

I N CHAPTER 1 WE EXAMINED THE SAYING OF SHIMON THE Righteous that appears in *The Sayings of the Fathers*: "The world stands on three things: the Torah, the Temple services, and acts of loving-kindness."[1] I emphasized the priority of the study of Torah over the Temple sacrifices, and noted this as a sign of the revolutionary change that had occurred in the Judaism of the day. The study of Torah became a general, public virtue—open to all. I linked this revolution with the activity of the Holiness School, the circle that, in my view, was responsible for editing the Torah and promulgating it among the entire people. This school of thought sought to blur—or to do away with completely—the barriers between the priesthood and the people and to allow the people as a whole to participate in the experience of studying Torah (including the Priestly Torah) and to participate in the Temple services. The integration of the Priestly heritage with elements of popular faith is the most striking characteristic of the Holiness School. In this sense, both the members of the Great Assembly, who stated that one ought to "raise many students" (*Avot* 1:1), and Shimon the Righteous, who gives priority to the study of Torah, continue the policy first implemented by the Holiness School.

As I mentioned in previous chapters, the issue of divine reward and punishment, on both the personal and the national level, was also central to the thought of the Second Temple period. The sage who studied under Shimon the Righteous and took his place after his death, Antigonos of Sokho, offers an interesting approach to this question. His saying appears immediately after that of Shimon the Righteous. But before discussing his ideas, I would like to draw attention to his name. It is clearly of Greek origin, and it indicates that Antigonos lived in the Hellenistic period, when the heirs of Alexander the Great ruled the Land of Israel, at about the year 200 B.C.E., or perhaps later. According to *Sayings of the Fathers*, he said: "Do not be as slaves who serve their master in order to receive allowance,[2] rather be as slaves who serve their master on the condition not to receive allowance"[3] (*Avot* 1:3). That is, the important value in the eyes of Antigonos of Sokho is the worship of God for its own sake. Worshiping God does not entail the expectation of any reward.[4]

Antigonos's saying seems to have caused a deep spiritual stir among his disciples. In *Avot de-Rabbi Natan*, an exposition of *Sayings of the Fathers*, we read: "Antigonos of Sokho had two disciples who repeated this doctrine to their disciples and their disciples to their disciples. They rose up and examined the matter, saying: 'Why did our predecessors say this? Is it right for a laborer to toil all day and not receive his reward in the evening?'" Is it possible for someone to work all day without reward? It is not, according to the disciples. Why then, they wondered, did Antigonos say that people ought to be as slaves who serve their master not in order to receive reward? "Had our predecessors known that there was another world and that the dead would be resurrected, surely they would not have said this," said his disciples. Apparently, they reasoned that Antigonos believed humans should not expect a reward because there truly is no reward. "They separated themselves from Torah. Two sects emerged from them: the Sadducees, named for Zadok; and the Boethusians, named for Boethus" (*Avot de-Rabbi Natan*, version A, chapter 5).

According to this source, the cause of the split in Judaism was the issue of divine reward and punishment. Is there a reward for the worship of the Lord? Should one expect reward, in this world or in the world to come? The sects that were founded in the Hellenistic period—the Sadducees and the Boethusians—disputed, according to the passage in *Avot de-Rabbi Natan*, the existence of a reward in this world or in the next. Though the tradition in *Avot de-Rabbi Natan* contains some aggadic elements[5] and might have been written in a later period,[6] its historical reliability is confirmed by an early Christian source.[7] According to this source, the Sadducees claimed that it is unworthy that God should be worshiped under the promise of a reward. This claim is actually almost identical to the saying of Antigonus.

The writings of Josephus Flavius confirm that it was the question of divine reward and punishment that served as the focal point of the schism within Second Temple Judaism. Josephus reports that there were three sects: the Pharisees, the Sadducees, and the Essenes. The fundamental argument among them had to do with the twin questions of divine providence and divine reward. According to Josephus, the Pharisees believed in both divine providence and reward. The Sadducees claimed that God does not know the actions of humanity; thus, there can be neither providence nor reward. The Essenes adopted a special position: they opposed the pharisaic conception of divine providence and punishment, but they believed that God predestined each person's fate and therefore everything is predetermined. Josephus's description of the controversy[8] bears some resemblance to the tradition in *Avot de-Rabbi Natan* where the Sadducees and the Boethusians, a group close to the Sadducees, are mentioned.[9] However, the ideology which is related to the Sadducees in both sources is similar.

THE BIBLICAL ORIGINS OF THE SECTS

It should be clear that the controversies between the different groups in the time of the Second Temple essentially continued the disputes of biblical times. We have already encountered the idea of worship for the sake of worship; Antigonos is not the first to propose this idea. In the second chapter, I discussed the Priestly Torah and noted that one of the central precepts of this system is the principle that one does not worship God in order to receive reward. The Priestly Torah emphasizes that the Temple services are not intended to bring about blessing or prosperity for the people. Indeed, there is not a single Temple ritual geared toward bringing bountiful rains, economic prosperity, or success on the battlefield within the Priestly Torah. The goal of worship is closeness to God, not material advantage. Antigonos of Sokho adopts the approach found in the Priestly Torah. He, too, advocates worship without regard for human needs, without concern for human distress. Worship of God has no goal save growing close to God. The Sadducees and the Boethusians, like Antigonus, follow the Priestly Torah, emphasizing the value of worship for its own sake, not for personal needs.[10]

In his description of the Sadducees, Josephus says that they "remove God beyond, not merely the commission, but the very sight of evil."[11] Here again we may see a continuity between the theology of the Priestly Torah and that of the Sadducees. We saw in the first chapter that the Priestly Torah claimed that God is not the source of evil. Evil, according to this conception, predates God's action as Creator. The Priestly Torah describes God as looking at the newly created world while ignoring the sight of the evil elements in the world; in this way, God may describe it as "perfectly good" (Gen. 1:31). In removing God "beyond the very sight of evil," the Sadducees can be seen as heirs to the Priestly Torah.

On the other side stand the Pharisees, heirs to the worldview championed by the Holiness School. The motto of the

Holiness School is found in the first verse of Leviticus 19: "Speak to the whole Israelite community and say to them: You shall be holy." The Sages interpret this verse as follows: "You shall be holy, this means—you shall be separate (pe-rushim)."[12] From their perspective, perishut (separation or distinctness) is the same as the concept of holiness, and it encompasses not only the priests, but all the people of Israel. This is a popular holiness that unites the people and the priests. Nowhere do we find the term holiness applied in Rabbinic literature to the pharisaic group (Havura);[13] rather the people of Israel as a whole are called holy (Yisrael kedoshim).[14]

These are the two main currents during the time of the Second Temple. The Pharisees represent one current, and the Sadducees and the Boethusians represent the other.[15] These currents propagate the biblical arguments between the elitist and isolated Priestly Torah and the Holiness School, which worked toward a synthesis of the Priestly and the popular views.[16]

THE DISPUTE BETWEEN THE SECTS AND ITS EXPRESSION IN THE TEMPLE WORSHIP

The dispute between the sects was not limited to the ideological realm; it had practical ramifications for the worship of the day. The site of worship at that time was the Temple, and it was only natural that most of the disagreements centered on issues concerning the Temple. The holy days when the people as a whole gathered at the Temple provoked the most controversy.

I will demonstrate this with the help of a number of events described in various sources. The most contested holiday was Sukkot (or Tabernacles), since the Pharisees incorporated into this holiday many ceremonies that have no basis in the Torah. These ceremonies were intended to voice the hope of the people that the Temple services provide them with material and agricultural prosperity. The ceremonies were incorporated into the Sukkot service because Sukkot is observed at a critical juncture in the agricultural year, falling just prior to the rainy season, a time in which farmers are about to sow their fields and are hoping for rain. For farmers, rain was a matter of life and death. How does one deal with this sort of anxiety? How does one go about enlisting the heavens?

The Pharisees maintained several ceremonies that were to be performed during the holiday of Sukkot whose sole purpose was to attempt to guarantee the rainfall.[17] One is the ceremony of the willow, a tree that is called the "willow of the brook" (Lev. 23:40). It is a symbol of water and of hope for timely rain. During the holiday, people would circle the altar while carrying willow twigs in their hands and reciting: "Please, Lord, redeem us, please, Lord, cause us to prosper."[18] After they finished circling, they would set the willows on the altar,[19] giving the altar the appearance of a green forest waiting for the timely rainfall. On the altar, now surrounded with willows of the brook, daily libations were made, using water drawn in a festive procession that went from the Temple to the Shiloah reservoir.[20] On a symbolic level, these ceremonies expressed the desire to ensure plentiful rains during the upcoming agricultural season.[21] Rabbi Akivah expressed this desire in the following manner: "The Torah teaches: bring water libations during the holiday that you be blessed with rain water."[22] The water libation is not mentioned in the Torah, but the Pharisee sages, through a series of interpretations, managed to uncover scriptural hints for the practice.[23] This is why Rabbi Akivah was able to preface his statement with "The Torah teaches."

The ceremonies of the willows and of the libation were very dear to the Pharisees. For the sake of these ceremonies, they were willing to discard certain controls that were enforced in the Temple throughout the year. During the rest of the year, the area of the Temple was clearly delineated. Each sector of the populace had an area into which it was permitted to enter. The general populace was permitted into the Courtyard of

Israel, while the entrance to the area between the Temple it-self and the altar in the Temple courtyard was restricted to priests. But during the holiday of Sukkot, the masses were allowed into this sanctified area between the Temple and the altar, in order to circle the altar and to cry out, "Please, Lord, redeem us, please, Lord, cause us to prosper."

Other rules, as well, were discarded in order to provide a venue of expression for the needs of the people. Throughout the year, pharisaic halakhah set very strict laws of purity and impurity and distinguished between associates (*haverim*)—those who observe these laws—and commoners (*Am Ha-Aretz*), who do not. Yet during the holidays (not only Sukkot), the Pharisees instated the rule that all people of Israel are like associates. During the pilgrimage to Jerusalem, even the people who knew nothing of the laws of purity and impurity and perhaps, in fact, even scorned these laws, were to be regarded as "associates," without their having to perform any sort of action. The very fact that they were gathered at the Temple in Jerusalem endowed them with the status of associates, and they were permitted to enter the Temple. The Sages grounded this ruling in their interpretation of the verse "Our feet stood inside your gates, O Jerusalem, / Jerusalem built up, a city knit together" (Ps. 122:23). The interpretation reads: "'a city knit together'—that is, a city that joins all the people of Is-rael together as associates" (Yerushalmi *Hagigah* 3:6).[24] All the strictures were dropped in order to cater to the needs and yearnings of the people and to integrate the people into the Temple services. On these holidays, a profound bond formed between the Temple, the priesthood, and the people. This is the pharisaic approach.

The Sadducees and the Boethusians opposed this approach and made every effort to disrupt the Pharisees' ceremonies. In the Tosefta, the story is told of how one year "Willow Day" (the seventh day of the holiday of Sukkot, in which the people circled the altar seven times) fell on a Saturday. So as not to desecrate the Sabbath, the Pharisees picked their willows in advance and set them in the Temple courtyard so that the willows would be ready for use on the morrow. The members of the sects tried to outwit them, reasoning as follows: the Sages of the Pharisees are known for their strict observance of Sabbath laws and will not carry heavy stones on the Sabbath. Let us cover the willows with heavy stones and the willow ceremony will not take place. Confounded, the Sages of the Pharisees would have begun debating whether or not it is permitted to carry heavy stones on the Sabbath. The problem was resolved when the common people came and carried off the stones. They did not observe the Sabbath laws very strictly and wanted the willow ceremony to take place in any case.[25]

Another tale is told regarding the water libation. Once, a high priest sympathetic to the Saducean or the Boethusian halakhah[26] took the libation flask and poured the water not on the altar, but onto his feet! Needless to say, this caused a great uproar among the people, who "pelted him with their citrons, and the corner of the altar was damaged."[27] Because the ceremony enjoyed such great popular support, the people would do anything to ensure that the ceremony took place and would harm anyone who tried to disrupt it. Conversely, we see the desire of the sects and their sympathizers among the priesthood to disrupt the pharisaic ceremony. They had theological objections to any ritual that was intended to bring rain and fertility, for they rejected divine providence and mandated worship of God without any anticipation of material reward.[28]

The very fact that the people were in the proximity of the Temple during the holidays was itself controversial. The pharisaic rule, which permitted all Israelites into the Temple courtyard irrespective of their degree of purity or impurity, was disputed. Disputes were particularly evident with regard to the custom of exhibiting the Temple vessels. This custom was instituted in order to link the people as a whole to the experience of holiness. All year long, the vessels were located within the Temple, and only a priest who had undergone ritual purification could approach and see them.[29] The Sages of the Pharisees allowed the table of the showbread and the menorah to be set outside,[30] apparently at the gate of the Temple. The people had full access to them, and some could not avoid touching them. Any such contact would have transmitted to the vessels the impurity found in the person who touched them, but this did not deter the pharisaic Sages.[31]

A coin minted during the Bar Kokhba period depicts the Temple and the table at its entrance.[32] The person who drew the picture lived during the time of the Bar Kokhba revolt, at least sixty years after the destruction of the Temple. But the coin maker or an informant had probably made the pilgrimage to Jerusalem as a child, and remembered the Temple and the table of that time. This must have been the summit of the pilgrimage: viewing the table and the menorah at the entrance to the Temple. The Tosefta tells that once the menorah became impure due to such public exhibition and had to be purified through immersion in water. The Sages of the Sadducees mocked the Pharisees, saying: "Come and see Pharisees immersing the light of the sun."[33] There is more than just scorn in these words; they are filled with anger and bitterness at the idea that the menorah, which symbolizes the sun, had become impure so that it had to be immersed.[34] In their eyes, this was sacrilege.

The Qumran document known as the Temple Scroll expresses a similar criticism of the pharisaic halakhah. This scroll, to be discussed in more detail later, reworks the text of the Torah and contains laws not mentioned there. In a section that deals with the table, we find a strict warning: "It shall not leave the Temple."[35] The Qumranic text, in essence, declares the pharisaic practice of removing the holy vessels, the menorah, and the table and displaying them outside for all the people to view was sacrilegious."

We find a great willingness on the part of the Pharisees to go to great measures—including the temporary lifting of interdictions and limitations—in order to have the people participate in the Temple services. This participation is expressed first and foremost in the ceremonies that aim at procuring prosperity and plenty for the land. This is the great point of connection between the Pharisees and the common people. Opposed to them are the Sadducees and the Boethusians, who reject the inclusion of the masses, reject the lifting of interdictions (a sacrilegious act, in their eyes), and reject the very legitimacy of ceremonies aimed at procuring plenty.

This bitter dispute can point us toward another issue, which is attested to in a number of different sources. There was an attempt made by the pharisaic Sages to form a bond between the people and the Temple throughout the year, not only at the time of the holidays. The Temple was the site of daily sacrifices, additional Sabbath sacrifices, and special sacrifices on the holidays. The pharisaic Sages agreed that these sacrifices could be purchased with donations taken up from the people as a whole. The donation consisted of half a shekel, which was collected once a year, before the month of Nisan. Collection was not limited to Jews in the Land of Israel, but included those living in the Jewish Diaspora. There is evidence of great caravans, which would come to Israel to bring the contributions of the Jews living in the Diaspora.[36] The significance of this contribution was that every Jew had a part in the Temple sacrifices. When any Jew came to the Temple and heard that sacrifices were being offered, that person participated in the sacrifices through contribution.

The halakhic approach of the Sadducees and the Qumran sect rejected this approach. The Sadducees ruled that the daily sacrifices could be funded by contributions of individuals (Bavli *Menahot* 65a).[37] Unlike the Pharisees, who interpreted biblical law regarding the contribution of half a shekel (Exod. 30:11–16) as an annual contribution, the Qumran Sect interpreted it as a contribution made once in a lifetime, when the person reached the age of twenty.[38] Here, too, the

Pharisees attempted to link the Temple service to the people by using their contribution for the daily cult. On the other side, the Sadducees and the Qumran sect viewed the Temple cult as a realm reserved exclusively for the priests and whatever elites they cultivated.[39]

Why did the people support the Pharisees? In a way, popular support of the Pharisees is surprising, considering their severe rulings on matters of purity and impurity, tithes, and other contributions. One could even say that these pharisaic strictures caused a schism in the nation, between the associates and the commoners. The people viewed the separation of the associates as an insult, and the result was bitterness and hatred toward the Pharisees, as is evident in some talmudic sources and, more clearly, in the New Testament. But we also learn from the New Testament, from Josephus, and from the writings of the Qumran sect, that most of the masses sided with the Pharisees. Why would the masses support the same Pharisees who caused a schism within the nation and elicited much anger and resentment with their stern rulings on issues of purity and impurity, tithes and contributions? While it is true that throughout the year the strictness of the Pharisees formed a divide between them and the general public, the same Pharisees allowed the people to express their anxieties and their yearnings during the critical holiday periods. During these times, the Pharisees drew the people closer to them and allowed them to express their feelings and needs through the Temple services.

This accounts for the popular support enjoyed by the Pharisees.[40] The other sects refused to acknowledge the needs of the people and did not permit them to express those needs in the Temple service They thus erected a barrier between the people and the Temple, and lost the support of the commoners. The willingness of the Pharisees to rule that "all the people of Israel are associates" for the duration of the holidays and to integrate the people in the Temple services garnered them the support of the people and allowed them to maintain their position as leaders of the nation, even after the destruction of the Temple.

THE MONOLITHIC APPROACH OF QUMRAN LITERATURE

In chapter 2, I argued that the pluralistic redaction of the Torah set the model for subsequent Jewish literature. This notion is correct only with regard to the pharisaic Rabbinic camp. In the sectarian literature found in Qumran, we see a wholly different trend.

The Qumran Temple Scroll[41] is in fact an "improved" edition of the Torah. In the Torah one can find, for instance, contradictory laws concerning how the Passover offering is to be prepared (roasted or cooked).[42] In contrast, in the Temple Scroll there is only one law of Passover, without any inner contradiction[43]. This is true throughout the Temple Scroll, wherein the formulation of the laws resolves all the inner tensions that exist in the Torah.

The Temple Scroll even blurs the stylistic difference between Deuteronomy, written as a speech of Moses, and the other four books of the Torah, which contain direct speeches of God. In the Temple Scroll, quotations from Deuteronomy are reworked in order to make them also the direct speech of the Lord.[44] For instance, the conclusion of the law of the idolatrous banned city from Deuteronomy 13:18 reads: "Let nothing that has been doomed stick to your hand, in order that the Lord may turn from His blazing anger and show you compassion, and in His compassion increase you as He promised your fathers on oath." However, in the Temple Scroll 55:10–12 these words are presented as a direct speech of God to Israel: "And nothing shall remain in your hands of what has been placed under the ban, so that I may desist from the heat of my anger and give you [my] compassion and be compassionate to you and increase you, as I said to your fathers."

The Temple Scroll can be seen as a monolithic edition of the pluralistic Torah. The same tendency to uniformity is to be found elsewhere in Qumran literature. In sharp contrast to Rabbinic literature, no inner disputes or debates over legal issues are recorded in Qumran's literature.[45] This seems to be the impact of the Qumranic conception that the true meaning of the Mosaic laws was revealed by God to the founders of their sect.[46] Given this direct line, there could be no place for human debate within the framework of revealed divine truth.

THE SCHOOL OF HILLEL AND THE SCHOOL OF SHAMMAI

Up until now we have treated the Pharisees as one group, and for a time they were. But circa 20 B.C.E., approximately one hundred years before the destruction of the Temple,[47] there was a break within the pharisaic camp. This was not a thoroughgoing break and did not result in the formation of two independent groups, but it did create two schools among the Pharisees. Ties of marriage and joint study were maintained,[48] but there were two schools nonetheless. They were named after their leaders: the School of Hillel and the School of Shammai. The disputes between these schools cover a great many halakhic, aggadic, and conceptual issues. We will see that they recapitulate many of the issues stemming from popular vs. elitist approaches to religion that we have explored in this book. We begin by examining the first dispute mentioned in the Mishnah, and, through this dispute, we will examine the spiritual worldview of each of the schools, which can be seen as a continuation of earlier trends in the pluralistic Torah.

The dispute concerns the proper way to recite the *Shema*. The recitation of the *Shema* is a central commandment that one has to observe daily, and it consists of reading the *Shema* passage (Deut. 5:4–9) and additional verses from the Torah twice a day, morning and evening. The question at hand is:

how exactly does one perform this commandment? The Mishnah describes the dispute as follows: "The School of Shammai says, 'In the evening everyone should recline in order to recite the *Shema* and in the morning they should stand. As it is written: "when you lie down and when you get up."' And the School of Hillel says 'Everyone may recite according to his own manner. As it is written "when you are walking along the way." If so, why does the verse say "when you lie down and when you get up?" At the time that people lie down and at the time that people get up'" (Mishnah *Berachot* 1:3). The School of Shammai claims that recitation requires a special posture: in the evening a person must bow and recite, and in the morning recite standing erect. The School of Hillel disagrees and rules that each person recites "according to his own manner," that is, there is no need to adopt a special posture when reciting.

What is the underlying significance of each of these ways of reciting the *Shema*? At the end of the Mishnah passage about the dispute over the recitation of the *Shema*, there is a short tale that may allow for a clearer understanding of the issue. "Rabbi Tarfon said: 'I was coming along the way and reclined to recite the *Shema*, and put myself in danger of robbers.' According to the School of Shammai, says Rabbi Tarfon, 'when I was riding along and the time to recite the *Shema* arrived, I had to dismount from my donkey in order to recline while I recited the *Shema*. Consequently, when I was standing by the roadside and a robber approached me, I put myself in danger....'"

We see from this story that the manner of reciting the *Shema* endorsed by the School of Shammai involves a cessation of whatever act one is engaged in. According to the School of Hillel, on the other hand, Rabbi Tarfon could have recited the *Shema* while riding his donkey. This is borne out by the final sentence of the passage, in which his friends, who adhered to Hillel's position, said to him: "You brought this upon yourself, that you violated the ruling of the School of

Hillel." The difference, then, is the manner in which the *Shema* is recited. The School of Shammai believes that the recitation of the *Shema* should be divorced from the continuum of daily activity. For the School of Hillel, the recitation of the *Shema* can be performed while one is engaged in regular activities. This is stated explicitly in an early Rabbinic saying not incorporated in the Mishnah: "The Rabbis have taught: The School of Hillel says, 'One may read when he is standing or when he is sitting or when he is walking by the way or when he is working.'"[49] That is, the recitation can be performed in any position, while performing any activity.[50]

The recitation of the *Shema* is described in the Mishnah as an acceptance of the kingship of heaven, i.e., the kingship of God.[51] In reciting the verse, "Hear, O Israel, the Lord is our God, the Lord is one," a person receives upon himself or herself the kingship of God. The discussion, then, is concerned with how one properly accepts the kingship of God. Does it have to occur in a ceremonial moment that stands outside the flow of one's worldly, mundane existence or does it constitute an integral part of life? Other sayings of Hillel and Shammai extend and clarify their respective positions.

A number of talmudic sources speak of a dispute between Hillel and Shammai regarding the value of the daily care of the body. "Let all your actions be for the sake of heaven," said Hillel. When Hillel went to a place, people would say to him: Where are you going? I am going to fulfill a commandment. Which commandment, Hillel? I am going to the baths. But is this a commandment? he answered: Yes, it is, in order to clean the body. Know, then, that this is a fact because if the [Roman] government gives an annual salary to the official in charge of washing and polishing the statues of kings and is even counted among the rank of the great men of the kingdom, then all the more we who were created in the image and likeness of God, as it is written: "for in His image did God make man." (*Avot de-Rabbi Natan*, version B, section 30).

For Hillel, then, care for the well-being of the body is a commandment. Shammai did not speak thus; rather "let us fulfill our obligations through that body."[52] According to Shammai, there is no commandment to take care of the body. Rather, there is an obligation to use the body to fulfill duties to the Lord.[53]

This dispute is related to another:[54] "They said of Shammai the Elder that throughout his life he would eat in honor of the Sabbath. If he found a fine animal he would say, 'This one is for Sabbath.' If he found one finer still, he would set aside the first and eat the second. But Hillel the Elder had a different standard: that all his actions be for the sake of heaven, as it is written, 'Blessed is the Lord day by day.'"[55] Shammai's position is clear, but what is the meaning of Hillel's statement? Hillel asserts that he is not occupied solely with the Sabbath feast. If one finds something pleasing to eat during the week, that too is a commandment. All actions are performed for the sake of heaven;[56] blessed is the Lord day by day. Not only the consumption of a Sabbath feast is a commandment; daily eating that nourishes the body is also a commandment.

We see here two distinct approaches to the value of the physical dimension of human existence. Hillel sees all of life as imbued with religious meaning and religious value. Since humans were created in the image of God,[57] it follows that all that people do to care for their bodies contains religious significance. Shammai opposes this approach: For him, there exists a separate dimension for the religious commandment, a separate dimension for holiness, and the rest is neutral from a religious point of view. His saying, "let us fulfill our obligations through that body" means that there is no religious value in caring for the body per se.[58] The body is only an instrument. There is even a hint of hostility toward the physical form in the words "that body."[59]

It is in this context that we should understand the dispute regarding the recitation of the *Shema*. Whoever views the continuum of human life as imbued with religious significance, as Hillel does, can accept the recitation of the *Shema*—the acceptance of God's kingship—even while one is busy with his work. In the Mishnah and the Tosefta to Tractate *Berachot*, examples are given of laborers perched atop a tree as they recite the *Shema*, or of someone working naked in the field who covers himself with some straw and then recites the *Shema*.[60] According to the School of Hillel, one can accept the kingship of God in this state as well. The School of Shammai, on the other hand, is shocked by this notion. To accept the kingship of God, one must cease working, dress, adopt a contemplative mood and only then, in fear and trembling, accept the kingship of God. These divergent approaches reflect different relationships between human beings and God. Among the School of Hillel there was a sense of intimacy with God,[61] while the School of Shammai felt awe, trembling, and fear. This difference is further reflected in other sayings and stories of the two schools and their leaders.

Rabbi Eliezer, one of the great sages of the School of Shammai, and a figure who will be discussed again below, would say:

> One should bring a suspensive guilt offering [אשם תלוי] any day and any time he wants, and this is called the guilt offering of the pious אשם חסידים. They said of Baba the son of Buti that he volunteered a suspensive guilt offering every day, save the day after Yom Kippur. (Mishnah *Keritot* 6:3)

The *asham taluy* (suspensive guilt offering) is a sacrifice that suspends a guilty feeling; it was offered when a person had a generalized feeling of guilt, but did not know of any particular sin that he or she had committed.[62] We see that Rabbi Eliezer and Baba the son of Buti, two of the central sages of the School of Shammai, wished to offer such a guilt offering every day except on the day following Yom Kippur. Why not on that day? Baba the son of Buti continues and says, "By the Temple! If they permitted it, I'd offer the sacrifice [on that day as well]." His friends admonish him, saying, "Wait until you enter into doubts."[63] By this they mean, yesterday was Yom Kippur, the day in which all your sins were atoned, so why bring a guilt offering so quickly? According to Baba the son of Buti, the guilt offering does not actually depend on any fear that a transgression was committed, but rather stems merely from the corporeal existence of man. Living in a material body that has physical desires creates in him a profound sense of guilt that requires atonement by means of the offering.

And indeed we find that there is a dispute between the two schools concerning the daily sacrifice. The daily sacrifice made in the Temple was perceived as an atonement sacrifice at the time of the Second Temple. The two schools disagreed on how to understand the atoning nature of the daily sacrifice. In the Torah, it is written that every day two lambs (kevasim) are to be offered (Exod. 29:38). The dispute between the two schools is expressed in the form of two interpretations of the word "lambs." The School of Hillel relates the Hebrew word for lambs (kevasim) to their function as purifiers (kovesim): that is, they purge Israel of their sins. The School of Shammai, on the other hand, ties the kevasim to the idea that they serve to subdue or suppress (koveshim) the sins of Israel.[64] According to the latter approach, the sacrifices do not dispense with the sins, but only suppress them, leaving behind a feeling of sin. There is thus a sense of a continuous, existential guilt before God that pervades the thinking of the School of Shammai.

The attitude adopted by the School of Hillel is far more easygoing, and features a far greater acceptance of the human condition. "For two and a half years the School of Shammai and the School of Hillel were in dispute: the former asserting that it were better for man not to have been created than to have been created, and the latter maintaining that it is better for man to have been created than not to have been created."[65] According to the School of Shammai, if humanity's very existence is tied to a guilty feeling, it would have been better not to have been created. In this statement, the School of

Shammai comes close to the atmosphere of the ideas promulgated by the Qumran sect: that humanity's very existence as a material creature and its standing before God as such, evoke a terrible self-abhorrence.

In the examples that I have presented—the recitation of the *Shema*, the status of bathing, the function and meaning of the guilt offering, the status of humanity vis-à-vis God—we see the fundamental divide between the School of Hillel and the School of Shammai. The teachings of Hillel promote an intimacy with God, and easily incorporate everyday experiences into a religious framework, while the teachings of Shammai keep human beings removed from God, in a state of awe mixed with guilt. Within this world of the Pharisees, then, we can see a line that goes back from the Shammaites to certain concerns of the Sadducees, and behind them to the school of the Priestly Torah, both of which preserved an elitist approach to a transcendent God, while the Hillelites recapitulate the spirit of the Holiness School, which opened Torah up to ethics and the experience of the people.

The controversy between the two schools continued for a long time, even after the destruction of the Second Temple. We know that at a certain time it took on political significance. Before the destruction of the Temple, there was a debate regarding the treatment of non-Jews that caused a great deal of agitation. Physical violence ensued, and the disciples of the School of Shammai killed some of the disciples of the School of Hillel and then forced the rest to accept, at sword point, a number of decisions against the Romans and against any cooperation with non-Jews in general.[66] For centuries, a fast was observed in the Land of Israel in remembrance of this event.[67] After the destruction of the Temple, in the Yavneh period (70–132 C.E.), matters settled down somewhat, only to be rekindled in the great controversy between Rabbi Eliezer—the greatest of the Shammaitic sages—and the sages of Yavneh—Rabbi Yehoshua, Rabbi Akivah, and Rabban Gamliel.

The dispute arose over a seemingly unimportant matter: Is a ringed oven pure or impure?[68] When Rabbi Eliezer saw that his was the minority opinion and that the majority of the Sages sided against him, he tried to buttress his argument by calling for supernatural verification (Bava *Metzi'a* 59b):

> On that day, Rabbi Eliezer gave them all the proofs in the world and they did not accept his position. He said to them: "If the law is as I say, let this carob tree bear witness to it." The carob tree uprooted and flew a hundred cubits. They said: "No proof is adduced from carob trees." Again he said to them: "If the law is as I say, let the aqueduct bear witness to it." The water in the aqueduct began flowing uphill. They said: "No proof is adduced from aqueducts." Again he said to them: "If the law is as I say, let the walls of the academy bear witness to it." The walls of the academy tilted, about to fall. Rabbi Yehosuha rebuked them saying: "Sages are discussing halakhah, what right have you?" They did not fall in deference to Rabbi Yehoshua and they did not aright themselves in deference to Rabbi Eliezer, and they are tilted to this very day. Again he said to them: "If the law is as I say, let the heavens bear witness to it." A voice came from the heavens and said: "What do you want with Rabbi Eliezer? Halakhah is decided according to his view in every case." Rabbi Yehoshua arose and said: "It is not in the heavens (Deut. 30:12), we do not obey a heavenly voice, for you have written in your Torah, 'side with the many' (Exod. 23:2)."

God has been trumped and in the story admits it: "My children have defeated Me." The Torah, then, is not in the heavens. The Rabbis say, You, God, have given it to us and now we must decide according to human criteria, that is, according to majority rule. God loses the right to intercede. The rules are written in the Torah and Jews follow them, according the Rabbinic majority's rules of interpretation. God has no say in the halakhic disputes of sages.

Rabbi Yehoshua cites the verse "It is not in the heavens," and thus denies the heavenly forces the right to intervene in the halakhic dispute. It is striking that he cites a verse from Deuteronomy that refers to the instruction (*mitzvah*) of God (Deut. 30:11–12). We mentioned above that, according to the Book of Deuteronomy, the Torah that lies within the Ark of the Covenant replaces the cherubs that are on the Ark of the

Priestly Torah. For the authors of Deuteronomy there is already no divine presence in the Ark. God's place is in heaven. We see, then, a conceptual link between the Book of Deuteronomy and the School of Hillel: For both, God is in heaven and the Torah is on earth, and it is up to human beings to determine halakhic questions without having to resort to God[69] (cf. Deut. 17:8–11).

The School of Hillel represents a tendency—it may be called rationalistic—that seeks an autonomous existence for man on earth. "The Heavens belong to the Lord, but the earth He gave over to man" (Ps. 115:16). The heavens cannot intervene in what happens on earth. Through this power of human autonomy and decision making, the great Sages who came forth from the School of Hillel, such as Rabbi Yehoshua and Rabbi Akivah, were able to lead the people of Israel through times of crisis: through the destruction of the Temple, the Bar Kokhba rebellion, and the Roman persecution that followed. They were able to set the pattern of leadership in Jewish society that preserved Jewish existence throughout the period of exile. This conception allowed them to legislate, innovate, renovate, and transform rules and laws in such a way as to ensure Jewish existence without a Temple, without prophecy, and without the manifest intervention of heavenly forces.

Postscript

W E ENDED THE LAST CHAPTER WITH THE DISPUTE between the School of Shammai and the School of Hillel. Concerning this controversy, it is said in the Talmud[1] that "both these and those are the words of the living God." We must recognize that various, and even contradictory, views can all be the true words of the living God. Throughout this book, we have seen how the Bible preserves, within itself, contradictory conceptions of great depth and uniqueness concerning such profound issues as humanity's place in the universe, the origin and meaning of evil, the purpose of reward and punishment, the role of free will and predestination in human affairs, the nature of the covenant, the character of worship, the function of the sanctuary, and the role of the political leader in the redemptive future of Israel. During the period we have surveyed, we see competing theologies emerging from parties and schools associated with elites and from those associated with the populace at large. We should not try to blur these disputes in order to achieve an artificial unity and harmony. Rather, we should enjoy the richness and complexity of the divine symphony that these different viewpoints and voices create in the Bible.

One of the major problems of our time is religious intolerance. A deep recognition and study of the different voices of the Bible, and of the many ideas that it inspired in the development of Judaism, may help to bring about an atmosphere of diversity and tolerance. By exposing and understanding the pluralistic character of the Bible, we can recognize that there is a place for, and significance to, the kind of debate in which the *other* view may also be a reflection of divine truth.

Abbreviations

AB	*The Anchor Bible*
ANET	*Ancient Near Eastern Texts*
ARE	*Ancient Records of Egypt*
ARW	*Archiv für Religionswissenschaft*
BASOR	*Bulletin of the American Schools of Oriental Research*
BiOr	*Bibliotheca Orientalis*
BZAW	*Beihefte zur Zeitschrift für die alttestamentliche Wissenschaft*
CBQ	*Catholic Biblical Quarterly*
CD	*Damascus Covenant (a Qumranic composition)*
CT	*Cuneiform texts from Babylonian tablets, etc., in the British Museum*
DSD	*Dead Sea Discoveries*
EM	*Encyclopedia Mikrait* (in Hebrew)
ErIs	*Eretz Israel*
ET	*Expository Times*
FRLANT	*Forschungen zur Religion und Literatur des Alten und Neuen Testaments*
HSM	*Harvard Semitic Monographs*

HTR	*Harvard Theological Review*
HUCA	*Hebrew Union College Annual*
ICC	*International Critical Commentary*
IDB	*Interpreter's Dictionary of the Bible*
IEJ	*Israel Exploration Journal*
JAOS	*Journal of the American Oriental Society*
JBL	*Journal of Biblical Literature*
JCS	*Journal of Cuneiform Studies*
JJS	*Journal of Jewish Studies*
JNES	*Journal of Near Eastern Studies*
JQR	*Jewish Quarterly Review*
JSOT	*Journal for the Study of the Old Testament*
JSOTsup	*Supplement to the Journal for the Study of the Old Testament*
JThC	*Journal for Theology and Church*
JTS	*Journal of Theological Studies*
NCBC	*New Century Bible Commentary*
OTL	*Old Testament Library*
OTS	*Oudtestamentische Studien*
PAAJR	*Proceedings of the American Academy of Jewish Research*
RQ	*Review de Qumran*
SBL	*Society of Biblical Literature*
SBT	*Studies in Biblical Theology*
SVT	*Supplement to Vetus Testamentum*
TDOT	*Theological Dictionary of the Old Testament*
ThLZ	*Theologische Literaturzeitung*
ThWAT	*Theologische Wörterbuch zum Alten Testament*
TSK	*Theologische Studien und Kritiken*
TZ	*Theologische Zeitschrift*
VT	*Vetus Testamentum*
WMANT	*Wissenschaftliche Monographien zum Alten und Neuen Testaments*
ZAW	*Zeitschrift für die alttestamentliche Wissenschaft*

Appendix A: Dating the Sources of the Torah

I T HAS LONG BEEN ACCEPTED BY SCHOLARS THAT THE Pentateuch is comprised of four principal sources. These sources are customarily denoted as follows: J, the source using the divine name "*YHWH*"; E, the "Elohist," who uses the name "Elohim"; P, the Priestly Source; and D, the Book of Deuteronomy. Within the Priestly Source, Leviticus 17–26 stands out in its linguistic and stylistic uniqueness. In some of the chapters the holiness of God is emphasized, and this is taken to imply a call to holiness addressed to all the Israelites. It has therefore been customary to call this section "The Holiness Code." The Holiness Code is denoted H, to distinguish it from the other parts of the Priestly Work, which are denoted P. In what follows, we will describe the development of the Pentateuchal sources against the background of the creation of biblical literature in general.

The results of archeological research point to the fact that literacy spread in the northern kingdom, Israel, in the first half of the eighth century B.C.E. and in Judea from the second half of that century.[1] Prior to this period, literacy was probably known mostly within elitist closed circles like the royal court and the Temple.[2] Thus, before the eighth century B.C.E., we can think of oral popular compositions on the one hand, and of written, elitist literature, on the other.

It seems that the earliest compositions remaining to us are the ancient poems that were first recited orally and only in a later period written down. The best example is the Song of Deborah (Judg. 5), which is probably dated to the first half of the eleventh century B.C.E.[3] Other ancient poems are preserved in the Torah,[4] but it is difficult to date them precisely.

In the tenth century B.C.E., kingship was established in Israel and Judea. We can assume that in the royal courts and temples in Israel and Judea there were scribes and priests involved in literary creativity. The literary activity of royal courts and temples of the ancient Near East includes the following types of literature: historical documents, wisdom literature, royal and cultic psalms, Priestly cultic rules and descriptions of the Creation of the world and of the first generations of humanity. We may suppose that similar literary compositions were written outside of the royal courts and temples of Judea and Israel.

We can confirm these assumptions at least with regard to the royal court and the Temple in Jerusalem. The prophet Isaiah lived in Jerusalem in the second half of the eighth century B.C.E. and was close to the circle of the court.[5] In his prophecy, there is a clear impact of the psalms[6] and of wisdom literature.[7] In this connection we can also mention the reference in the Book of Proverbs[8] to the redaction of wisdom literature in the court of Hezekiah, who was the king of Judea in Isaiah's time.

While the Book of Psalms and the Book of Proverbs are both collections of materials from different periods,[9] we can infer from Isaiah's prophecies that parts of these books were written before Isaiah's time (i.e., before the second half of the eighth century B.C.E.).

From another source, contemporary with Isaiah, we can learn about Priestly literary activity in Jerusalem prior to the second half of the eighth century B.C.E. The Holiness Code (Lev. 17–26)[10] was based on an earlier stage of Priestly literature, the Priestly Torah.[11] The Priestly Torah was probably written in the Temple in Jerusalem between the building of the Solomon Temple in the tenth and the first half of the eighth centuries.

The Priestly Torah is mainly a literature of cultic rules, similar in literary form to other compositions of cultic rules in the ancient Near East.[12] It also includes a description of the Creation (Gen. 1:1–2:4a) and a schematic list of the first generations of humanity (Gen. 5), both of which are typical in the literature of scribes and priests in the ancient Near East. In all respects, then, the Priestly Torah resembles other Priestly literary compositions of the ancient Near East, while the Holiness Code has a character all its own.

We may summarize these conclusions so far by saying that the earliest premonarchic stage of biblical literal creativity is the oral formation of the ancient poems like the Song of Deborah.[13]

The second stage, which appears after the establishment of kingship in the tenth century B.C.E., is the literature created in the royal courts and temples of Israel and Judea. In this category we can list some of the psalms now included in the Book of Psalms, parts of the Book of Proverbs, and the Priestly Torah.

The spread of literacy in the eighth century B.C.E. brought with it new types of literature. For the first time there was a broader public who could read and appreciate written compositions. It was at this time that written prophecies first appeared. Active during this period were Hosea and Amos in the north and Isaiah and Micah in the south. The exact time and the way in which their words were written is not known, but we have clear reference to writing in the books of both Hosea and Isaiah.[14]

The second type of literature, which was probably first formed in the eighth century B.C.E., is biblical prose. While we have several prosaic units in the Priestly Torah, they are written in a schematic fashion resembling the style of cultic rules.[15] Real biblical prose was probably written for the first time in the eighth century B.C.E.

The first stage of prose literature was created in the northern kingdom of Israel in the first half of the eighth century B.C.E. To this stage belong the E source of the Pentateuch[16] and some of the traditions related to the north, which are preserved now in the historical books Joshua, Judges, Samuel,[17] and Kings.[18] The first step of the creation of non-Priestly legislation took place probably at the same time and in the same area. This legal collection, known as the Covenant Code,[19] is now embodied in Exodus 20: 19–23.[20]

The Assyrians destroyed the northern kingdom during the second half of the eighth century B.C.E. Many of its inhabitants were expelled and scattered by the Assyrians; others escaped to Jerusalem.[21] Those refugees probably brought with them the literary compositions of the north. A unique group redacted the E source in Jerusalem and is also responsible for the composition of the J source of the Pentateuch.[22] We have several stories in the book of J about altars erected by the Patriarchs in various parts of the land. Only with regard to the Jerusalem altar,[23] however, do we have a story about a sacrificial act.[24] We can infer from this that the J source objects to sacrificial worship outside of Jerusalem,[25] as did the cultic reformation of King Hezekiah, which was directed mainly against sacrificial altars outside of Jerusalem.[26] In his reforming zeal, Hezekiah smashed the bronze serpent that Moses had made,[27] to which until that time the Israelites had been offering sacrifices.[28] The abasement of the serpent in J's story in Genesis 3:14 can similarly be seen as a reflection of Hezekiah's act. Thus, we locate the J source in Jerusalem in the time of Hezekiah, i.e. the last quarter of the eighth century B.C.E.

The Jerusalem of Hezekiah is probably also the background of the stories about David and Solomon in Samuel and Kings. The grandeur of Jerusalem in the David and Solomon stories reflects the reality of Hezekiah's time rather than the reality of the city of David, which was far more modest.

The occupation of the northern kingdom, Israel, by the Assyrians in the second half of the eighth century B.C.E. stopped the literary creation of that kingdom. Judea was not fully conquered by the Assyrians, though Sennacherib's campaign against Hezekiah in 701 B.C.E. led to huge destruction in Judea. After Hezekiah died in 698 B.C.E., his son Manasseh ruled as a syncretist who introduced idolatry to the Jerusalem Temple.[29] These events probably put an end to the great literary activity happening in Jerusalem during Hezekiah's time.

The renewal of this activity took place only in the time of Manasseh's grandson, Josiah, who was devoted to the worship of the God of Israel. In the eighteenth year of his rule, 622 B.C.E., Josiah asked the priests to repair the Temple. During the work, a book of the Torah was found in the Temple.[30] This book was the basis for the cultic reformation led by Josiah.[31] Biblical scholarship identifies this book as Deuteronomy. Some scholars think that an early version of Deuteronomy had already been written in the north before the fall of the kingdom of Israel[32] and was brought to Jerusalem and expanded there. On the basis of the laws of Deuteronomy (12, 16), Josiah abolished all the cultic sites outside of Jerusalem and celebrated the Passover in Jerusalem (2 Kings 23:1–24).

The school that wrote the Book of Deuteronomy is also responsible for the composition of the historical books, Joshua, Judges, Samuel, and Kings.[33] As noted above, some of the traditions related to the north, which are preserved in the historical books, were already written in the north in the eighth century B.C.E. The editors of the historical books known as Deuteronomistic because of their affinity with the ideology and language of Deuteronomy, used these traditions and other historical documents preserved in the archives of the court and of the Jerusalem Temple.[34] It appears that there were two separate editions of the historical books: The first was done in Jerusalem in the time of Josiah, and the second in Babylon after the exile.[35] The prophet Jeremiah, who started his prophetic activity in the time of Josiah, was ideologically aligned with the Deuteronomistic School.[36]

The tragic death of Josiah in the year 609 B.C.E. marked the decline of the Kingdom of Judea. The Babylonian Empire that defeated the Assyrians became the great power of the ancient Near East. In the year 597 B.C.E., King Yehoiachin was exiled to Babylon together with the elite circles of Jerusalem. In 586 B.C.E., the Babylonians destroyed Jerusalem and its temple and exiled many of the inhabitants of Jerusalem and Judea to Babylon.

The prophet Ezekiel was a prominent religious figure among those who were exiled from Judea. He belonged to the Priestly circle of Jerusalem, and his style is close to that of the Holiness School.[37] The cultic legislation in Ezekiel 40–48 is similar to that of the Priestly sources of the Pentateuch but differs on several issues.[38]

In the year 539 B.C.E., Cyrus conquered Babylon and allowed the Jews to go back to Judea. Many did so, but others stayed on in Babylon, and it appears that the redaction of the Torah started in Babylon during this period.[39] The style of the editors is that of the Holiness School,[40] and the unique character of that school prepared its members for this significant project. On the one hand they were experts in Priestly traditions, but on the other they had an affinity with popular traditions as well. They were uniquely suited to integrate the Priestly Torah and the popular traditions of E and J into one composition.

The editors of the Torah left the book of Deuteronomy unchanged[41] and made it the conclusion of the Pentateuch, placing before it the material that is now contained in the first four books. These books are interwoven from the other Pentateuchal sources mentioned above: P, E, J, and H.

We do not know precisely when the great enterprise of the redaction of the Torah was finished, but it doubtless took years. It reached its apogee with Ezra's publication of the Torah before the assembly of the people, as described in the

Book of Nehemiah.[42] This event probably took place in the mid-fifth century B.C.E. Biblical scholars consider this to be the occasion on which the Torah was publicly promulgated among the people for the first time.[43]

We can now tell the supposed evolution of the Torah literature in one brief chronology:

1. The process starts in the premonarchic time with the oral composition of poems now embodied in the Torah.
2. The writing of the Priestly Torah takes place in Jerusalem, between the tenth and the eighth centuries B.C.E.
3. The composition of the E source and the Covenant Code (Exod. 20:19–23:33) in the northern kingdom of Israel occurs in the first half of the eighth century B.C.E.
4. In the second half of the eighth century B.C.E., the stage moves back to Jerusalem, where the Holiness Code (Lev. 17–26) and the J source are composed and the E is redacted by the J circle.
5. In 622 B.C.E., the Book of Deuteronomy is published by Josiah in Jerusalem.
6. After the exile in 586 B.C.E., the activity moves to Babylon, where the final redaction of the Torah takes place.
7. The last act is the publication of the Torah by Ezra in Jerusalem in the middle of the fifth century B.C.E.

Appendix B: List of the Main Scriptural Passages of the Priestly Torah (PT) and the Holiness School (HS)[1]

HS Corpus	PT Corpus
GENESIS[2]	
	1:1–2:4
	5:1–28, 30–32[3]
	6:922[4]
	8:15–19
	9:1–17
	17:1–27
	35:9–13
	48:3–6
EXODUS	
	2:23–25
6:2–7:6[5]	
	7:8–13
	8:12–15

HS Corpus	*PT Corpus*
EXODUS *(continued)*	
	9:8–12
12:1–20, 43–49	
	25–30[6]
31	
34:29–35	
35–40	
LEVITICUS	
	1–16[7]
17–26[8]	
NUMBERS	
1:1–5:10	
	5:11–6:21[9]
6:22–10:28	
13:1–16[10]	
14:26–35	
15	
16:1–11,16–24,26–7,35[11]	
17–18	
	19[12]
20:1–13[13], 2229	
25:618	
27	
	28–29[14]
30–31	
32:6–15[15]	
33:52–53, 55–56[16]	
35–36	
DEUTERONOMY	
32:48–52	

Notes

NOTES TO INTRODUCTION

1. On the division of the first four books of the Torah between these sources, see S. R. Driver, *An Introduction to the Literature of the Old Testament*, Gloucester, MA 1972: 1–68, 116–159. For a more popular representation of the sources, see R. E. Friedman, *Who Wrote the Bible*, San Francisco 1987.

2. J. Wellhausen, *Prolegomena to the History of Ancient Israel*, trans. J. S. Black and A. Menzies, New York 1957; idem, *Die Composition of the Hexateuchs und der Historischen Bucher des Alten Testament*, Berlin 1899.

3. For a summary of the criticism of Wellhausen's theory in his generation, see R. J. Thompson, *Moses and the Law in a Century of Criticism*, SVT 8 (1963): 60–62. For scholars who claim for the antiquity of the P in our time, see Y. Kaufmann, *The Religion of Ancient Israel*, trans. M. Greenberg, Chicago 1960: 153–211; M. Haran, *Temples and Temple Service in Ancient Israel*, Oxford 1978: 132–148; M. Weinfeld, "Social and Cultic Institutions in the Priestly Source against Their Ancient Near Eastern Background," *Proceedings of the Eighth World Congress of Jewish Studies, Bible Studies, and Hebrew Language*, Jerusalem 1981: 95–129; idem, *Deuteronomy 1–11, AB*, New York, 1991: 25–36; J. Milgrom, *Leviticus 1–16, AB*, New York 1991: 13–34; idem, "The Antiquity of the Priestly Source: A Reply to Joseph Blenkinsopp," *ZAW* 111 (1999): 10–22.

4. For the argument about the lateness of J, see J. Van Seters, *Abraham in History and Tradition*, New Haven 1975; idem, *In Search of History*, New Haven 1983; idem, *Prolog to History: The Yahwist as Historian in Genesis*, Louisville 1992; idem, *The Life of Moses: The Yahwist as Historian in Exodus-Numbers*, Louisville 1994; H. H. Schmid, *Der sogenante Jahwist*, Zurich 1976; E. Blum, *Die Komposition der Vatergeschichte, WMANT* 57, Neukirchen 1984. For the lateness of the historical books, see G. Garbini, *History and Ideology in Ancient Israel*, London 1988; P. R. Davies, *in Search of Ancient Israel*, Sheffield 1992; T. L. Thompson, *Early History of the Israelite People: From the Written and*

Archeological Sources, Leiden 1992; idem, *The Mythic Past: Biblical Archeology and the Myth of Israel*, New York 1999; N. P. Lemche, *Early Israel*, SVT 37, Leiden 1985; idem, *The Israelite in History and Tradition*, 1998; N. P. Lemche and T. L. Thompson, "Did Biran Kill David," *JSOT* LXIV (1994): 3–3; L. L. Grabbe (ed.), "Can a History of Israel Be Written," *JSOTSup* 245, Sheffield, MA 1997. For the critique of Van Seters, see B. Halpern, *The First Historian*, San Francisco 1988; E. Nicholson, *The Pentateuch in the Twentieth Century*, Oxford 1998: 132–160; W. H. Schmidt, "A Theologian of the Solomonic Era? A Plea for the Yahwist," *Studies in the Period of David and Solomon and other Essays*, T. Ishida (ed.), Tokyo 1982: 55–73. For critique of the "Copenhagen School," see B. Halpern, "Erasing History: The Minimalist Assault of Ancient Israel," *Bible Review*, 1995; A. Hurvitz, "The Historical Quest for 'Ancient Israel' and the Linguistic evidence of the Hebrew Bible: Some Methodological Observations," *VT*, XLVII (1997): 301–315; idem, "The Relevance of Biblical Hebrew Linguistics for the Study of Ancient Israel," *Proceedings of the Twelfth World Congress of Jewish Studies, Division A—The Bible and Its World*, Jerusalem 1999: 21–34; S. Japhet, "Can the Persian Period Bear the Burden? Reflections on the Origins of Biblical History," *Proceedings of the Twelfth World Congress of Jewish Studies, Division A—The Bible and Its World*, Jerusalem 1999: 35–46.

5. See appendix A.

6. See Kaufmann, 60–61.

7. For more on the inscription "YHWH and his ASHERAH," see J. A. Emerton, "YHWH and his ASHERAH: The Goddess or Her Symbol," *VT* 49 (1999): 315–337.

8. The idea that the Torah was written by several prophets or authors, some of them later than Moses, was already expressed by classical and medieval Jewish sources. See I. Knohl, "Between Faith and Criticism" (in Hebrew), *MEGADIM* 33 (2001): 123–126.

NOTES TO CHAPTER ONE

1. Cf. A. Dillmann, *Die Bucher Numeri, Deuteronomium und Josua*, KeH, Leipzig 1886: 666–667; J. Begrich, "Die priesterliche Torah", *BZAW* 66 (1936): 63–88; H. L. Ginsberg, *New Trends in the Study of the Bible (Essays in Judaism 4)*, New York 1967: 23; M. Weinfeld, "Theological Currents in the Pentateuchal Literature," *PAAJR* 37 (1969): 118, 122–123; M. Haran, *Temples and Temple Service in Ancient Israel*, Oxford 1978: 11, 143; Ch. Cohen, "Was the P Document Secret?" *JANES* 112 (1969): 39–44.

2. On the process of the redaction see: A. Kuenen, *An Historico-Critical Inquiry into the Origin and Composition of the Hexateuch*, London 1886: 313–342; R. E. Friedman, "Sacred History and Theology: The Redaction of Torah," *The Creation of Sacred Literature*, Berkeley 1981: 25–34; Knohl, ibid.: 101–103, 200–203.

3. The legal codes were each kept in separate place in the Torah; see Y. Kaufmann, *History of the Religion of Israel*, vol. IV, New York 1977: 393–394. The policy regarding epic parts seems to be that in cases where it was possible,

different versions were put side by side (for instance, the two creation stories in Gen. 1–3); where there was a fear of duplication (like in the Flood story), the different traditions were mingled and redacted together.

4. Cf. J. Wellhausen, *Prolegomena zur Geschichte Israels*, Berlin 1905: 404–409; S. Mowinkel, *Studien zur dem Bucher Ezra-Nehemiah* III, Oslo 1965: 121–141; J. A. Sanders, *Torah and Canon*, Philadelphia 1974: 50–53. There are scholars who claim that the Book of Ezra was not identical to the known Pentateuch. Cf. Kuenen (above, n. 2), 303; U. Kellerman, "Erwagungen zum Esragesetz," *ZAW* 80 (1968): 373–375; M. Noth, *The Laws in the Pentateuch*, London 1966: 2, 76; J. Blenkinsopp, "Ezra-Nehemiah," *OTL*, London 1989: 152–157. On the references to the Torah in Ezra-Nehemiah see S. Japheth, "Law and 'the Law' in Ezra-Nehemiah," *Proceedings of the Ninth World Congress of Jewish Studies, Panel Sessions*, Jerusalem 1988: 99–104.

5. See L. W. Batten, "Ezra and Nehemiah," *ICC*, Edinburgh 1913: 357–358; J. M. Myers, *Ezra and Nehemiah, AB*, Garden City, New York 1965: 154; K. Koch, "Ezra and the Origins of Judaism," *JJS* 19 (1974): 182; Blenkinsopp (above, n. 4), 289.

6. Similar claims are made about the celebration of Passover during the reign of King Josiah, upon the publication or "finding" of the Book of Deuteronomy in 2 Kings 23:22 and the reforms of King Hesekiah in 2 Chron. 30:26 and Josiah in 2 Chron. 35:18.

7. See I. L. Seeligmann, "The Beginnings of Midrash in the Book of Chronicles" (in Hebrew), *Tarbiz* 49 (1980): 31–32; M. Fishbane, *Biblical Interpretation in Ancient Israel*, Oxford 1985: 135–136; S. Japhet, *I & II Chronicles, OTL*, London 1993: 1053; M. Z. Brettler, *The Creation of History in Ancient Israel*, London 1995: 24.

8. On this law see Knohl, *Sanctuary*, 216–218.

9. The law in Deuteronomy also refers to the law in Leviticus. See S. Japhet, "The Relationship Between Legal Corpora in the Pentateuch in Light of Manumission Laws," in S. Japhet (ed.), *Studies in Bible, Scripta Hierosolymitana 31*, Jerusalem 1986: 63–89.

10. See *Sifra* Behukotay 8:12.

11. See Neh. 8:7–8, cf. Fishbane (above, n. 7): 107–109.

12. See Seeligmann (above, n. 7): 14–32; Fishbane, ibid., 91–207.

13. *The Temple Scroll*, ed. Y. Yadin, Jerusalem 1983. The Temple Scroll is in fact an "improved" edition of the Torah. In the Torah one can find, for example, several laws that contradict each other regarding Passover. In contrast, in the Temple Scroll, there is only one law of Passover, without any inner contradiction. See Temple Scroll, 11QT 17:6–16. This is true for all other laws that were unified within the Temple Scroll while resolving all the inner tensions that exist in the Torah. The Temple Scroll even blurs the stylistic difference between Deut. and the other four books of the Torah.

14. *Midrash on Psalms*, Buber edition, 493.

15. *Mishnah* Berachot 1:1.

16. אלו ואלו דברי אלהים חיים Bavli *Eruvin* 13a.

17. See above, n. 1.

18. Cf. Fishbane (above, n. 7), 296–298; Japhet (above, n. 7), 101.

19. Bavli *Gittin* 57b. Cf. S. Zeitlin, "Sameas and Polion," *Journal of Jewish Lore and Philosophy* 1 (1919): 61–67.

20. All we know about Akivah's father is that his name was Joseph. He probably was a poor peasant; cf. L. Finkelstein, *Akiba: Scholar, Saint and Martyr,* New York 1978, 18–20. We don't even know the name of Rabbi Meir's father. He was probably also a descendant of converts; cf. N. G. Cohen, "Rabbi Meir, A Descendant of Anatolian Proselytes," *JJS* 23 (1972): 51–59.

21. According to some Rabbinic sources, he lived at the time of Alexander the Great, and indeed met with him. According to other sources, he lived at a later date, well into the Hellenistic period. On the legend about the meeting between Shimon and Alexander, see J. Gutmann, "Alexander the Great in Palestine" (in Hebrew), *Tarbiz* 11 (1940): 284–287; J. A. Goldstein, "Alexander and the Jews," *PAAJR* 59 (1993): 59–101. Cf. G. F. Moore, "Simeon the Righteous," *Jewish Studies in Memory of Israel Abrahams,* New York 1927, 348–364; J. C. VanderKam, "Simon the Just: Simon I or Simon II?" in D. P. Wright et al. (eds.), *Pomegranates & Golden Bells (J. Milgrom jubilee volume),* Winona Lake, IN 1995: 303–318.

22. See Begrich (above, n. 1).

23. See Knohl, *Sanctuary,* 101–103. My argument for the editing of the Torah by this school was accepted by J. Milgrom, *Leviticus, AB,* New York 2000: 1332–1345.

24. See chapter 4.

NOTES TO CHAPTER TWO

1. See J. A. Wilson's comment on the theology of Memphis in his book *The Burden of Egypt,* Chicago 1951: 59 (cf. G. Sarton, *A History of Science,* New York 1965: 134–135.)

2. For a list of the scriptural passages that belong to the Priestly Torah, see I. Knohl, *The Sanctuary of Silence,* Philadelphia 1995: 104–106; and appendix B.

3. Ibid., 220 ff; see also appendix A.

4. These traditions were written, in my view, in a later period (see appendix A): however, they seem to reflect the reality of the premonarchic period.

5. See 2 Sam. 15:35–36, 17:15–17, 19:12.

6. 1 Kings 1:7–8, 38–39.

7. This singular exception of Jehoiada (2 Kings 11:4–20) was probably provoked by the religious threat posed by Athaliah's actions to YHWH worship in Jerusalem.

8. We do not know exactly what the Urim and Thummim were, but it is clear that they served as a form of communication with and entreaty of God. See A. M. Kitz, "The Plural Form of Urim and Thummim," *JBL* 116 (1997): 401–410. Often during wartime the king or the general would ask whether the nation should go to war, and if so, from which direction the army should attack. There is evidence for this throughout the early period, that is, in the days of the judges, and throughout battles of Saul and David (see Judg. 1:1; 20:18, 1 Sam. 14:36–37, 2 Sam. 5:19, 23, and elsewhere).

9. The priests of Shilo entered the battlefield with the Ark of the Covenant (1 Sam. 4:3–6). In the story of David and Bathsheba, the narrator recounts David's attempts to convince Uriah to go home to Bathsheba, as part of David's attempt to cover up his own sin. But Uriah refuses and says to David, "The Ark and Israel and Judah are located at Succoth...how can I go home and eat and drink and sleep with my wife?" (2 Sam. 11:11). From this we learn that down to the time of David, the Ark goes out to war, and the priests doubtless accompany it. Cf. 2 Sam. 15:25.

10. In the later monarchic era, when Jehosaphat seeks counsel on the night before he is to make war with Edom, he does not turn to the priest, but to the prophet (2 Kings 3:11). The prophet has taken the place of the priest as military adviser.

11. See Deut. 17:9, 3:10; Ezek. 44:24.

12. See M. Weinfeld, "Social and Cultic Institutions in the Priestly Source against their Ancient Near Eastern Background," *Proceedings of the Eighth World Congress of Jewish Studies, Panel Sessions, Bible Studies, and Hebrew Language,* Jerusalem 1983: 95–129; idem, "Traces of Hittite Cult in Shiloh, Bethel, and in Jerusalem," B. Janowski et al. (eds.), *Religionsgeschichtliche Beziehungen zwischen Kleinasien, Nordsyrien und dem Alten Testament,* Freiburg 1993: 456–457; D. P. Wright, "The Disposal of Impurity," *SBL Dissertation Series 101,* Atlanta 1987; J. Milgrom, "The Shared Custody of the Tabernacle and Hittite Analogy," *JAOS* 90 (1970): 202–209; idem, "The Concept of MAAL in the Bible and the Ancient Near East," *JAOS* 96 (1976): 236–247; J. Moyer, "Hittite and Israelite Cultic Practices: A Selected Comparison," in W. Hallo et al. (eds.), *Scripture in Context II* , Winona Lake, IN 1983: 19–38; M. Greenberg, "Hittite Royal Prayers and Biblical Petitionary Psalms," in K. Seybold and E. Zenger (eds.), *Neue Wege der Psalmenforschung (W. Beyerlin Festschrift),* Freiburg 1994: 15–27; A. M. Kitz, "The Plural Form of Urim and Thummim," *JBL* 116 (1997): 401–410.

13. See B. Mazar, "The Early Israelite Settlement in the Hill country," in S. Ahituv and B. A. Levine (eds.), *The Early Biblical Period, Historical Studies,* Jerusalem 1986: 35–48.

14. See Wright's discussion of the scapegoat, above, n. 12, 49–60.

15. The Jebusites probably migrated from the north after the destruction of the Hittite empire in the first half of the twelfth century B.C.E.; see Mazar, above, n. 13.

16. For a detailed discussion of the Priestly account of Creation, see W. H. Schmidt, *Die Schopfungsgeschicte der Priesterschrift,* Neukirchen 1964; Y. Amit, "Creation and the Calendar of Holiness" (in Hebrew), in M. Cogan, B. L. Eichler, and J. Tigay (eds.), *Tehilla le-Moshe—Biblical and Judaic Studies in Honor of M. Greenberg,* Winona Lake, IN 1997: 13–29. Amit claims that this account stems from the Holiness School. Her main argument is based on the importance of the Sabbath in Gen. 2:1–3. While Amit's article is interesting, I do not think that there is sufficient evidence for ascribing this chapter to the Holiness School. Had the passage come from this school, we should expect to hear something about prohibition of work as in Exod. 31:14–15; 35:2–3 (on the origins of these laws in the

Holiness School, see Knohl, *Sanctuary*, 15–18) and Lev. 19:3; 23:3; 26:2. J. Milgrom has claimed recently that all Priestly traditions in Gen. 1–11 stem from the Holiness School (J. Milgrom, *Leviticus 17–22, AB*, New York 2000: 1440–1441). His claim is based mainly on the polemics against Babylonian mythology, which he takes as evidence that these traditions were written by the final editors of the Torah who belonged to the Holiness School and who worked during the Babylonian exile. While I am happy to see that Milgrom follows my view that the Torah was edited by the Holiness School at the time of the exile and the return (see *Sanctuary*, 101–103, 200–204, 224), I cannot accept his argument regarding the Priestly tradition in Gen. 1–11. It is true that there are polemics against the myths of Mesopotamia in these traditions. Yet, it has been argued that the Mesopotamian conceptions of creation could have been known in Israel at a much earlier date (see E. A. Speiser, *Genesis, AB*, New York 1981: liv–lvii; G. J. Wenham, *Genesis 1–15, Word Biblical Commentary*, Waco, TX 1987: 9). Furthermore, the Holiness School has a typical style, distinct from that of the Priestly Torah (see *Sanctuary*, 106–110), and there is no sign of this style in Gen. 1–11.

17. See H. Gunkel, *Genesis*, trans. M. E. Biddle, Macon, GA 1997: 103; S. R. Driver, *The Book of Genesis, Westminster Commentary*, London 1904: 3; U. Cassuto, *A Commentary on the Book of Genesis*, Jerusalem 1961: 19–20; C. Westermann, *Genesis 1–11*, trans. J. J. Scullion, Minneapolis 1984: 93–7. According to this view, Gen. 1:1 serves as a heading to P's description of Creation in 1:1–2:4a. It is typical in the Priestly writings to start or to end units with titles or colophons that summarize the unit; see M. Fishbane, "Biblical Colophons: Textual Criticism and Legal Analogies," *CBQ* 42 (1980): 438–449.

18. The view that it is subordinate to verse 2 was held by Ibn Ezra and, in our time, by W. Gross, "Syntaktische Erscheinungen am Anfang althebräischer Erzählungen: Hinterground und Vorderground," *SVT* 32 (1981): 131–145. The view that it is subordinate to verse 3 was held by Rashi. Among modern commentators it is held by J. Skinner, *Genesis, ICC*, Edinburgh 1994: 12; E. A. Speiser, *Genesis, AB*, New York 1981: 12; N. Sarna, *The JPS Torah Commentary*, Philadelphia 1989: 3. If we see verse 1 as a temporal clause, it should be translated, "When God began to create the heavens and the earth."

19. See Gunkel (above, n. 17), 104, Westermann (above, n. 17), 108–110. Wenham (above, n. 16), 11; B. S. Childs, *Myth and Reality in the Old Testament*, London 1968: 2; J. D. Levenson, *Creation and the Persistence of Evil*, San Fransisco 1988: 121.

20. See Westermann, ibid., 110.

21. See especially Deut. 32:10; Isa. 45:18; Ps. 107:40; Job 6:18; 12:24; and Westermann's discussion (above, n. 17, 102–113).

22. We have already seen that *tohu* is a designation of the desert and uninhabited areas. According to the Priestly Torah, these areas are places of impurity and evil; see Lev. 14:53, 16:10, 21. On darkness as evil, see the parallelism in Isa. 45:7. As was suggested by Gunkel (above, n. 17, 105) and by many other scholars, the word *tehom* (deeps) should be understood in light of the Mesopotamian goddess Tiamat, the female dragonesque representation of the aggressive forces of chaos. In contrast to the Mesopotamian Tiamat, the *tehom* in

Gen. 1:2 is a passive entity; it does not contend against God's Creation. This fits to the general conception of impurity and evil in the Priestly Torah as passive entities (see Kaufmann, ibid., 542–545).

23. See for instance Isa. 45:7: "I form light and create darkness, / I make weal and create woe— / I the Lord do all these things."

24. Isa. 27:1, 51:9–10; Hab. 3:8–15; Pss. 29:3, 46:3–6, 65:8, 68:22–23, 74:13–14, 77:17–20, 89:10–11, 93:3–4, 104:6–8, 104:3; Job 7:12, 26:12–3, 38:8–11. The basic discussion is by H. Gunkel, *Schöpfung und Chaos in Urzeit und Endzeite*, Göttingen 1895.

25. For רוח אלהים as "spirit of God" or "wind of God," see Wenham (above, n. 16), 17, who writes "The phrase does really express the powerful presence of God moving mysteriously over the face of the waters."

26. See Levenson, *Creation*, 122–123.

27. See Cassuto (above, n. 17, 50–51).

28. Cf. 27–28; J. Hempel, "Glaube, Mythos und Geschichte im Alten Testament," *ZAW* 65 (1953): 126–128; J. L. Mckenzie, "Myth and the Old Testament *CBQ* 21 (1959): 277; A. S. Kapelrud, "The Mythological Features in Genesis Chapter 1 and the Author's intention," *VT* 24 (1974): 184. Levenson, *Creation*: 54–55.

29. See Levenson, *Creation*, 122–123.

30. *Talmud Yerushalmi, Hagigah* 2:1 (77c) *Bereshit Rabah* 1:1 (J. Theodor and Ch. Albeck, eds.), Jerusalem 1965: 3. Cf. the saying of *Bar Kapara* recorded in these sources that claims heaven and earth were formed out of the *tohu v' vohu*.

31. Cf. H. J. Stipp, "Alles Fleisch hatte seinem Wandel auf die Erde verdorben (Gn 6,12)," *ZAW* 111 (1999): 167–186.

32. For this interpretation of Gen. 6:11, see Jubilees 5:2 and H. C. Brichto, "On Slaughter and Sacrifice, Blood and Atonement," *HUCA* 47 (1976): 20; cf. P. J. Harland, "The Value of Human Life," *SVT* 64 (1996): 37–40.

33. On Azazel and parallel rituals in the ancient Near East, see H. Tawil, "The Prince of the Steep: A Comparative Study," *ZAW* 92 (1980): 43–59; D. P. Wright, *The Disposal of Impurity, SBL Dissertation Series 101*, Atlanta 1987: 15–74; J. Milgrom, *Leviticus 1–16, AB*, New York 1991: 1071–1079; B. Janowski and G. Wilhelm, "Der Bock, der die Sunden hinaustragt," in B. Janowski et al. (eds.), *Religionsgeschichtliche Beziehungen zwischen Kleinasien, Nordsyrien und dem Alten Testament*, Freiburg 1993: 109–160; M. Weinfeld, "Traces of Hittite Cult in Shiloh, Bethel and in Jerusalem," in B. Janowski et al. (eds.), *Religionsgeschichtliche Beziehungen zwischen Kleinasien, Nordsyrien und dem Alten Testament*, Freiburg 1993: 456–457; S. A. Geller, *Sacred Enigmas*, New York 1996: 68–74.

34. "*Azazel*, i.e. the hardest of mountains," quoted from Bavli *Yoma* 67b. It is interesting to note that after this explanation the Talmud gives another explanation: "The School of R. Ishmael taught: *Azazel* it was called because it obtains atonement for the affair of Uza and Azazel." This is a reference to the legend of the falling angels in Gen. 6. According to the Book of Enoch, Asael or Azazel was one of the leaders of these rebellious angels (see Enoch 6:8, 8:1, 10:4). Thus this talmudic tradition preserves the mythological meaning of the name (contrary to the apologetic interpretation of Y. M. Grintz, *Studies in Early Biblical Ethnology and History* [in Hebrew], no. 217, Tel Aviv 1961: 218). The mythic image of

Azazel as Samael is to be found also in the Midrash *Pirke de Rabbi Eliezer* 45, G. Friedlander (ed.), New York 1970: 363–364.

35. This spelling is to be found in the Samaritan version of Lev. 16:10 in the Temple Scroll of Qumran 26:13, in 4Q180 Fragment 1, lines 7,8 (DJD V 78) and in the Vatican 66 MS of the Sifra, see S. Naeh, "Notes to Tannaitic Hebrew Based on Codex Vat. 66 of the Sifra," M. Bar-Asher (ed.), *Language Studies*, Jerusalem 1990: 272–275.

36. See Wright, above, n. 33.

37. See 2 Sam. 12:31; 1 Kings 3:25; Ps. 136:13; Dan. 2:34.

38. For *eretz gezera* used to denote the death of a person, see Isa. 53:8; Ezek. 37:11; Ps. 88:6; Lam. 3:54. For the death of an animal, see Hab. 3:17.

39. See Milgrom, ad. loc.

40. See above, n. 33.

41. "Baal and Mot," J.C.L. Gibson (ed.) (orig. ed. G. R. Driver), *Canaanite Myths and Legends*, Edinburgh 1977: col. II, 11. 16–17.

42. "Baal and Mot,"col. IV, 11. 18–23.

43. See M. Smith, "Interpreting the Baal Cycle," *Ugaritica* 18 (1986): 314–316.

44. See J. Milgrom, *The JPS Torah Commentary: Numbers*, Philadelphia 1990: 438–443.

45. In this we see the great difference between Azazel and the active evil spirits discussed by B. Levine, " Kippurim" (in Hebrew), *ErIs* 9 (1969): 88–95.

46. I. Knohl, "The Priestly Torah versus the Holiness School: Sabbath and the Festivals," *HUCA* 58 (1987): 86–87.

47. Milgrom accepted and followed my theory. See *Leviticus 1–16, AB*: 1062–1063.

48. See above, n. 38. For a discussion of the fight of the sea in Ugaritic myth and its biblical parallels, see S. E. Lowenstamm, "The Ugaritic myth of the Sea and its Biblical Counterparts" (in Hebrew), *ErIs* 9 (1969): 96–101.

49. See P. J. Karney, "Creation and Liturgy: The Predaction of Exodus 25–30," *ZAW* 89 (1977): 280; M. Weinfeld, "Sabbath, Temple and the Enthronement of the Lord—The Problem of the *Sitz im Leben* of Genesis 1:1–2:3," in A. Caquot and M. Delcor (eds.), *Melanges Henri Cazelles*, Neukirchen 1981: 503; Levenson, *Creation*, 83–86.

50. Gen. 1:31–2:3, Exod. 39:32,43. The last verses are, in my view, from the Holiness School; see *Sanctuary*, 66–68.

51. See Knohl, *Sanctuary*, 137–148.

52. Gen. 17:1–7. Abraham is asked by God to "Walk before me and be blameless" (Gen. 17:1). This is a condition of the covenant. Thus, I can't accept the view that the Priestly covenant is unconditional; see J. J. P. Valeton, "Bedeutung und Stellung of des Wortes ברית im Priestercodex," *ZAW* 12 (1982): 501–512; J. Begrich, "Berit-Ein Beitrag zur Erfassung einer alttestamentlichen Denkform," *ZAW* 60 (1944): 7.

53. This verse indeed does not stem from the Priestly Torah, but rather from the other Priestly school, the Holiness School (see *Sanctuary*, 61). However, the concept of this verse originates in the Priestly Torah.

54. See *Sanctuary*, 125–128.

55. On the suppression of anthropomorphism in the Priestly Torah, see *Sanctuary*, 128–137. The avoidance of anthropomorphic descriptions of God in the Priestly Torah is only with regard to the name "YHWH" used in the time of Moses; the personal God of the Genesis period, which is symbolized by the name "Elohim," has an image similar to that of man (Gen. 1:26–7).

56. The impersonality and lack of anthropomorphism in the punishment descriptions of the Priestly writings were noted by A. Rofe, *The Belief in Angels in the Bible and in Early Israel* (in Hebrew), Jerusalem 1979: 172–176.

57. In other sources this juxtaposition is regularly found in the formulas הי אלהים, הי אלהיר, הי אלהיכם.

58. See my debate with J. Milgrom in *Sanctuary*, 225–230.

59. See *Sanctuary*, 139–140; I. Knohl, "Between Cult and Morality: Theological Transitions in the Torah," *S'VARA* 2 (1991): 29–34; idem, "The Guilt Offering of the Holiness School" (forthcoming), *Tarbiz* 71 (1992).

60. R. Otto, *The Idea of the Holy*, J. W. Harvey (trans.), Oxford 1958: 1–59.

61. See Jon. 3:8. On the meaning of חמס as a violation of the social-moral order, see G. von Rad, *Old Testament Theology*, vol. 1, D. M. G. Stalker (trans.), Edinburgh 1973: 157; Speiser (above, n. 18), 117; Westermann (above, n. 17), 559; H. Haag, "חמס," *ThWAT* 2 (1977): 1056–1060; Harland (above, n. 32), 37–40.

62. See Gen. 2:3, Exod. 26:33–34, 28:4,36,38,41, 29:1,6,21,27,29,30,33,36–37, 30:10,13,25,29–32,36–7, 31:11; Lev. 5:15–16, 6:9,11,18–20,22–23, 7:1,6, 8:9–12,15,30, 10:3–4,12–13,17, 12:2, 16:2–4,16–17,20,23–4, 23:4,7–8,24,27,35–37; Num. 5:17, 6:5,8,11,20, 28:7,18,25–26, 29:1,7,12.

63. This is the usual character of holiness in the Hebrew Bible; see H. Ringren, *The Prophetical Conception of Holiness*, Upsala 1948: 23. On the exceptional cases, Lev. 19 and Isa. 5:16, where holiness has a moral significance, see *Sanctuary*, 180–181, 213–214.

64. See Deut. 30:15 and the comment of S. R. Driver, *Deuteronomy, ICC*, Edinburgh 1973: 331–332.

65. See O. Eissfeldt, *El in ugaritichen Pantheon*, Leipzig 1951; M. Pope, "El in Ugaritic Texts," *SVT* 2 (1955); F. M. Cross, *Canaanite Myth and Hebrew Epic*, Cambridge, MA 1973: 13–24.

66. See F. M. Cross, "The Song of the Sea and Canaanite Myth," *JThC* 5 (1968): 2; R. J. Clifford, "The Tent of El and the Israelite Tent of Meeting," *CBQ* 33 (1971): 221–227.

67. The interpretation of the Ugaritic *dd* as "tent" was suggested by Clifford, ibid. There are some problems involved with this interpretation. See F. Renfroe, *Arabic-Ugaritic Lexical Studies*, Munster 1992: 97–99; M. S. Smith, *The Ugaritic Baal Cycle*, I, Leiden 1994: 187–188.

68. The Ugaritic term is *krs*, which is cognate with the Hebrew קרש used in the description of the Priestly Tabernacle; see Exod. 26:15–29. A similar term was used in Mari; see D. F. Flaming, "Mari's Large Public Tent and the Priestly Tent Sanctuary," *VT* 50 (2000): 484–498.

69. See A. Herdner, *Corpus des tablettes en cuneiforms alphabétiques*, Paris 1963: 4, 20–24. Translation by Cross, *Canaanite Myth*, 36.

70. *Sinai and Zion*, San Francisco 1987: 138–139.

71. See also Ezek. 47:1–12 .

72. R. J. Clifford, *The Cosmic Mountain in Canaan and the Old Testament*, Cambridge, MA 1972: 158; J. D. Levenson, *Theology of the Program of Restoration of Ezekiel 40–48*, Harvard Semitic Monograph Series, Missoula, MT 1976: 11.

73. Levenson, ibid., 11–12.

74. See Pss. 128:5, 132:13–15, 134:3. Cf. R. E. Clements, *God and Temple*, no. 1d., Oxford 1965: 49.

75. See Exod. 29:7.

76. Not only El's, but also the symbolism of Baal's shrine on Mount Sapon was adapted to Jerusalem and its Temple. The reference to the "dew of Hermon" can thus be interpreted as a transference of a Canaanite fertility motif to Zion. See Ps. 48:3 and the discussions by H. J. Kraus, *Worship in Israel*, Oxford 1962: 201 ff.; M. Dahud, *Psalms I, AB*, Garden City, NY 1965: 289–290; Clements, *God and Temple*, 10–11; Clifford, *The Cosmic Mountain*, 142; A. Robinson, "Zion and Saphon in Psalm XLVIII 3," *VT* 24 (1974): 118–121; J. D. Levenson, *Sinai and Zion*, Minneapolis 1985: 124.

77. Isa. 33:20.

78. To see this mobility of a "divine exile," see B. D. Sommer, "Conflict Constructions of Divine Presence in the Priestly Tabernacle," *Biblical Interpretation 9* (2001): 60–61. However, I tend to see this mobility as mainly polemic.

79. Clements, *God and Temple*, 120. Cf. T. E. Fretheim, "The Priestly Document: Anti-Temple?" *VT* 18 (1968): 319.

80. J. Milgrom (*Leviticus 17–22, AB*, 1428–1429) claims, against my view, that the cult of the Priestly Torah is not concerned with human welfare. He bases his arguments on the antiquity of the Priestly blessing (Num. 6:22–26) and the well-being offering (שלמים). Regarding the Priestly blessing, the text is from the Holiness School (see *Sanctuary*, 89). The date of the silver plaques with a similar text found in Jerusalem is late seventh or early sixth century B.C.E., and this fits well with the time of the Holiness School's activity, (from the second half of the eighth century onward; see *Sanctuary*, 204–220). However, it might be that the roots of this text go back to an earlier period. We must remember that besides the circle of the Priestly Torah, there were other Priestly circles with different conceptions. Such was the Priestly house of Shilo. While the Priestly Torah, does not refer to any involvement of the holy Ark or the priests in the time of war (*Sanctuary*, 140, 156), the priests of Shilo carried the Ark to the war field (1 Sam. 4:4). In light of this difference between the priest of Shilo and the views of the Priestly Torah, I cannot accept the suggestion of M. Haran ("Shilo and Jerusalem: The Origin of the Priestly Tradition in the Pentateuch," *JBL* 81 [1962]: 14–24) and Milgrom (*Leviticus 1–16, AB*, New York 1991: 30–35) that the origins of the Priestly Torah are in Shilo. In my view, we should better look to Bethel. As for the well-being offering, it is part of the individual worship that the Priestly Torah tolerates (see *Sanctuary*, 23–27, 163). However, nowhere do we find this sacrifice as a part of the public cult of the Priestly Torah. In contrast, within the laws of

the Holiness School, which has a different theology, we do indeed have a well-being sacrifice as a part of the public ritual of the first-fruits festival (1 Lev. 23:19–20, cf. *Sanctuary*, 25 and n. 48).

81. See G. von Rad, *Old Testament Theology*, vol. 1, D. M. G. Stalker (trans.), Edinburgh 1973: 135; F. M. Cross, *Cannanite Myth and Hebrew Epic*, Cambridge, MA 1973: 318–320.

82. W. Zimmerli, "Sinaibund und Abrahambund," *TZ* 16 (1960): 277.

83. Zimmerli, ibid., 268-280 and subsequently R. E. Clements, *Abraham and David*, London 1967: 74–75; N. Lohfink, "Die Priesterschriftliche Abwertung der Tradition von Offenbarung des Jahwenamens an Mose," *Biblica* 49 (1968): 1; D. J. McCarthy, *Old Testament Covenant*, Oxford 1972: 48; H. Cazelles, "Alliance du Sinai, Alliance de l'Horeb et Renouvellement de l'Alliance," in *Beitrage zur Alttestamentlichen Theologie* [Festschrift W. Zimmerli], Göttingen 1977: 69–79

84. See A. Toeg, *Lawgiving at Sinai* (in Hebrew), no. 114, Jerusalem 1977: 149.

85. *The Laws in the Pentateuch and other Studies*, D. R. Apt-Thomas (trans.), Edinburgh 1966: 91–93.

86. See M. Haran, *Temples and Temple Service in Ancient Israel*, no. 12, Oxford 1978: 143.

87. See my argument, *Sanctuary*, 15–17. Cf. B. J. Schwartz, "The Priestly Account of the Theophany and Lawgiving in Sinai," M. V. Fox et al. (eds.), *Texts, Temples and Traditions—A Tribute to Menahem Haran*, Winona Lake, IN 1996: 130–132. While I agree with Schwartz (ibid., no. 61) that the divine indwelling is conditional according to the Priestly Torah, this does not give the laws a framework of mutual bilateral relationship since, as Schwartz himself admits (ibid., n. 59), "the blessing and curses are actually quite absent from the Priestly law code once the Holiness stratum is subtracted."

88. See Exod. 25:21–22. Schwartz (ibid., 126) claims on the basis of 2 Kings 11:12 that the עדות was an object, not a document. However, the עדות in 2 Kings is enigmatic. Some scholars see it as a reference to a document; see G. von Rad, "Das judische Konigsritual," *ThLZ* 72 (1947): 211–216; M. Cogan and H. Tadmor, *II Kings, AB*, New York 1988: 128; J. J. M. Roberts, "Whose Child is This? Reflections on the Speaking Voice in Isaiah 9:5," *HTR* 90 (1997): 211–216. It is more reasonable to connect the Priestly עדות with similar terms in the psalms (see M. Parnas, *SHNATON* 1 [1977]: 235–246).

89. On treaty forms in the ancient Near East and their impact on the Bible, see G. E. Mendenhall, "Covenant Forms in Israelite Tradition," *Biblical Archeologist* 17 (1954): 49–76; D. J. McCarthy, *Treaty and Covenant (Analecta Biblica 21)*, Rome 1963; M. Weinfeld, *Deuteronomy and the Deuteronomic School*, Oxford 1972: 59–157; H. Tadmor, "Treaty and Oath in the Ancient Near East: A Historian's Approach," G. M. Tucker and D. A. Knight (eds.), *Humanizing America's Iconic Book—SBL Centennial Addresses*, Chico, CA,1982: 149–163.

90. See H. Tadmor, "The Aramaization of Assyria: Aspect of Western Impact," H. G. Nissen and J. Renger (eds.), *Mesopotamien und Seine Nachbaren*, Berlin 1982: 455.

91. The one-sided nature of the *ade* was emphasized by I. J. Gelb, "Review of D. J. Weisman, 'The Vassal Treaties of Esarhaddon,'" *BiOr* 19 (1962): 160–162.

92. The blessings of Leviticus 26 belong to the Holiness Code and represent the different view of the Holiness School; see *Sanctuary*, 173–174.

93. Similar worldview is expressed in the Book of Job; see below, chapter 7.

94. See M. Weinfeld, "ברית," *TDOT* 2 (1977): 763.

95. On this contrast, see N. Sarna, *Understanding Genesis*, New York 1966: 14–16; M. Greenberg, *On the Bible and Judaism: A Collection of Writings*, Tel Aviv 1985: 16–20.

96. On the link between the Priestly concept of holiness and the tendency toward an impersonal understanding of God, see W. Eichrodt, *Theology of the Old Testament*, vol. 1, J. Baker (trans.), London 1961: 407.

97. Besides Exod. 8:19 and Lev. 2:13, the only other case where the name "Elohim" is used in the Priestly Torah in the Moses period is in Num. 6:7. For discussion of this verse, see *Sanctuary*, 161–162.

NOTES TO CHAPTER THREE

1. Jubilees 3:3; see O. S. Wintermute, *The Book of Jubilees*, in J. H. Charlesworth (ed.), *The Old Testament Pseudepigrapha*, vol. 2, New York 1985: 58. Cf. *Midrash Bereshit Rabba*, 17:4, ed. J. Theodor and Ch. Albeck, Jerusalem 1965: 156, line 5.

2. Cf. G. J. Wenham, *Genesis 1–15, Word Biblical Commentary*, Waco, TX 1987: 71–72.

3. See Exod. 4:3, 7:10, Isa. 27:1.

4. See Y. Kaufmann, *History of Israelite Religion*, vol. 2, Jerusalem–Tel Aviv 1960: 411–412.

5. For some different interpretations of this concept, see H. Gunkel, *Genesis*, M. E. Biddle (trans.), Macon, GA 1997: 14–15; G. von Rad, *Genesis, OTL*, London 1972: 88–90; C. Westermann, *Genesis 1–11*, J. J. Scullion (trans.), Minneapolis 1984: 240–248.

6. See Gunkel, ibid.; U. Cassuto, *A Commentary on the Book of Genesis*, Jerusalem 1961, 112–113; cf. W. M. Clark, "A Legal Background to the Yahwist's use of 'Good and Evil' in Genesis 2–3," *JBL* 88 (1969): 275–276.

7. Cf. H. C. Berichto, *The Names of God*, New York 1998: 94–96.

8. See Ricoeur, *The Symbolism of Evil*, Boston 1967: 239.

9. See Gunkel (above, n. 5), 29.

10. See Bavli *Berachot* 17a, for the concluding personal prayer of R. Alexandri: "Sovereign of the Universe. It is known full well to Thee that our will is to perform Thy will, and what prevents us? The yeast in the dough and the subjection to foreign Powers. May it be Thy will to deliver us from their hand, so that we may return to perform the statutes of Thy will with a perfect heart" (Soncino trans.).

11. See Clark (above, n. 6), 268–269; T. N. D. Mettinger, *King and Messiah*, Lund, Sweden 1976: 240–244.

12. See H. Frankfort, *Kingship and the Gods*, Chicago 1948: 238–239.

13. See S. E. Loewenstamm, "Man as Image and Son of God," *Tarbiz* 27 (1957): 1–2; H. Wildberger, "Das Abbild Gottes, Gen 1:26–30," *TZ* 21 (1965): 253–255, 484–488.

14. Loewenstam, ibid.; Wildberger, ibid., 257–259; Tryggve N. D. Mettinger, "Unbild oder Urbild? 'Imago Dei' in traditionsgeschictlicher Sicht," *ZAW* 86 (1974): 403–424 and the bibliography on 403, n. 1; J. D. Levenson, *Creation and the Persistence of Evil*, New York 1988.

15. See Gunkel (above, n. 5), 31.

16. See the discussion of Mettinger, *King and Messiah* (above, n. 11), 270–272; H. G. May, "The King in the Garden of Eden: A study of Ezekiel 28:12–19," in B. W. Anderson and W. Harrelson (eds.), *Israel's Prophetic Heritage, Essays in honor of J. Muilenburg*, London 1962: 166–176; R. R. Wilson, "The Death of the King of Tyre: The Editorial History of Ezekiel 28," in J. H. Marks and R.M. Good (eds.), *Love and Death in the Ancient Near East, Essays in Honor of M. H. Pope*, 1987: 211–218; J. van Seters, "The Creation of Man and the Creation of the King," *ZAW* 101 (1989): 333–342.

17. See *ARE* 2, 75–100, 334.

18. See H. Frankfort (above, n. 12), 299–301.

19. On the Israelite King as son of God, see G. Cook, "The Israelite King as Son of God," *ZAW* 73 (1961): 202–225; "Whose Child Is This? Reflections on the Speaking Voice in Isaiah 9:5," *HTR* 90 (1997): 115–129.

20. For קניתי as "I have created," see Cassuto (above, n. 6), 201; Westermann (above, n. 5), 290. For the meaning of את as "together with," see J. Skinner, *A Critical and Exegetical Commentary of Genesis, ICC*, Edinburgh 1910: 102 ff.; Westermann, ibid., 292.

21. See Skinner, ibid., 102–103; E. Lipinski *ThWAT* קנת VII (1993): 63–71.

22. Skinner (above, n. 20), 105.

23. See H. Bloom, *The Book of J*, New York 1991: 188.

24. See J. D. Levenson, *The Death and resurrection of the Beloved Son*, New Haven, CT 1993: 69–81.

25. Gen. 4:14, see also Westermann (above, n. 5), 310.

26. Above, n. 23, 188.

27. Cf. M. I. Gruber, "The Tragedy of Cain and Abel: A Case of Depression," *JQR* 69 (1978–9): 89–97.

28. I agree with W. Hallo, "Antediluvian Cities," *JCS* 23 (1970): 64; Westermann (above, n. 5), 327; and N. Sarna, *Genesis, The JPS Torah Commentary*, Philadelphia 1989, 36, who maintain that J sees the founding of the first city as an achievement of human civilization. For a different view, see G. Wallis, "Die Stadt in den Uberlieferungen der Genesis," *ZAW* 78 (1966): 133–148; F. S. Frick, *The City in Ancient Israel*, Missoula, MT 1977: 205–207; R. Coot and D. Ord, *The Bible's First History*, Philadelphia 1989: 80–81; H. Bloom (above, n. 23), 188. Cf. T. Hiebert, *The Yahwist's Landscape*, New York 1996: 42–43.

29. For a discussion of parallel traditions in the ancient Near East and the seven sages who lived before the Flood, see R. R. Wilson, *Genealogy and History in the Biblical World*, New Haven, CT 1977: 149–154.

30. See Gen. 2:12 and, for the connections, M. Greenberg, *Ezekiel 21–37, AB,* New York 1997: 581–582.

31. Cf. Ps. 82:7 and the Ugaritic text Keret 125:17–23 discussed by Mettinger (above, n. 11), 273.

32. The scholarly literature is vast. See Westermann (above, n. 5), 363–364; M. and R. Zimmermann, "Heilige Hochzeit der Gottersohne und Menschen-tochter," *ZAW* 111 (1999): 327–328.

33. See Westermann, ibid., 272.

34. See Gunkel (above, n. 5), 56–57; B. S. Childs, "Myth and Reality in the Bible," *SBT* 27 (1962); Westermann, ibid., 371–372; Wenham (above, n. 2), 140.

35. See Westermann, ibid., 374.

36. See J. Wellhausen, *Die Composition des Hexateuchs und der historischen Bucher des Alten Testament,* Berlin 1889: 306–308; Gunkel, (above, n. 5), 57–58; Westermann, ibid., 378.

37. The connection between Gen. 6:1–4 and Isa. 14 was pointed out by Westermann, ibid., 382.

38. See J. D. Levenson, *Creation and the Persistence of Evil,* San Francisco 1985.

39. On the connection between the tower story and Gen. 3:20–22, 6:1–3, see Skinner (above, n. 20), 29.

40. See Gunkel (above, n. 5), 98–99; Sarna (above, n. 28), 75–76, suggests that what lies behind Gen. 11:2–4 is not an actual ziggurat but the passage in Enuma Elish, VI 62 (*ANET* 69): "They raised the head of Esagila toward Apsu." Apsu is, among other things, a poetic term for the sky.

41. See, Sarna ibid.; V. Hurowitz, *I Have Built you an Exalted House,* Sheffield, MA 1991.

42. On שם as eternal memory achieved by building of monuments, see 2 Sam. 18:18, Isa. 56:5, cf. Gunkel (above, n. 5), 96; S. Talmon, "Yad Wasem: An Idiomatic Phrase in Biblical Literature and Its Variations," *Hebrew Studies* 25 (1984): 8–17. The objection of Westermann (above, n. 5), 548, that there is a difference between a king and the common people does not hold. As I have noted, it is the trend of J to democratize monarchic conception.

43. The search for divinity is also expressed by the description of the tower as a monument whose top is in the heavens (Gen. 11:4).

44. Cf. G. von Rad, *Old Testament Theology,* vol. 1, New York 1962: 161–165.

NOTES TO CHAPTER FOUR

1. For scholars who date the song to the eighth century B.C.E., see the list made by S. R. Driver, *Deuteronomy, ICC,* Edinburgh 1896: 346–347; for earlier dates see F. M. Cross, *Cannanite Myth and Hebrew Epic,* Cambridge, MA 1973: 264, n. 193.

2. For a discussion of possible Canaanite motives in these verses, see O. Eissfeldt, "El and Yahwe," *JSS* 1 (1956): 25–37; idem, *Das Lied Moses, Deut. 32, 1–43 und Lehrgedicht Asaphs, Psalm 78,* Berlin 1958; A. Rofe, *The Belief in Angels in the Bible and in Early Israel* (in Hebrew), Jerusalem 1979: 66–78; S. E. Loewenstamm, נחלת הי in S. Japhet (ed.), *Studies in the Bible, Scripta Hierosolymitana* 16, Jerusalem 1986: 177–187.

3. See *RASHI*, ad. loc.

4. See P. W. Skehan, "A Fragment of the 'Song of Moses' (Deut. 32) from Qumran," *BASOR* 136 (1954): 12–15; idem, "Qumran and the Present State of OT Studies," *JBL*, 78 (1959): 21; U. Ulrich et al., *Qumran Cave 4 IX, DJD XIV*, Oxford 1995: 90.

5. κατα αριθμον αγγελων Θεου, according to the number of the angels of God.

6. El, the Canaanite head of the pantheon, had seventy sons. For other reflections of this tradition in the Bible, see the seventy sons of Gideon, also called Jerubaal, in Judg. 8:29–32, 9:1–56; see also T. H. Gaster, "Sons of God," *IDB* 4: 426.

7. Cf. Rofe (above, n. 2), 88–89; I. Knohl, "Biblical Attitude to Gentile Idolatry" (in Hebrew), *Tarbiz* 64 (1994): 5–12; J. Tigay, *Deuteronomy, The JPS Torah Commentary*, Philadelphia 1996: 435–436. Compare also Deut. 29:25.

8. See Y. Kaufmann, *The Religion of Israel*, Chicago 1960: 358.

9. I take here the meaning of the word ונהרו (Isa. 2:2) as "they shall go." For other possible translations and their implications, see B. J. Schwartz, "Torah from Zion: Isaiah Temple Vision (Isa. 2:1–4)" in A. Houtman et al., *Sanctity of Time and Space in Tradition and Modernity*, Leiden 1998: 11–26. For possible late redaction of the passage, see H. G. M. Williamson, *The Book Called Isaiah*, Oxford 1994: 144–155.

10. Kaufmann (above, n. 8), 346.

11. On the relationship between Isaiah's words and the Assyrian propaganda, see P. Machinist, "Assyria and Its Image in the First Isaiah," *JAOS* 103 (1983): 719–737.

12. B. Oded, "Mass Deportation in the Neo-Assyrian Empire"(in Hebrew), *SHNATON* 3 (1978–9): 159–173; idem, *Mass Deportations and Deportees in the Neo-Assyrian Empire*, Wiesbaden 1979.

13. See Machinist (above, n. 11), p. 725.

14. The Hebrew is וכבד משאה. My translation is based on the commentaries of Ibn Ezra and Luzzatto to the Book of Isaiah. Cf. S. D. Luzzatto, *A Commentary to the Book of Jesaiah*, Tel Aviv 1970: 239.

15. The only other case is Ps. 20:2, "the name of Jacob's God keep you safe." Here we have probably a reference to the magic power of the divine name; cf. Ps. 20:8 and the recent discussion of W. F. Smelik, "The Use of הזכיר בשם in Classical Hebrew: Josh. 23:7; Isa. 48:1; Amos 6:10; Ps. 20:8; 4Q504 iii 4; 1QS 6:27," *JBL* 118 (1999): 321–332. Some exegetes consider "the name of YHWH" to be an addition; however, see the contra argument of W. A. M. Beuken, *Isaiah II, Historical Commentary on the O.T.*, Leuven, Belgium 2000: 177–178. On the origins of Isa. 30:27–33 in the pre-exilic period, see H. G. M. Williamson, *The Book Called Isaiah*, Oxford 1994: 231–232.

16. Cf. Ps. 140:4.

17. See Isa. 6:4, cf. also J. Milgrom, *The JPS Torah Commentary: Numbers*, Philadelphia 1990: 459–460.

18. See Num. 21:8, Isa. 14:29, 30:6; cf. K. R. Joines, "Winged Serpents in Isaiah's Inaugural Vision," *JBL* 86 (1967): 410–415.

19. On the connection between God's name and the angel, see Exod. 23:20–21.

20. This picture is of course dramatically different from Isaiah's fundamental doctrine of the remnant; cf. G. B. Gray, *Isaiah I–XXVII, ICC,* Edinburgh 1912: 110. Some scholars suggest that we have here a verdict of the Divine Court; see R. Knierim, "The Vocation to Isaiah," *VT* 18 (1968): 57–64; M. Tsevat, "Isaiah 6," in B. Z. Luria (ed.), *Zer Liwgevurot—The Z. Shazar Jubilee Volume,* Jerusalem 1973: 161–172. For the motive of hardening the heart, see H. Wildberger, *Isaiah 28-39,* translated by T. H. Trapp, Minneapolis 2002: 624-629.

21. Further destruction is proclaimed in verse 13. For the meaning of this verse as prediction of disaster, see J. A. Emerton, "The Translation and Interpretation of Isaiah VI. 13," in J. A. Emerton and S. C. Reif (eds.), *Interpreting the Hebrew Bible—Essays in Honor of E. I. Rosenthal,* Cambridge 1982: 104–105. Later generations tried to take out the severity of this verse; see C. A. Evans, "The Text of Isaiah 6:9–10," *ZAW* 94 (1982): 415–418.

22. For Topheth, see 2 Kings 23:10. On the Molech cult, see M. Weinfeld, "The Molech Cult in Israel and its Background" (in Hebrew), *Proceedings of the Fifth World Congress of Jewish Studies,* vol. 1, Jerusalem 1969: 52–61, 154; P. G. Mosca, *Child Sacrifice in Canaanite and Israelite Religion,* dissertation, Harvard 1975; G. C. Heider, "The Cult of Molek: A Reassessment," *JSOTSup* 43, Sheffield 1985; J. Day, *Molech—A God of Human Sacrifice in the Old Testament,* Cambridge 1989; J. D. Levenson, *The Death and Resurrection of the Beloved Son,* New Haven, CT 1993: 3–31; B. J. Schwartz, *The Holiness Legislation—Studies in the Priestly Code,* Jerusalem 1999: 187–196; J. Milgrom, *Leviticus 17–22, AB,* New York 2000: 1552–1565, 1586–1591, 1728–1738, 1768–1785.

23. Cf. Mosca (above, n. 22), 212; Heider (above, n. 23), 324–325; Milgrom, ibid., 1560; and reservation of Levenson (above, n. 22), 10.

24. See Milgrom, ibid., 1768–1785.

25. Isaiah's condemnation of the covenent with death (28:18) should be seen in light of his objection to the conception of death as an independent force; on this covenant, see J. Blenkinsopp, *Isaiah 1–39, AB,* New York 2000: 391–395.

26. See Y. Kaufmann, *History of of Israelite Religion* (in Hebrew), Jerusalem–Tel Aviv 1968: vol. 3, 12–14.

27. Cf. S. Spiegel, *Amos vs. Amaziah* (Essays in Judaism Series 3), New York 1967.

28. For the various interpretations to this verse, see W. R. Harper, *Amos and Hosea, ICC,* Edinburgh 1904: 136; M. Haran, "Amos," *EM* 6 (1971): 284–285; F. I. Andersen and D. N. Freedman, *Amos, AB,* New York 1989: 531–532; S. Paul, *Amos, Hermeneia,* Minneapolis 1985: 193–194; M. Weiss, *The Book of Amos* (in Hebrew), Jerusalem 1992: 182–184.

29. One hundred years later, Jeremiah also mounted an uncompromising attack on the Temple services. Coming to the courtyards of the Temple he says: "Add your burnt offering to your other sacrifices and eat the meat!" (Jer. 7:21). The Priestly Torah distinguishes between two types of sacrifice: a burnt offering (*olah*), which is offered in its entirety to God, and sacrifice (*zebah*), which is partially eaten by the bearer of the sacrifice. Jeremiah disparages the Priestly rituals and says, in essence, take the burnt offerings and eat them along with the sacri-

fices; have a feast. "For when I freed your fathers from the land of Egypt, I did not speak with them or command them concerning burnt offerings or sacrifice"(Jer. 7:22). Haran (ibid.) thinks that Jeremiah followed Amos. He claims that their argument is based on the traditions of the JE source, which tell about a few sacrifices in Egypt (Exod. 12:21–27) and at Sinai (Exod. 17:15, 18:12, 24:4–8, 32:5–6), but no sacrifices were done on the long way from Sinai to Israel. Furthermore, the old legal law, the Book of Covenant (Exod. 21–23), does not deal with sacrifices. M. Weinfeld claims that Jeremiah refers to the absence of a commandment on sacrifices from the Ten Commandments. See M. Weinfeld, "Jeremiah and the Spiritual Metamorphosis of Israel," ZAW 88.

30. Isa. 6:1–8

31. The reference here is mainly to P. As I have argued in the introduction, in my view, P was formed before Isaiah.

32. See W. Eichrodt, Theology of the Old Testament (J. Baker, trans.), London 1961: 1:278.

33. N. H. Snaith, The Distinctive Ideas of the Old Testament, New York 1964: 53. Ringgren points out that the idea of moral holiness is also rare among later prophets, see H. Ringgren, The Prophetical Conception of Holiness, Uppsala 1948: 23.

34. See above, chapter 2.

35. For dating the Holiness Code to the second half of the eighth century, see B. D. Eerdmans, Das buch Leviticus, Giessen 1912: 101; L. E. Elliot-Binns, "Some Problems of the Holiness Code," ZAW 76 (1955): 38; M. Haran, "The Holiness Code" (in Hebrew), EM v. 5 (Jerusalem 1968): 1098; J. Milgrom, Leviticus 1–16, AB, New York 1991: 26–27; Knohl, Sanctuary, 204–212.

36. The German term is "Heiligkeitsgesetz"; it was coined by Klostermann, who identified this code. See A. Klostermann, Der Pentateuch, Leipzig 1893: 368–413. For the Holiness School as the School behind this code and other parts of the Priestly legislation, see Knohl, Sanctuary, 6, 101–110; 168–198, 204–220.

37. See Gen. 2:3, Exod. 26:33–34, 28:2,36,41, 29:1,21,29,34,36–37, 30:25, 29–32,36–37; Lev. 2:3,10, 5:15–16, 6:10–11,18–22, 7:1,6, 8:9–12,15,30, 10:12–13,17–18, 12:4, 16:2–4,16–17,19,23–24; Num. 5:17, 6:5,8,20, 28:18,25–26, 29:1,7,12.

38. Cf. Lev. 19: 5–13,35–36.

39. Lev. 19:3,14–15.

40. For other connections between Isaiah and the Holiness School, see Knohl, Sanctuary, 212–214.

41. Amos 8:4–6.

42. See Amos 6:4.

43. Cf. M. Weinfeld, "Sabbatical Year and Jubilee in the Pentateuchal Laws and Their Ancient Near Eastern Background," in T. Veijola (ed.), The Law in the Bible and its Environment, Publications of the Finnish Exegetical Society 51, Göttingen 1990: 39–62; idem, Social Justice in Ancient Israel and in the Ancient Near East, Jerusalem 1995: 75–96.

44. Non-Israelites can still be enslaved according to the Holiness Code; see Lev. 25:44–46.

45. See B. Uffenheimer, 'Utopia and Reality in Biblical Thought," *Immanuel* 9 (1979): 9.

46. Lev. 2:14–17. Cf. Knohl, *Sanctuary*, 24.

47. Milgrom claims that the fact that according to the Holiness School this festival and its rites were held in a public form in the central Temple should be seen as an evidence that this school deprived the individual farmer from "the experiential joy of presenting his private offering to his God"; see J. Milgrom, "Firstfruits of Grain and the Composition of Leviticus 23:9–21," in M. Cogan, B. L. Eichler and J. H. Tigay (eds.), *Tehilla le-Moshe, Biblical and Judaic Studies in Honor of Moshe Greenberg*, Winona Lake, IN 1997, 88, n. 18. However, in my view the results of the centralization of the cult should not be taken as an indication of an intention to harm the popular cult; rather there is here an effort of integration of popular customs within the cult of the central Temple.

48. Cf. Exod. 28:3 ff.

49. See U. Cassuto, *A Commentary on the Book of Exodus*, Jerusalem 1967, 383.

50. Cf. J. Milgrom, *The JPS Torah Commentary: Numbers*, Philadelphia 1990: 413–414.

51. See below, chapter 8.

NOTES TO CHAPTER FIVE

1. For Egypt, see Pritchard, *ANET*, 324; for Mesopotamia, 331–342; for the Hittites, 346–356. The evidence of the Ugaritic texts is more fragmentary, but note the two prayer texts, which, according to H. L. Ginsberg (כתבי אוגרית Jerusalem 1936: 88–92), were said during sacrificial acts.

2. In the description of the Solomonic Temple, there is the mention of מזמרות, probably a musical instrument (see 1 Kings 7:50, 2 Kings 12:14, 25:14), but this does not change the nonverbal character of the cult.

3. Translated and abridged by M. Greenberg, Chicago 1960: 303–304.

4. Cf. N. Sarna, "The Psalm Superscription's and the Guilds," in S. Stein and R. Loewe (eds.), *Studies in Jewish Religion and Intellectual History Presented to Alexander Altmann on Occasion of his Seventieth Birthday*, University of Alabama 1979: 281–300.

5. H. Levine, *Sing Unto God a New Song: A Contemporary Reading of the Psalms*, Indiana University Press 1995: 28–29.

6. Kaufmann, *Religion*, 303.

7. It may be thought that the Priestly blessing represents a third instance, but as I have stated above (chapter 2, n. 80), its text (Num. 6:22–27) derives, in my opinion, from the Holiness School. In any case, the Priestly blessing took place *after* the completion of the sacrificial act (Lev. 9:22).

8. The verbal contents of this confession are not given by the Torah; however, it is interesting that the formula of confession by the High Priest on the Day of Atonement, as documented in Rabbinic literature, includes a definite element of adjuration by the "Name," which is close to the world of magic. See G. Alon, *Jews, Judaism and the Classical World*, Jerusalem 1977: 235–251; S. Lieberman,

Texts and Studies, New York 1974: 23–25; idem, Tosefta *Ki-fshuta*, vol. 7, New York 1967: 393. The confession mentioned in Lev. 5:5 is not made by a priest and it may have been done outside the Priestly precinct.

9. For an analysis of the scapegoat ritual, see Wright (above, chapter 2, n. 33).

10. On the ceremony of the wayward woman, see J. Licht, *A Commentary on the Book of Numbers I–X* (in Hebrew), Jerusalem 1985: 166–169.

11. Num. 5:21, which breaks the original flow of the formula of adjuration, came from an additional editing. The redactors, who were suspicious of the quasi-magical dimension of the original formula of oath, inserted v. 21, which represents God as punishing the woman directly (see Knohl, *Sanctuary*, 88).

12. My own position regarding the existence of prayer and song in the outer circle is similar to that of Kaufmann (*Religion*, 305). Unlike Milgrom's claim (*Lev. 1–16, AB*, 19, 60–61; *Lev. 17–22, AB*, 1426–1428), I never argued that prayer and hymn were not part of the activity in the Temple and its courtyards. My argument, like that of Kaufmann, refers exclusively to the silence of the Priestly act per se, as reflected in the laws of the Priestly Torah. However, Milgrom's objection (a similar claim was made by M. Fishbane, "Accusation of Adultery: A Study of the Law and Scribal Practice in Numbers 5:11–31," *HUCA* 45 [1974]: 27–28) that the Priestly Code contains no explicit statement barring speech during the time of offering sacrifices, requires a reply. As has been demonstrated by Fishbane himself, as well as by other scholars, the cultic laws of the Priestly Torah are formulated in a manner remarkably similar to that of the Priestly rules in the ancient Near East (See Fishbane [chapter 2, n. 17]; C. Cohen, "Was the P Document Secret?" *JNES* 1 / 2 [1969]: 39–44. In the instructions addressed to the priests of ancient Near Eastern temples, the rules regarding cultic activities include specific orders for various recitations intended to accompany the cultic act (see the texts referred to above, n. 1). The fact that the corresponding instructions in the Priestly Torah do not include any directions concerning speech accompanying the cultic act cannot be viewed as mere chance, given that they are so similar in external form and in literary pattern to other cultic rules in the ancient Near East.

13. A similar situation existed in the time of the second temple (see I. Knohl, "Between Voice and Silence: The Relationship between Prayer and Temple Cult," *JBL* 115 [1996]: 21–23. On sacrifice and song as two complementary modes of ritual performance, see H. Levine [above, n. 5], 32–78).

14. For the meaning of מבקש הי see Deut. 4:29, Ps. 27:8. It is not clear if this communication was done through prayer, prophecy, or both.

15. See Num. 11:16–17, 24–29; for the sources and redaction of this chapter, see B. D. Sommer, "Reflecting on Moses: The Redaction of Numbers 11," *JBL* 118 (1999): 601–624. Num. 12:4–5,9–10.

16. This is depicted in Num. 12:9–10.

17. On the outer Tent of Meeting, cf. M. Haran, *Temples and Temple Service in Ancient Israel*, Oxford 1978: 260–275; I. Knohl, "Two Aspects of the Tent of Meeting," in M. Cogan et al. (eds.), *Tehila le-Moshe, Biblical and Judaic Studies in Honor of Moshe Greenberg*, Winona Lake, IN 1997: 73–79.

18. The issue of prophecy is also critical in Num. 12, which belongs to the same tradition.

19. Cf. R. Rendtorff, "Jakob in Bethel: Beobachtungen zum Aufbau zur Quellenfragge in Gen. 28:10–22," *ZAW* 94 (1982): 511–523.

20. On the significance of this dream, cf. H. Klein, "Ort und Zeit der Elohist," *Evangelische Theologie* 37 (1977): 248–251.

21. On Gen. 31:11 see A. Rofe, *The Belief in Angels in the Bible and in Early Israel* (in Hebrew), Jerusalem 1979: 226–228, 237. As was suggested by Rofe, we have here an effort to identify the local God "Bethel" (see Jer. 48:13), with the God of Israel or with his angel; cf. O. Eissfeldt, "Der Gott Bethel," *ARW* 28 (1930): 1–30.

22. See Rofe, ibid., 236–238.

23. See n. 20.

24. These traditions in Gen. are usually designated to the E source. According to Coote, E was written in the court of Jeroboam; see R. B. Coote, *In Defense of Revolution—The Elohist History*, Minneapolis 1991: 2.

25. See G. I. Davis, *Hosea, NCBC*, Grand Rapids 1992: 24–25; A. A. Macintosh, *Hosea, ICC*, Edinburgh 1997: xxxiii.

26. See 1 Kings 19:18. The custom of kissing the calf of Bethel is mentioned in "Aramaic Text in Demotic Script"; see R. C. Steiner, "Aramaic Text in Demotic Script," in W. W. Hallow (ed.), *The Contest of Scripture: Canonical Compositions from the Biblical World*, Leiden 1997: 310, 313.

27. See also Gen. 31:11–13 and the detailed discussion of Rofe (above, n. 22), 239–254.

28. See M. Abberbach and L. Smolar, "Aaron, Jeroboam and the Golden Calves," *JBL* 86 (1967): 129–140; Alan W. Jenks, *The Elohist and North Israelite Traditions, SBL Monograph Series*, Missoula, MT 1977: 50–52, 103–106.

29. The tone of these verses is dramatically different from the positive representation of the angel in Exod. 23:20–25.

30. Rashi, following the Midrash, explains this act as a wish of Moses to distance himself from the unfaithful people.

31. See Jenks (above, n. 28), 53–54.

32. Cf. R. Fidler, *The Dream Theophany in the Bible* (in Hebrew), Ph.D. dissertation, The Hebrew University, Jerusalem 1996: 53–55. In Jer. 23:25–27 we find harsh criticism of the prophetic dream. On the reserved attitude of Deuteronomy to dreams, see A. Rofe, *Introduction to Deuteronomy*, Jerusalem 1988: 61–62. On the importance of dreams in the traditions designated to E in Genesis, see K. Jaros, *Die Stellung des Elohisten zur kanaanaischen Religion*, Göttingen 1974: 70–98; Coote (above, n. 25), 11–113; Fidler, 237–251.

33. F. M. Cross (*Canaanite Myth and Hebrew Epic*, Cambridge, MA 1973: 198–207) suggested that the origin of this opposition is the Mushite priesthood of Shiloh. This assumption is possible. However, I can't accept the classification of this tradition as "Elohistic" (for this classification, see Jenks (above, n. 28, 50–55). As we saw above, there are sharp differences between this tradition and the traditions of Genesis, which are usually designated to the E Elohistic source. The E traditions in Genesis are very positive regarding Beth-el, angels, and dreams. In contrast, the traditions of the calf and of the prophetic Tent of Meeting criticize the main cultic symbol of Beth-el, the calf, and see angels and dreams as inferior religious phenomena. Hence, it is impossible that they come from the same source. Thus, it is mistaken to date the E source (see Jenks, 103–106) on the basis of the opposition to Beth-el, which comes from another source.

34. A fragment of this tradition was preserved in Deuteronomy.

35. This and similar formulas reflect the Deuteronomistic ideology of the centralization of the cult: cf. Y Zakovitch, "'To Cause His Name to Dwell There'— and 'To Put His Name There'" (in Hebrew), *Tarbiz* 41 (1972): 338–340; B. Halpern, "The Centralization Formula in Deuteronomy," *VT* 31 (1981): 20–38; N. Lohfink, "Zur deutronomischen Zentralisationsformel," *Biblica* 65 (1984). On the cultic centralization in Deut. 12, see B. M. Levinson, *Deuteronomy and the Hermeneutics of Legal Innovations,* Oxford 1997: 23–52.

36. On the image of the Ark in Deuteronomy and Jeremiah, see M. Weinfeld, "Jeremiah and the Spiritual Metamorphosis of Israel," *ZAW* 88 (1976): 25–26.

37. See Deut. 7:21, 9:3, 20:4, 23:15.

38. See G. von Rad, *Studies in Deuteronomy,* D. Stalker (trans.), London 1953: 38–39; M. Weinfeld, *Deuteronomy and the Deuteronomic School,* Oxford 1972: 191–209; idem, *Deuteronomy 1–11, AB,* New York 1991: 37–44.

39. The passage has been reworked by the editors of the Pentateuch. Cf. A. Rofe, "Textual Criticism in light of Historical Literary Criticism: Deuteronomy 31:14–15," in *ErIs* 16 (H. Orlinsky Volume, 1982): 171–176.

40. For the assumption about the northern roots of Deut., see M. Weinfeld, "Deuteronomy and Its Northern Roots," in *Deuteronomy 1–11, AB* , New York 1991: 44–57.

41. See also Deut. 11:18–20, 17: 9, 31:11–13.

42. See 1 Kings 8:29–49 and J. A. Montgomery, *The Book of Kings, ICC,* New York 1951: 193–194.

43. See further J. D. Levenson "From Temple to Synagogue: 1 Kings 8," in B. Halpern and J. D. Levenson (eds.) *Traditions in Transformation,* Winona Lake, ID 1981: 143–166.

44. See Knohl (above, n. 11), 26–28.

NOTES TO CHAPTER SIX

1. H. Frankfort, *Kingship and the Gods,* Chicago 1948: 5.

2. The idea of the king as son of the gods existed also in Mesopotamia. However, there was some difference between the two cultures with regard to these notions; see Frankfort, ibid., 42–47, 77–8, 157–161, 171–80, 299–302.

3. *ARE* 2, 75–100, 334; *ARE* 3, 12–19, A. H. Gardiner, "The Coronation of King Haremhab," *JEA* 39 (1953): 13–31.

4. See Frankfort (above, n. 1), 58.

5. See Frankfort, ibid., 162–212.

6. See also Ps. 89:28 and the Septuagint version of Ps. 110:3.

7. For this rendering of the Hebrew אל גיבור see J. Day, "The Canaanite Inheritance of the Israelite Monarchy" in J. Day (ed.), "King and Messiah in Israel and the Ancient Near East," *JSOT* 270, Sheffield, MA 1998: 84.

8. See Weinfeld, *Social Justice in Ancient Israel and in the Ancient Near East,* Jerusalem and Minneapolis 1995: 45–56.

9. See ibid., 57–74.

10. Y. Kaufmann (*History of Israelite Religion,* vol. 3, Jerusalem–Tel Aviv 1969: 467, n. 62) rejects the Massoretic version and suggests, following the

Septuagint, the reading יוצדק. However, the Septuagint version seems to be a correction intended to avoid the problem of calling a human being by the Tetragrammaton. For a discussion of the possibility of an allusion here to Zedekiah, see W. McKane, *Jeremiah, ICC*, Edinburgh 1986: 564–565.

11. See Dan. 9:25–6.

12. 1 Sam 10:1, 15:17, 16:12–13, 24:6,10, 26:9,15; 2 Sam. 1:16, 5:3, 12:7, 23:1; 1 Kings 1:34,39,45; 2 Kings 9:3,6, 11:12.

13. See Pss. 2:2, 45:5, 89:39,52. There are two references in the Hebrew Bible to the anointing of prophets (see 1 Kings 19:16 and Isa. 61:1). In both cases this is a metaphorical use and there is no real act of anointing with oil. The same is true with the references to anointing with regard to foreign kings (1 Kings 19:16; Isa. 45:1).

14. 2 Sam. 6:17–18; see further 1 Kings 8:63–64, 2 Kings 16:12–13; see also 1 Sam 13:9, 1 Kings 3:4,15, 12:32–3, and the discussion of Day (above, n. 7), 75.

15. The JPS translation obscures this point: "You are a king forever, a rightful king by My decree." See the review of the scholarly debate on this verse by Day (above, n. 7), 73–74.

16. See S. E. Loewenstamm, "Man as Image and Son of God" (in Hebrew), *Tarbiz* 27 (1957): 1–2.

17. See Loewenstamm, ibid.; H. Wildberger, "Das Abbild Gottes, Gen. 1:26–30," *TZ* 21 (1965): 257–259.

18. See Gen. 1:26–27, 5:1, 9:6.

19. See Weinfeld (above, n. 9), 75–96.

20. See Weinfeld, ibid.; R. Westbrook, *Property and the Family in Biblical Law*, Sheffield 1991: 36–57; J. Milgrom, *Leviticus 23–27, AB*, New York 2001: 2166–2170.

21. One cannot argue that the omission of the king is due to the fact that in the desert period there was no king in Israel. After all, this law refers to the much later reality of the land of Israel where there are fields, houses, and slaves.

22. Lev. 4:3. See further 6:15, 16:32; 21:10.

23. In my view, this story stems from the Holiness School; see *Sanctuary of Silence*, 76–81.

24. The Book of Chronicles usually follows here the view of the separate Priestly sources of the Pentateuch with regard to cultic issues; see E. L. Curtis, *Chronicles, ICC*, Edinburgh 1910: 452.

25. See Lev. 13:45. On the story of Uzziah, see E. L. Greenstein, "An Inner–Biblical Midrash of the Nadav and Avihu Episode" (in Hebrew), *Proceedings of the Eleventh World Congress of Jewish Studies*, Jerusalem 1994: 71–88.

26. For the evidence that Canaanite kings could also be priests, see Day (above, n. 7), 74–75.

27. S. Mowinkel, *The Psalms in Israel's Worship*, vol. 1, Nashville 1967: 59. Ps. 45:7 is a particularly challenging verse in this regard. Depending on how one parses the verse, it could read either: "Your throne, O God, is everlasting" or "Your divine throne is everlasting" (JPS). For support for the first reading, see "Psalm xlv7", *JTS*, n.s. (1961): 51–53; ibid., 83–84.

28. See Mowinkel, ibid., 50–60.

29. The Book of Chronicles was compiled in the Second Temple period, when there was no kingship, so the conflict must date from the period referred to in the story, the eighth century B.C.E.

30. Y. Kaufmann, *The Religion of Israel* (translated and abridged by M. Greenberg), Chicago 1960: 60.

31. Kaufmann, 77. A similar claim from the silence of the prophets is made by Day (above, n. 7), 82.

32. Frankfort (above, n. 1), 342–343.

33. Frankfort, 342, is aware of these stories and explains them by saying: "The king created the conditions which made a given form of the cult possible: David's power allowed him to bring the Ark to Jerusalem; Solomon's riches enabled him to build the temple...But the king played little part in the cult. He did not as a rule sacrifice; that was the task of the priests." It must be said that this description is not accurate; David, Solomon, and Jeroboam did sacrifice in the dedication rites of their new cultic centers. The above mentioned incident concerning Uzziah in 2 Chron. 26:16–20 can also attest to kings' acquiring or seeking to acquire Priestly functions. Ps. 110 shows that this is not only a struggle for power. The reference to the priesthood of Melchizedek may suggest a wish to adopt the model of the ancient Near East, where the king is at the same time the political and the cultic leader.

34. On the two messiahs in the Qumran literature, cf. D. Goodblatt, *The Monarchic Principle*, Tübingen 1994: 65–71; J. J. Collins, *The Scepter and the Star*, New York 1995: 74–101; M. Abegg, "The Messiah at Qumran: Are We Still Seeing Double?" *DSD* 2 (1995): 125–144; J. VanderKam, "Messianism in the Scrolls," in E. Ulrich and J. VanderKam (eds.), *The Community of the Renewed Covenant: The Notre Dame Symposium on the Dead Sea Scrolls*, Notre Dame 1994: 212–234; F. M. Cross, "Notes on the Doctrine of the Two Messiahs at Qumran," in D. W. Parry and S. D. Ricks (eds.), *Current Research and Technological Developments on the Dead Sea Scrolls*, Leiden 1996: 1–4; W. M. Schniedewind, "Structural Aspects of Qumran Messianism in the Damascus Document," in D. W. Parry and E. Ulrich (eds.), *The Provo International Conference on the Dead Sea Scrolls*, Leiden 1999: 523–536.

35. See the discussions and bibliography in G. F. Moore, *Judges, ICC*, Edinburgh 1895: 230; M. Elat, *Samuel and the Foundation of Kingship in Ancient Israel*, Jerusalem 1998: 60–72.

36. See M. Buber, *Kingship of God* (English translation by R. Scheimann), Prometheus Books, Amherst, MA 1964: 29–36. Buber claimed that the same view of negation of kingship was held by the Torah. However, as was already pointed out by Y. Kaufmann in his review of Buber's book (*Kirjat Sefer* 10 [1934]: 64), nowhere in the Torah do we see a negation of human kingship. This idea is reflected only in the books of Judges and Samuel. (Besides the above mentioned verses, see also 1 Sam. 10:19 and 12:12).

37. See Josephus, Ant. 18:23–25 and M. Stern, "Zealots," *Encyclopedia Judaica Year Book*, Jerusalem 1973: 133–152. While it is true that it is the dominion of the Romans that was negated by the Scarri, in Josephus's description of their philosophy, there is a negation of any human dominion.

38. See I. Knohl, *The Messsiah before Jesus,* Berkeley 2000: 5–23.

39. See ibid., 24–26.

40. See ibid., 87–101.

41. For Hillel's chronology, see the recent discussion by H. Shapira, "Beit ha-Midrash (the House of Study) during the Late Second Temple Period and the Age of the Mishnah: Institutional and Ideological Aspects" (in Hebrew), dissertation, the Hebrew University, Jerusalem 2001: 80–81.

42. See ibid., 63–65.

43. On Hillel's ideology and its legal implications, see Y. Lorberbaum, "Imago Dei, Rabbinic Literature, Maimoneades and Nahmanides" (in Hebrew), dissertation, The Hebrew University, Jerusalem 1997: 96–268.

NOTES TO CHAPTER SEVEN

1. See 2 Kings 21:6.

2. See 2 Kings 23:24–27.

3. Jeremiah says, "In those days, they shall no longer say, 'Parents have eaten sour grapes and children's teeth are blunted. But every one shall die for his own sins: whosoever eats sour grapes, his teeth shall be blunted'" (Jer. 31:29–30). On the relationship between this prophecy and Ezek. 18, see G. A. Cook, *The Book of Ezekiel, ICC,* Edinburgh 1936: 197; Y. Kaufmann, *The History of Israelite Religion* (in Hebrew), vol. 3, Tel Aviv 1962: 554–555; W. Zimmerli, *Ezekiel, Hermeneia,* Philadelphia 1969: 378; W. Eichrodt, "Ezekiel," *OTL,* London 1970: 236; M. Weiss, *Scriptures in their own Light* (in Hebrew), Jerusalem 1987: 480–486; G. Brin, *Studies in the book of Ezekiel* (in Hebrew), Tel Aviv 1975; 102–103; M. Greenberg, *Ezekiel 1–20, AB,* New York 1983: 340. On the relationship among Ezek. 18, Jer. 31:29–30, and Deut. 24:16, see M. Weinfeld, "Jeremiah and the Spiritual Metamorphosis of Israel," *ZAW* 88 (1976): 35–39.

4. Cf. Weiss, ibid., 489–510.

5. See 2 Chron. 33:12–19, 36:12–17; and Kaufmann (above, n. 3), vol. 4, 474; S. Japhet, *The Ideology of the Book of Chronicles and its Place in Biblical Thought,* Frankfurt am Main 1989: 163.

6. See Kaufmann (ibid.), 554–556; Greenberg (above, n. 3), 341; Joyce, "Divine Initiative and Human Response in Ezekiel," *JSOTSup* 51, Sheffield, MA 1989: 42–55.

7. See Ezek. 18:21–24.

8. The claim that the Children of Israel practiced idolatry in Egypt does not appear in the Pentateuch; it is mentioned, however, in Josh. 24:14.

9. For a possible source of "laws that were not good" in the laws of the Pentateuch, see M. Fishbane, *Biblical Interpretation in Ancient Israel,* Oxford 1985, 181–187; J. D. Levenson, *The Death and Resurrection of the Beloved Son,* New Haven 1993: 43–56. B. J. Schwartz claims that if the Israelites had repented at any stage, God would have had to accept their penitence. In order to hold the decree of exile, God commanded them "laws that were not good and rules by which they could not live" (Ezek. 20: 25), meaning, to sacrifice their children; see B. J. Schwartz, "Repentance and Determinism in Ezekiel," *Proceedings of*

the Eleventh World Congress of Jewish Studies Division A—The Bible and Its World, Jerusalem 1994: 128. While this interpretation is possible, as Fishbane rightly commented, still the Israelites in the time of the exile "live out the consequence of earlier sins"; thus "the theological core of Ezek. 20 is diametrically opposed to the teaching of Chapter 18." See M. Fishbane, "Sin and Judgment in the Prophecies of Ezekiel," *Interpretation* 38 (1984): 142–144.

10. See also Jer. 19:5.

11. See Gen. 4:3–5 and 8:20–21.

12. The only source in the Book of Genesis that uses the name "YHWH" is the J source. This source also uses at times the name "Elohim." Hence we may see the story of the binding as part of the J tradition.

13. See Gen. 18:17–19.

14. See Levenson, *The Death of the Beloved Son*, 114–117, for a summary of the arguments that the *Akedah* serves as an etiology of the sacrificial service in the Jerusalem Temple.

15. On the relationship between Ezek. 36 and Jer. 31:31–34, see M. Greenberg, *Ezekiel 21–37, AB*, New York 1997: 336–337.

16. For a survey of the different explanations to this phenomena, see Schwartz, "Repentance and Determinism in Ezekiel," 124–126.

17. The declaration took place in the year 538 B.C.E. For the exact date, see H. Tadmor in H. Tadmor and I. Eph'al (eds.), *The Restoration—The Persian Period* (in Hebrew), Jerusalem 1983: 15.

18. On the debate about "third Isaiah," see B. Sommer, *A Prophet Reads Scripture*, Stanford 1998: 187–195.

19. Many candidates have been suggested for King Uzziah; see K. Dietz, *Ussiah der Knecht Gottes*, Abhandlungen und Vortrage hrausgegeben von der Bremer Wissenschaftlichen Geselschaft 4 (1929); for King Yehoiachin, see Rothstein's review of Sellin's *Studien zur entstehungsgeschichte der Judischen Gemeinde* in *TSK* LXXV (1902): 282 ff.; for Jer., see. F. A. Farley, "Jeremiah and the Suffering Servant," *ET* (1926–7), 521 ff.; for Moses, see E. Sellin, *Mose und seine bedeutung fur die israelitisch-judische Religionsgeschichte*, Leipzig 1922: 81 ff.; and others.

20. Cf. E. Burrowes, *The Gospel of the Infancy and Other Biblical Essays*, London 1940: 59 ff.

21. C. C. Torey, *The Second Isaiah*, New York 1928: 409–422; A. S. Peak, *The Servant of Yahwe*, 1931; O. Kaiser, *Der Konigliche Knecht, FRLANT* vol. 70, Göttingen 1959: 129–139; Tryggve N. D. Mettinger, *A Farewell to the Servant Songs*, Lund, Sweden 1983; and many others.

22. Y. Kaufmann, *The Babylonian Captivity and Deutero-Isaiah*, C. W. Efroymson (trans.), New York 1970: 149–162.

23. Torrey, ibid., 409–412; Mettinger, ibid., 37–46.

24. See S. R. Driver, *Deuteronomy, ICC*, lxxiii–lxxvii.

25. See B. Oded, "Mass Deportation in the Neo-Assyrian Empire" (in Hebrew), *SHNATON* 3 (1978–1979): 159–173; idem, *Mass Deportations and Deportees in the Neo-Assyrian Empire*, Wiesbaden 1979; R. Zadok, *The Jews in Babylonia during the Chaldean and Achaemenid Periods*, Haifa 1979: 35–37, 99–101.

26. See the Assyrian documents dealt with by H. Tadmor, "The Aramaization of Assyria: Aspects of Western Impact," in H. J. Nissen and J. Renger (eds.), *Mesopotamien und Seine Nachbaren*, Berlin 1982: 451 and n. 33.

27. See Eph'al in Tadmor and Eph'al (above, n. 17), 25–27.

28. See C. C. Torrey (above, n. 21), 143–146; see also H.G. M. Williamson, *Variations on a Theme, King, Messiah and Servant in the Book of Isaiah*, London 1998: 125.

29. On this law, see J. Milgrom, *Cult and Conscience*, Leiden 1976: 74–76; Knohl, *Sanctuary*, 152.

30. Mettinger (above, n. 21), 41, sees the servant as a scapegoat; however, the scapegoat is not killed according to biblical law and he is not a substitute sent to Azazel to suffer in the place of the Israelite community (see D.Wright, *The Disposal of Impurity*, Atlanta 1987: 24). Hence, the ram of guilt offering is in my view a better model for the servant.

31. See M. Greenberg, "The Biblical Concept of Asylum," *JBL* 78 (1959): 129–130; J. Milgrom, *Numbers*, Philadelphia 1990: 294; in this connection, we should also consider the high priest's expiation for the people on the Day of Atonement.

32. The example of the high priest proves that the idea of "vicarious suffering" of the righteous has a place in biblical thought, contra Kaufmann (above, n. 3), 140–147, and Orlinski (H. M. Orlinski, "The So-Called 'Servant of the Lord' and 'Suffering Servant' in Second Isaiah," *VTS* 14 [1967]: 51–59). See also Y. Muffs, "The Prophets' Prayer," in A. Shapiro (ed.), *Torah Nidreshet* (in Hebrew), Tel Aviv 1984: 80–82.

33. This new understanding of the exile is not reflected in other prophecies of Second Isa., where the exile is perceived as a punishment for Israel's sins (see Orlinski, ibid., 23–27).

34. See M. Tsevat, "The Meaning of the Book of Job," *HUCA* 37 (1966): 99–100; G. M. Tucker, 'Rain on a Land Where No One Lives," *JBL* 116 (1997): 12–16.

35. Regarding this interpretation of the meaning of the revelation to Job, see R. Otto, *The Idea of the Holy*, Oxford 1958: 77–80; Y. Leibowitz, *Judaism, Human Values, and the Jewish State*, Cambridge, MA 1992: 48–53; M. Greenberg, *On The Bible and Judaism: A Collection of Writings* (in Hebrew), Tel-Aviv 1985: 238–239.

36. Cf. Driver and Gray, *The Book of Job, ICC*, Edinburgh 1921: 2–3; M. Pope, *Job, AB*, New York 1965: 3–4.

37. On Job 1:4–5, see M. Weiss, *The Story of Job's Beginning*, Jerusalem 1983: 44–45.

38. See Driver and Gray (above, n. 36) introduction, 56; E. Dhorme, *Commentary to the Book of Job* (trans. H. Knight), London 1926: 20–21; Y. Kaufmann, (above, n. 3), vol. 2 (in Hebrew), 619–620; Pope (above, n. 36), xxxviii .

39. N. H. Torczyner claims that in God's answer to Job (38:1ff.) the Tetragrammaton was revealed to Job (*The Book of Job* [in Hebrew], Jerusalem 1941: 536–537). For this reason, he understands the Book of Job to be "a song of proselytism." Y. Kaufmann (ibid., 620, n. 16), however, was correct in rejecting this

theory. He claimed that there is no hint of it in the text, pointing to the lack of any mention of the Tetragrammaton in God's words to Job.

NOTES TO CHAPTER EIGHT

1. *Avot* 1:2

2. The word "allowance" stands here for the Hebrew word פרס. The exact meaning here is the measured allowance that was given to slaves; cf. E. Bickerman, *Studies in Jewish and Christian History*, vol. 2 , Leiden 1980: 270–272.

3. This translation follows the version שלא על מנת לקבל פרס. This version is attested to in the best manuscripts, see S. Sharvit, "Textual Variants and Language of the Treatise *Avot*" (in Hebrew), dissertation submitted to Bar-Ilan University, Ramat Gan 1976: 291; M. Kister, *Studies in Avot de-Rabbi Natan: Text, Redaction and Interpretation* (in Hebrew), Jerusalem 1998: 156, n. 195.

4. E. Bickerman (ibid., 282) suggests that the saying was uttered shortly before or during the religious persecution of Antiochus Epiphanes. As I will argue later in this chapter, in my view, we do better to look for an influence of both the old Priestly tradition and of Greek philosophy as the possible background for this saying.

5. The claim that the Sadducees are named after Zadok, who was Antigonos's disciple, is probably not historical. See A. Geiger, *Urschrift und Ubersetzungen der Bible*, Breslau 1857: 101–106, cf. J. Le Moyne, *Les Sadduceens*, Paris 1972: 155–163.

6. According to Kister (above, n. 3), 32–34, 155–157, the tradition in version B of *Avot de-Rabbi Natan* is earlier than the one in version A.

7. Pseudo-Clementines, *Recognitiones*, 1, 54. On this source, see George Strecker, *Das Judenchristentum in Pseudoklementinen*, Berlin 1981; idem, "The Pseudo Clementines," in W. Schneemelcher (ed.), *New Testament Apocrypha*, vol. 2, Cambridge, England 1992: 483–484. Cf. D. Flusser, "Some of the Precepts of Torah from Qumran (4QMMT) and the Benediction Against the Heretics" (in Hebrew), *Tarbiz* 61 (1992): 355–356; M. Kister, "Studies in 4Q MIQSAT MAASE Ha-Torah and Related Texts: Law, Theology, Language and Calendar" (in Hebrew), *Tarbiz* 68, (1999): 326.

8. See Josephus, *Bellum* II, 119–166, *Ant.* XIII, 171–173. For one Greek source that could serve Josephus, see S. Pines, "A Platonistic Model for Two of Josephus' Accounts of the Doctrine of the Pharisees Concerning Providence and Man's Freedom of Action," *Immanuel* 7 (1997): 38–43; D. Flusser, "Josephus on the Sadducees and Menander," in his collected works *Judaism and the Origins of Christianity*, Jerusalem 1998: 610–616. In general, the Rabbis followed the Pharisaic view, cf. E. E. Urbach, "Studies in Rabbinic Views Concerning Divine Providence," in M. Haran (ed.), *Yehezkel Kaufmann Jubilee Volume* (in Hebrew), Jerusalem 1960: 122–148.

9. On the different views regarding the identity of this group, see M. D. Herr, "Who Were the Boethusians?" *Proceedings of the Seventh World Congress of Jewish Studies: Studies in the Talmud, Halacha and Midrash*, Jerusalem 1981: 1–20; Y. Sussmann, "The History of *Halacha* and the Dead Sea Scrolls," *Tarbiz*

59 (1990): 48–60; Kister (above, n. 3), 156, n. 200; A. Schremer, "The Name of the Boethusians: A Reconstruction of Suggested Explanation and Another One," *JJS* 48 (1997): 298–299.

10. By claiming biblical roots for the conceptions of Antigonos and the Sadducees, I do not want to exclude the possibility of an influence of Epicurean thought (cf. E. Baneth, *Ursprung der Sadokaer und Boethosaer*, Dessau 1882). The two may go together. On the general phenomenon of the flourishing of Jewish Sects in this period, see A. I. Baumgarten, *The Flourishing of Jewish Sects in the Maccabean Era: An Interpretation.*, Leiden 1997: cf. his recent discussion: "Legal Disputes as a Cause of Sectarian Schism," in G. Brin and B. Nitzan (eds.), *Fifty Years of Dead Sea Scroll Research—Studies in Memory of Jacob Licht*, Jerusalem 2001: 155–165.

11. Bellum II, 164.

12. *Sifra* Kedoshim, first section.

13. The original meaning of the name פרושים is unknown: see A. I. Baumgarten, "The Name of the Pharisees," *JBL* 102 (1983): 411–428. Our comments here refer mainly to the ideology of the sect rather than to the original meaning of its name.

14. Here we see a clear contrast to the Qumran literature, where the term בית קורש לישראל is applied to the Qumranic sect (1QS VIII 5–6). However, in some Qumranic documents there is a tendency to extend purity and holiness to all the people. Cf. M. Himmelfarb, "Sexual Relations and Purity in the Temple Scroll and the Book of Jubilees," *DSD* 6 (1999): 11–36.

15. The Qumran community shares some of the views of the Sadducees; cf. I. Knohl, "Post Biblical Sectarianism and the Priestly Schools of the Pentateuch: The Issue of Popular Participation in the Temple Cult on Festivals," in J. Trebolle Barrera and L. Vegas Montaner (eds.), *The Madrid Qumran Congress*, Leiden 1992: 601–609 and n. 20 on 609.

16. According to Josephus, the sects existed "from the most ancient times" (Ant. 18.11). This statement can be understood as an indication that he had no explicit information on when the sects were formed (See A. Baumgarten, *The Flourishing of Jewish Sects in the Maccabean Era: An Interpretation*, Leiden 1997: 19–20). Apart from any possible historical connection, what we are emphasizing here is the striking ideological continuity.

17. On these ceremonies, cf. R. Patai, *Man and Temple In Ancient Jewish Myth and Ritual*, New York 1967: 24–53; H. Fox, "The Joy of the Place of Drawing," *Tarbiz* 55 (1986): 173–216; J. Rubenstein, *The History of Sukkot in the Second Temple and Rabbinic Periods*, Atlanta 1995: 103–162; J. Tabory, *Jewish Festivals in the Time of the Mishna and Talmud* (in Hebrew), Jerusalem 1995: 175–200.

18. אנא הי הושיעה נאת נא, אנא הי הצליחה נא Mishnah *Sukkah* 4:5

19. Mishnah *Sukkah* 4:5.

20. Mishnah *Sukkah* 4:9

21. Cf. Patai (above, n. 17), 33–47; Rubenstein (above, n. 17), 122–131.

22. Tosefta *Sukkah* 3:18.

23. Cf. Tabory (above, n. 17), 198–199.

24. Yerushalmi *Hagigah* 3:6.

25. See Tosefta *Sukkah* 3:1. As several scholars have claimed (cf. C. Albeck, *Commentary to the Mishnah*, vol. 2, Jerusalem 1952: 255); it seems that the Boethusians rejected the ritual per se, not only its performance on the Sabbath.

26. According to Tosefta *Sukkah* 3:16, he was a Boethusian, and according to the Talmud (Bavli *Sukkah* 48b, Yerushalmi *Sukkah* 4:8 54d), a Sadducee (cf. Sussmann, above, n. 9, 48–53). Josephus Flavius tells a similar story about Alexander Yannai, the Hasmonean king who was also a high priest (*Ant.* 13:372); the high priest in the Talmudic sources is anonymous.

27. Tosefta *Sukkah* 3:16.

28. Rubenstein (above, n. 17), 121, n. 67, and in his study "The Sadducees and the Water Libation," *JQR* 84 (1994): 417–444, argues against the common view that the Sadducees rejected the ritual of the water libation because it has no explicit source in the Torah. He rightly claims that the view that the Sadducees rejected "the Oral Torah" and that this comprised the essential debate between the groups oversimplifies matters; cf. Sussmann (above, n. 9), 57, n. 185. However, I cannot accept his conclusion that the Sadducees did not reject the legitimacy of the libation, but had only different views as to how the ritual should be performed.

29. According to the Priestly laws of the Pentateuch, nonpriests who look at the holy vessels that are within the temple will die (Num. 4:18–20); cf. M. Haran, *Temples and Temple-Service in Ancient Israel*, Winona Lake, IN 1985: 178.

30. Mishnah *Hagigah* 3:5, Yerushalmi *Hagigah* 3:8 (79:4), Bavli *Hagigah* 26:2.

31. In *Oxyrhynchus Papyri* 5, 840, there is a report about a discussion between a high priest and Jesus. The high priest rebukes Jesus and his disciples who come to view the sacred vessels, though not properly purified (see B. Grenfell and A. S. Hunt, *Fragments of an Uncanonical Gospel from Oxyrhynchus*, Oxford 1908). As has been correctly noted by A. Buechler, "The New Fragment of an Uncanonical Gospel," *JQR*, o.s., 20 (1908): 338–339, this discussion should be understood on the background of the above mentioned Rabbinic texts. Although the papyrus states that the high priest was a Pharisee, this statement should be attributed to the polemical, anti-Pharisaic tendency of the composition. We know that most of the high priests in the late Second Temple Period were Sadducees. Thus, if this story does reflect a historical reality, it probably preserves the echo of Sadducee criticism of the custom of displaying the vessels to the populace.

32. See the studies of D. Barag, "The Table of the Showbread and the Facade of the Temple on Bar Kokhba Coins," *Qadmoniyot* 20 (1977–78): 22–25; and A. Grossberg, "Response to D. Barag," *Qadmoniyot* 21 (1978–79): 81–82.

33. Tosefta *Hagigah* 3:35.

34. See Sussmann (above, n. 9), 68.

35. See *The Temple Scroll*, ed. Y. Yadin, 306.

36. Cf. S. Safrai, "Relations between the Diaspora and the Land of Israel," in S. Safrai and M. Stern (eds.), *The Jewish People in the First Century*, Assen 1974, 188–192.

37. See Bavli *Menahot* 65a. In MS Michal 388 of the *Scholion* to *Megillat Ta'anit*, this view is related to the Boethusians. See H. Lichtenstein, "Die Fastenrolle Eine Untersuchung zur Jüdisch-Hellenististischen Geschichte,"

HUCA VIII–IX (1931–32): 323. Cf. V. Noam, *"Megillat Ta'anit* and the *Scholion*: Their Nature, Period and Sources, Accompanied by a Critical Edition," dissertation submitted to the Hebrew University, Jerusalem 199:, 65–67.

38. See John M. Allegro, *Discoveries in the Judean Desert*, 5, Oxford 1968: 7. Cf. J. Liver, "The Half-Shekel in the Scrolls of the Judean Desert Sect" (in Hebrew), *Tarbiz* 31 (1961): 18–21; D. Flusser, "Matthew XVII, and the Dead Sea Sect" (in Hebrew), *Tarbiz* 31 (1961): 150–156; M. Beer, "The Sect and the Half–Shekel," *Tarbiz* 31 (1962): 298–299.

39. Cf. E. Bickerman, "Notes on the Megillath Ta'anit," *Zion* 1 (1936): 351–356; idem, *Studies in Jewish and Christian History*, Leiden 1980: 161–172. J. Liver, "The Half Shekel Offering in Biblical and Post-Biblical Literature," *HTR* 56 (1963): 173–198; H. Mantel, *The Men of the Ancient Synagogue*, Jerusalem 1983: 214–217; Sussmann (above, n. 9), 67, n. 220; E. and H. Eshel, "4Q471 Fragment 1 and Ma'amadot in the War Scroll," in J. Trebolle Barrera and L. Vegas Montaner (eds.), *The Madrid Qumran Congress*, Leiden 1992: 617–620.

40. Cf. Sussmann (above, n. 9), 66–68.

41. On the Temple Scroll as a product of the Qumran community, see I. Knohl, "Biblical Paraphrases," to be published in a volume on the Dead Sea Scrolls, by Yad Ben-Zvi, Jerusalem.

42. See chapter 1.

43. The Temple Scroll 17:6–16

44. See M. Weinfeld, "God versus Moses in the Temple Scroll," *RQ* 15 (1991): 175–80; L. H. Schiffman, "The Deuteronomic Paraphrases of the Temple Scroll," *RQ* 15 (1992): 543–568.

45. There are some differences between the legal compositions, but nowhere is there an explicit saying about a debate over legal issues within the sect.

46. CD, III, 12–16; Ch. Rabin, *The Zadokite Document*, Oxford 1954: 13.

47. The exact time of the activity of Hillel and Shammai is not clear. It seems that they acted in the later years of the dominion of King Herod (37–4 B.C.E.); cf. I. Ben-Shalom, *The School of Shammai and the Zealots' Struggle against Rome* (in Hebrew), Jerusalem 1993: 69–109.

48. Cf. Tosefta *Yevamot* 1:10, ed. S. Lieberman, New York 1967: 3.

49. Bavli *Berachot* 11a.

50. This conception is reflected in chapters 2–3 of the Mishnah tractate *Berachot*, which were formulated according to the view of the house of Hillel, cf. I. Knohl, "A Parasha Concerned with Accepting the Kingdom of Heaven" (in Hebrew), *Tarbiz* 53 (1983): 27–30.

51. Mishnah *Berachot* 2:2.

52. נעשה חבותינו מך הגוף הזה, see M. Kister, *Prolegomenon to Avoth de-Rabbi Nathan Solomon Schechter Edition*, New York-Jerusalem 1997: 26, n. 24.

53. Kister, ibid.

54. The connection between the two disputes was pointed out first by S. Schechter in his edition of *Avot de-Rabbi Natan* (New York–Jerusalem 1997: 66, n. 17), cf. E. E. Urbach, *The Sages—Their Concepts and Beliefs*, Jerusalem 1979: 339–340.

55. Bavli *Beza* 16a.

56. Cf. Tosefta *Berachot* 4:1, ed. S. Lieberman, New York 1955: 18; and Lieberman's discussion, Tosefta *Ki-fshutah*, vol 1, New York 1995: 56.

57. On the significance of the conception of creation in the image of God in the School of Hillel, see Y. Lorberbaum, *Imago Dei: Rabbinic Literature, Maimonides and Nahmanides* (in Hebrew), dissertation submitted to the Hebrew University, Jerusalem 1997: 96–268.

58. See Kister, above, n. 52.

59. In the hostility to the carnal realm of life, there is some similarity between the School of Shammai and the Qumran writings; cf. Knohl (above, n. 50), 22–26.

60. Tosefta *Berachot* 2:8,12, ed. S. Lieberman, New York 1955: 7, 9.

61. Cf. D. Flusser, *Judaism and the Origins of Christianity*, Jerusalem 1988: 509–514; idem, "Hillel and Jesus: Two Ways of Self-Awareness," in J. H. Chalesworth and L. L. Johns (eds.), *Hillel and Jesus: Comparative Studies of Two Major Religious Leaders*, Minneapolis 1998: 71–107.

62. See Lev. 5:17–19.

63. Mishnah *Keritut* 6:3.

64. *Pesiktah De Rab Kahana*, Mandelbaum edition, 120.

65. Bavli *Eruvin* 13b.

66. See Yerushalmi *Shabbat* 1:7,3c; and see S. Lieberman, *Hayerushalmi Kiphshuto* (in Hebrew), Jerusalem 1934: 38.

67. See S. Lieberman, *Shkiin*, Jerusalem 1970: 22–23, 101.

68. See Bavli *Bava Metzi'a* 59b and the discussions by I. England, "The 'Oven of Akhnai': Various Interpretations of an Agada" (in Hebrew), *Annual of the Institute for Research in Jewish Law*, 1 (1974): 45–57; B. Jackson, "Human Cognition and Divine Knowledge in Biblical and Early Rabbinic Law" (in Hebrew), *Annual of the Institute for Research in Jewish Law*, 6–7 (1979–80): 69–70; S. Handelman, *The Slayers of Moses: The Emergence of Rabbinic Interpretation in Modern Literary Theory*, Albany 1982: 40 ff.; M. Fisch, *Rational Rabbis*, Bloomington, IN 1997: 78–88; cf. the bibliography in J. L. Rubenstein, *Talmudic Stories*, Baltimore 1999: 314–315, n. 1–3.

69. Compare Deut 17:8–11 on bringing legal matters to the priest or magistrate "in charge at the time."

NOTE TO POSTSCRIPT

1. See Bavli *Eruvin* 13a.

NOTES TO APPENDIX A

1. See D. W. Jamieson-Drake, "Scribes and Schools in Monarchic Judah," *JSOTsup* 109, Sheffield, MA 1991:147–159; N. Na'aman, "Historiography: The Fashioning of Collective Memory and the Establishment of Historical Consciousness in Israel in the Late Monarchial Period" (in Hebrew), *Zion* 60 (1995): 449–472; idem, *The Past That Shapes the Present—The Creation of Biblical Historiography in the Late First Temple Period and After the Downfall*, Yeriot, *Essays and Papers in the Jewish Studies* 3 (in Hebrew) (2002): 13–25.

2. Na'aman, ibid., 25–29, 77.

3. See I. Singer, "Egyptians, Canaanites and Philistines in the Iron I" (in Hebrew), in N. Na'aman and I. Finkelstein (eds.), *From Nomadism to Monarchy*, Jerusalem 1990. Many scholars date it to the last quarter of the 12th century B.C.E.; see R. G. Boling, *Judges, AB*, New York 1975: 116.

4. Gen. 49:1–27; Exod. 15:1–19; Num. 21:17–18; 23:7–10,18–24; 24:3-9; 15–24; Deut. 32:1–43; 33:1–29. Another piece of ancient poetry was preserved in Hab. 3.

5. See H. Wildberger, *Isaiah 28–39* (trans. T. H. Trapp), Minneapolis 2002: 570–572.

6. See M. Zeidel, *Biblical Studies* (in Hebrew), Jerusalem 1978: 1–97; Wildberger, ibid., 579–589.

7. Zeidel, ibid., 98-108; Wildberger, ibid., 597–609.

8. See Prov. 25:1 and the discussions of M. Weinfeld, *Deuteronomy and the Deuteronomistic School*, Oxford 1972: 161; H. L. Ginsberg, *The Israelian Heritage of Judaism*, New York 1982: 36–37.

9. On the linguistic criteria as a tool for distinguishing late psalms, see A. Hurvitz, *The Transition Period in Biblical Hebrew* (in Hebrew), Jerusalem 1972: 67–176.

10. For dating of the Holiness Code to the second half of the eighth century, see the literature in n. 35 of chapter 4.

11. See I. Knohl, *The Sanctuary of Silence*, Minneapolis 1995: 8–123.

12. See M. Fishbane, "Biblical Colophons: Textual Criticism and Legal Analogies," *CBQ* 42 (1980): 438–449.

13. It seems that the ancient poem in Deut. 33:1–3,5,25–29 belongs to the same phase; see I. L. Seeligmann, "A Psalm from Pre-Regal Times," *VT* 14 (1964): 75–92. A similar date should be given probably to the "Song of the Sea," F. M. Cross, *Canaanite Myth and Hebrew Epic*, Cambridge, MA 1973: 121–125; M. S. Smith, *The Pilgrimage Pattern in Exodus*, Sheffield, MA 1997: 222–226.

14. See Hos. 8:12 and the discussion of Ginsberg (above, n. 8), 21; Isa. 8:1. It remains uncertain whether we have another reference to writing in Isa. 8:16; see the discussion of H. Wildberger, *Isaiah 1-12*, Minneapolis 1991: 365–356.

15. See M. Paran, *Forms of the Priestly Style in the Pentateuch*, Jerusalem 1989: 14–21.

16. See H. W. Wolff, "The Elohistic Fragments in the Pentateuch," *Interpretation* 26 (1972): 158–173.

17. Josh. 24, Judg. 4:1–12:15 and 1 Sam. 1–12 stem probably from a northern source; see A. Rofe, "Ephraimite versus Deuteronomistic History," in D. Garrone and Felice Israel (eds.), *Storia e Tradizioni di Israele*, Brecia 1991.

18. See M. Cogan and H. Tadmor, *II Kings, AB*, New York 1998: 4.

19. The Covenant Code is a composite unit and may not have been composed in one generation. On the question of what is the earlier nucleolus of this collection and whether we have here indeed a legal code, see the debate between S. M. Paul, "Studies in the Book of the Covenant in the Light of Cuneiform and Biblical Law," *VTS* 18 (1970); and A. Toeg, *Lawgiving at Sinai* (in Hebrew), Jerusalem 1977: 80–94.

20. Some scholars point to the absence of a reference to the king in the "Covenant Code" as a proof for the dating of this collection to the premonar-

chic time; see M. Haran, "Covenant Code" (in Hebrew) *EM* 5 (1978): 1089. In my view this absence is another aspect of the general reservation of the Torah toward the institute of kingship (see chapter 6).

21. See M. Broshi, "The Expansion of Jerusalem in the Reign of Hezekiah and Manasseh," *IEJ* 24 (1974): 21–26.

22. On the redaction of E by J, see T. Yoreh, "The Elohistic Source: Structure and Unity" (in Hebrew) dissertatio, submitted to the Hebrew University, Jerusalem 2003.

23. See Gen. 22:2 and 2 Chron. 3:1

24. Gen. 22:13.

25. This was pointed out by T. Yoreh in his master's thesis: "The Time of the J Source and His Relation to the E Source" (in Hebrew), The Hebrew University, Jerusalem 2001: 62–70.

26. See 2 Kings 18:1,22.

27. Num. 21:8–9.

28. 2 Kings 18:4. It is worth noting that a serpent was engraved on one of the stones of an alter in Be'er Sheva that was dismantled during Hezekiah's reform; see B. Halpern, "Jerusalem and the Lineages in the Seventh Century B.C.E." in B. Halpern and D. W. Hobson (eds.), "Law and Ideology in Monarchic Israel," *JSOTsup* 124, Sheffield, MA 1991: 67.

29. 2 Kings 21:6–7.

30 2 Kings 22:8.

31. 2 Kings 23:1–24.

32. See A. Alt, "Die Heimat des Deuteronomiums," in *Kleine Schriften*, II, Munich 1953: 250–275.

33. See M. Noth, "The Deuteronomistic History," *JSOTsup* 15, Sheffield, MA 1981.

34. See Na'aman, *The Past that Shapes the Present* (above, n. 1); 76–88.

35. See Cross (above, n. 13), 274–289; R. E. Friedman, "The Exile and Biblical Narrative," *HSM* 22, Chico, CA 1981; R. D. Nelson, "The Double Redaction of the Deuteronomistic History," *JSOTsup* 18, Sheffield, MA 1981.

36. See M. Weinfeld, "Jeremiah and the Spiritual Metamorphosis of Israel," *ZAW* 88 (1976): 17–56.

37. See S. R. Driver, *An Introduction to the Literature of the Old Testament*, Edinburgh 1913: 145–149.

38. See M. Haran, "Ezekiel's Code (Ezek. xl-xlviii) and Its Relation to the Priestly School" (in Hebrew), *Tarbiz* 44 (1974): 43–53.

39. See Knohl (above, n. 11), 201–203.

40. See ibid., 101–103.

41. There were minor changes in the concluding chapters; see Knohl, ibid., 95, 103.

42. See Neh. 8:1–12.

43. Cf. J. Wellhausen, *Prolegomena zur Geschichte Israels*, Berlin 1905: 404–409; S. Mowinkel, *Studien zur dem Bucher Ezra-Nehemiah III*, Oslo 1965: 121–141; J. A. Sanders, *Torah and Canon*, Philadelphia 1974: 50–53. There are scholars who claim that the book of Ezra was not identical to the known Penta-

teuch; cf. A. Kuenen, *The Origin and Composition of the Hexateuch* (trans. P. H. Wicksteed), London 1886: 303; U. Kellerman, "Erwagungen zum Esragesetz," *ZAW* 80 (1968): 373–375; M. Noth, *The Laws in the Pentateuch*, London 1966: 2, 76; J. Blenkinsopp, *Ezra-Nehemiah*, OTL, London 1989: 152–157. On the references to the Torah in Ezra-Nehemiah, see S. Japhet, "Law and 'the Law' in Ezra-Nehemiah," *Proceedings of the Ninth World Congress of Jewish Studies, Panel Sessions*, Jerusalem 1988: 99–104.

NOTES TO APPENDIX B

1. For detailed discussion, see I. Knohl, *The Sanctuary of Silence*, 8–110.

2. There are several verses in the Book of Genesis that probably belong to the HS editors; see Knohl, ibid., 104.

3. Gen. 5:29 originated in the J source; see I. Knohl, "Cain—The Forefather of Humanity," to be published in *M. Weinfeld Jubilee Volume*.

4. There are additional PT verses in Gen. 7:6-8:14; however, they are interwoven with J verses.

5. These verses are part of the editorial stratum of the Ten Plagues story. For other HS verses that belong to this stratum, see Knohl, *Sanctuary*, 62, n. 7.

6. There are several HS verses that were added to these PT chapters; see Knohl, ibid., 104.

7. There are several HS verses that were added to these PT chapters; see Knohl, ibid., 105.

8. Lev. 23 is a composite chapter that also has a PT layer; see Knohl, ibid., 1–45.

9. There are several HS verses that were added to these PT units; see Knohl, ibid., 87–89.

10. There are additional HS verses in Num. 13:17–14:25; however, they are interwoven with J verses.

11. HS verses are interwoven with J verses in Num. 16; see Knohl, ibid., 73–85.

12. There are several HS verses that were added to this PT unit; see Knohl, ibid., 92–4.

13. HS verses are interwoven with J verses in Num. 20:113; see Knohl, ibid., 94–96.

14. There are several HS verses that were added to this PT unit; see Knohl, ibid., 14–45.

15. HS verses are interwoven with J verses in Num. 32; see Knohl, ibid., 98.

16. Num. 33:54, together with 3:50-1, is probably from PT; see Knohl, ibid., 98–99.

Index of Biblical Passages and Other References

19:16, 180n13
19:18, 178n26
25:14, 176n2

2 Kings, Book of
3:11, 163n10
10:16, 78
10:29, 78
17:6, 55
17:24, 55
18:4, 191n28
21:6, 102
23:1-24, 153
23:10, 174n22
23:24-27, 102

1 Samuel, Book of
4:3-6, 163n9
4:4, 168n80
8:4-9, 98
10:19, 181n36
12:12, 181n36

2 Samuel, Book of
6:7, 21
6:17-18, 91
7:13, 89
7:14, 89, 93
8:18, 91
11:11, 163n9
14:17, 41
18:18, 172n42

Amos, Book of
2:8, 61
5:21, 62
5:24, 62
5:25, 62
6:3-6, 60
6:10, 173n15
7:12, 62
8:5-6, 61

2 Chronicles
13:5, 32
26:16-20, 94, 181n33
35:13, 3

Daniel, Book of
9:25-6, 90

Ezekiel, Book of
18:2, 102
18:3-4, 102
18:21-24, 103
18:30, 103
18:31, 103, 110
20, 108–109
20:8, 104
20:23-24, 104
20:25, 108, 182n9
20:25-26, 105
28:2, 42
28:6-9, 46
28:14, 42
28:16-18, 46
28:18, 42
36:25, 109
36:26, 109
36:27, 109
40-48, 154

Haggai, Book of
2:11, 5

Hosea, Book of
5:5, 79
5:6, 81
5:15, 79
8:13, 81
12:4-5, 80
13:2, 79

Isaiah, Book of
1:1-9, 13
1:11, 61
1:14, 61
1:15, 62, 63
1:16-17, 62
2:1-4, 173n9
2:2-3, 13, 54
2:4, 56
5:8, 67
5:16, 63, 65
6:3, 57
6:9-10, 58

6:11-12, 58, 174n20
6:13, 174n21
9:5, 89
10:13, 56
10:14, 31, 55
11:6, 54
11:8, 54
11:9, 54
14:13-15, 45
27:1, 13
28:18, 174n25
30:27, 57
30:33, 59
31:8-9, 59
33:20-22, 25
42:6-7, 114
45:1, 180n13
45:20-23, 114
48:1, 173n15
51:9-10, 13
53, 114
53:3, 111
53:4-6, 111
53:5, 115
53:7, 10, 115
53:10, 115
56:5, 172n42
61:1, 180n13

Jeremiah, Book of
7:21, 174n29
7:22, 174n29
7:31, 105
23:6, 90
23:25-27, 178n32
31:29-30, 182n3

Job, Book of
1:1, 120
2:9, 116
7:12, 47
27:5, 116
38:25-27, 117
39:9-11, 118
40:25-29, 118
41:25-26, 118
42:5-6, 116, 119

Subject Index

Aaron, 27
  relation to Jeroboam, 80
  in the tabernacle, 62–63
Abel, 44
Abraham (patriarch)
  Binding of Isaac (*Akedah*),
    105–107
  covenant of, 29
  revelation of God, 20,
    166n52
  God and, 49
Abtalyon, 6
Adam
  Cain's offering and, 44–45
  loneliness of, 38
  moral judgment, 40
  sexual awareness, 40
Akedah (Binding of Isaac),
  105–107
Akivah (Rabbi), 128, 141,
  162n20
Am Ha-Aretz (commoners), 129
Amos, Book of
  Sabbath observance, 61
  social polarization in, 60–61
andurarum, 93
angels
  E source and, 178n33
  "knowing good and evil," 41
anthropomorphism
  in Deuteronomy, 82–83
  in Genesis, 77
  of God, 20, 28, 167nn55, 56

of God in Priestly Torah,
    83–84
  in God–Moses encounters,
    76–77
Antigonos of Sokho
  Hellenism's influence of, 124
  on the reward of worship,
    124, 126, 185n5, 186n10
  Sadducees and, 185n5
asham taluy (suspensive guilt
    offering), 139–140
Assyria
  conquest of kingdom of
    Israel, 55–56, 113, 152
  covenants, 30–31
  king in image of Bell (god),
    92
  Sennacherib, 153
atonement. *see also* sacrifices
  Azazel ritual, 16–17, 72–73,
    165nn33, 34
  Day of, 18, 176n8
  guilt offering, 114–115
Azazel
  atonement ritual, 16–17,
    72–73, 165nn33, 34
  death as, 17–18, 59
  Hittites and, 17
  Mot (Canaanite god of
    death), 17–18
  name, origin of, 166n35
  passivity of, 18
  in the Talmud, 165n34

as imperfect (J source), 38
Job on, 116–121
morality, 33–34

D. *see* Deuteronomy, Book of
David, King
Bathsheba and, 163n9
in Priestly role, 90–91, 181n33
wise woman of Tekoa, 41
Day of Atonement, 18, 176n8
death
Azazel as symbolic of, 17–18,
59
impurity, 18
J source on, 60
mortality and, 41–43
Mot (Canaanite god of death),
17–18
in Priestly Torah, 59
Sheol, 45
YHWH and, 60
Deuteronomy, Book of
as book of Torah found, 153
boundaries of peoples in,
52–53
calf cult in, 83
dreams in, 178n32
God's presence in, 52–53, 56,
82–83
historical books and, 153
on idol worship, 112–113
kingship in, 91–93
nations detached from God,
113–114
Paschal Law in, 3
prayer in, 84–85
publication by Josiah, 155
Song of Moses in, 52, 172nn1, 2
Sons of God in, 52–53
spatial distance in, 84–85
Tent of Meeting, outer, 83
on Torah study, 84
women slaves, 4, 161n8
worshiping God in, 52
YHWH in, 84–85
divine punishment, 21
divine qualities
evil as, 38–39, 57
good as, 39
kings, 41, 42–43, 45–46

"knowing good and evil,"
40–41
knowledge as, 38–39
royal divine wisdom in J
source, 40–42
sexuality, 39
Tower of Babel, 48–49,
172nn42, 43
divine reward and punishment,
125
Dragon, 47
dreams
revelation, 82
Tent of Meeting, 81–82,
178n33

Egypt. *see also* Pharaoh
Israel's idolatry in, 104, 182n8
kings in, 87–88
Marenptah, 88
Pharaoh, 43, 87–88
El (Canaanite god)
Elohim, 24
seventy sons of, 173n6
tent of, 24, 25–26, 167nn67,
68
Eliezer, Rabbi
asham taluy (suspensive guilt
offering), 139–140
on purity of ringed oven, 142
on treatment of non-Jews, 141
Elijah (prophet), 78
Elohim
in Binding of Isaac (*Akedah*),
106, 107
covenant (*berit*) and, 32
Creation and, 106
El (Canaanite god) and, 24
ethical attributes of, 106,
107–108
in the Flood, 15, 19–20
morality of, 22
and Noah, 19–20
as nurturing Creator, 27
as personal god, 19–20, 23,
166n52
in Priestly Torah, 19–20
YHWH and, 21, 167n57
Elohist code, xii, 151–152, 155,
178n43

Omer offering in, 68
on pact (*edut*) between Israel
  and God, 1, 31
physical dimensions of God,
  9, 21
popular customs of, 68
revelation in, 19
ritual and morality separated
  in, 64–65
rituals and, 27, 63–65, 168n80
sacrifices (*olah/zebah*),
  174n29
sea monsters in, 38, 47–48
on Sinai revelation as pact
  (*edut*), 28
speech in priestly rituals,
  72–73, 176n8, 177nn11, 12
Tabernacle in, 71–72, 176n2
transition of faith in, 119
on worship, 126
YHWH in, 20, 83–84,
  167nn55, 56
priests
  and cultic roles for kings,
    93–94, 180n23
  cult of, xiii–xvi
  as elites, xiii
  Hittites and, 11
  king as, 90–91
  literary creativity of, 150
  Melchizedek as, 94
  monarchy and, 10, 162nn8, 9
  morality in, xiii–xvi
  political involvement of, 10
  prophets' critiques, xiii–xvi
  rulings of, 5–6
  sacrifices, importance of, 7
  sectarianism and, 130,
    187nn26, 31
  Solomon's Temple, 10
  Temple vessels, 130–131,
    187n31
  Torah defined by, 7
  in war time, 10, 162n8,
    163n9, 168n80
prophets, anointing of, 180n13
prose literature, 151–152
Proverbs, Book of, 150
Psalms, Book of, 150
  deification of kings in, 96

juridic role of kings in, 89–90
King David's priestly functions in, 90–91
kings as priests in, 91
Levites, 72
priests, 72
prophecies of Isaiah and, 150
punishment
  destruction of Temple in
    Jerusalem, 101–102
  foreigners looking on, 112,
    113–114
  of "laws that were not good,"
    105, 182n9
  of sinners, 102–103, 182n3
purity
  daily sacrifice of two lambs
    (*kevasim*), 140
  of people of Israel, 129–131
  Temple vessels and, 130–131,
    187nn29, 31

Qumran
  anointed king and anointed
    priest models in, 97
  boundaries of peoples in, 52
  on funding of sacrifices,
    132–133

rainfall, 118, 126

Sabbath observance, 61, 66
sacrifices. *see also* worship
  Akedah (Binding of Isaac),
    105–107
  Amos on, 61
  asham taluy (suspensive guilt
    offering), 139–140
  of Cain, 44–45
  child, 58–59, 108, 174nn21, 22
  criticism of, 61
  of the first born, 22
  first fruit offering, 68, 176n47
  God and, 44–45
  half-shekel donations for, 132
  immorality and, 61
  Jeremiah on, 174n29
  to Molech, 58–59, 174n22
  moral behavior and, 62–63
  olah, 174n29